MAGIC
IN THE
ANCIENT WORLD

Fritz Graf

Translated by Franklin Philip

HARVARD UNIVERSITY PRESS

Cambridge, Massachusetts, and London, England

First Harvard University Press paperback edition, 1999

First published as *Idéologie et Practique de la Magie dans l'Antiquité Gréco-Romaine,* copyright
© 1994 by Les Belles Lettres

Publication of this volume was assisted by a grant from the French Ministry of
Culture and Communication.

Library of Congress Cataloging-in-Publication Data

Graf, Fritz.
  [Magie dans l'antiquité gréco-romaine. English]
  Magic in the ancient world / Fritz Graf ;
translated by Franklin Philip.
      p.   cm. — (Revealing antiquity ; 10)
  Includes bibliographical references and index.
  ISBN 0-674-54151-0 (cloth)
  ISBN 0-674-54153-7 (pbk.)
  1. Magic, Ancient.
  2. Rome—Religious life and customs.
  I. Title.
  II. Series.
BF1591.G7213   1997
133.4′3′093—dc21   97-20985

Revealing Antiquity

· 10 ·

G. W. Bowersock, General Editor

CONTENTS

Acknowledgments   *vi*

1   Introduction   *1*

2   Naming the Sorcerer   20

3   Portrait of the Magician, Seen from the Outside   61

4   How to Become a Magician: The Rites of Initiation   89

5   Curse Tablets and Voodoo Dolls   118

6   Literary Representation of Magic   175

7   Words and Acts   205

Notes   235

Bibliography   303

Index   308

ACKNOWLEDGMENTS

THE LAST DECADE has seen a steadily growing interest in the subject discussed in this book, not the least in the United States. Without the scholarly work of many people, this account would have been impossible. It started as a series of seminars at the École Pratique des Hautes Études (section des sciences religieueses) in Paris, developed into a book in French, transformed itself into a significantly changed German version, and now presents itself in English. During this series of metamorphoses, I have derived enormous benefits from friends and colleagues. John Scheid in Paris invited me to the École and helped with the French edition, as did Evelyne Scheid-Tissinier, Magali Tongas, and Didier Mertens. The participants in my seminars helped by clarifying several tricky issues. Jan Bremmer, Christopher Faraone, Sarah Iles Johnston, David Jordan, and Henk Versnel contributed by discussing and debating various points. I thank each of them. I especially thank Sarah Iles Johnston for the invaluable help she gave in the production of the book. Scholarship, unlike magic, is not the business of a solitary figure.

1

INTRODUCTION

THE PRACTICE OF magic was omnipresent in classical antiquity. The contemporaries of Plato and Socrates placed voodoo
dolls on graves and thresholds (some of these dolls can
be found in modern museums), Cicero smiled upon a
colleague who said that he had lost his memory under the
influence of a spell, and the Elder Pliny declared that
everybody was afraid to fall victim to binding spells. The
citizens of classical Teos cursed with spells whoever attacked the city; the Twelve Tables legislated against magical transfers of crops from one field to another; and the
imperial law books contain extensive sanctions against all
sorts of magical procedures—with the sole exception of
love spells and weather magic. The accusation of having
worked magic was wielded against many a prominent
Greek and Roman, from Republican senators to the philosopher Boethius in the sixth century of our era; had
Socrates lived in a place other than Athens, he would
certainly have incurred the same risk. Ancient magic lived
on: Greek spells from Egyptian papyrus books reappear
in Latin guise in astrological manuscripts at the time of

Christopher Columbus; the story of the sorcerer's apprentice, told in Lucian, is famous in European literature and music; and the image of the modern witch is unthinkable without Greek and Roman antecedents. Magic, in a certain sense, belongs to antiquity and its heritage, like temples, hexameters, and marble statues.

Ancient magic had more facets than just the harm done through spells and curses. Magical rites not only helped to harm enemies and rivals but also gave access to a higher spirituality. These rites could open the way to the supreme god, or at least to an intimate dinner with Helios or an encounter with Seth. Magicians had a direct link to the divine world, and magic was seen as a gift from the gods as early as Pindar's time. Anyone with a charismatic personality could be seen as a magician as well: Apollonius of Tyana, the philosopher Plotinus, and the orator Libanius, as well as Moses and Jesus, were thought to have powers well beyond those of ordinary people.

But magic is a bit like a black hole; to many people, it seems invisible. Contemporary social anthropologists doubt whether magic exists at all. The debate about the distinction between magic and religion has been long and bitter, and without a clear solution; scholarship, anyway, continued a discussion already begun by theology. For a long time the science of antiquity ignored the phenomenon. Despite the revival of interest in ancient religion, interest in ancient magic remains marginal— curse tablets, papyrus books, and voodoo dolls are much less appealing than are mythological scenes on Attic vases or the papyrus fragments of Sappho. This situation is understandable and, to a certain degree, perfectly justified; nevertheless, scholarly interest in ancient societies should not be fastidious. This book gives a general account of ancient magic, from the invention of the term in the last years of the sixth century B.C. to the end of antiquity.

THE SOURCES

The study of ancient magic, like the study of all religious problems in the civilizations of antiquity, must draw on all possible sources from literature to the texts on papyri and in inscriptions, as well as the (rarer) visual material. Besides these documents that are common to the whole history of ancient religions, there are those specific texts of magic papyri and curse tablets (primarily engraved on thin sheets of lead) found throughout the ancient world, from classical Greece to Greco-Roman Egypt. Among these sources, however, the texts preserved on papyrus are certainly the most surprising, and thanks to their highly detailed ritual scenarios, they constitute the most important source of information. Thus, it is with them that we shall begin.[1]

Among these magic texts on papyrus gathered in the two volumes of Preisendanz's *Papyri Graecae Magicae*,[2] distinctions must be made. First we possess small pieces of papyrus—whose number, moreover, is still growing—comprising magic texts that are, so to speak, applied: charms against illnesses, formulas for sympathetic magic (spells), and especially binding spells or *defixiones*.[3] Only the fact that these binding spells, which come from all of Greco-Roman Egypt, are written on papyrus distinguishes them from other similar and much more numerous texts that the epigraphers call *tabulae defixionum*. These texts, which are mostly inscribed on small metal sheets, have been found in almost every part of what was the ancient world. The great majority of them are on lead.[4] It must be assumed that such magic texts also had existed on papyrus outside of Egypt; however, with rare exceptions, the ancient papyri have been preserved only in the extremely dry soil of the Nile Valley.

Besides the short texts, there are in Preisendanz's collection several long texts on papyrus. These long texts are of considerable interest, for they represent real magical books, collections of recipes and instructions for procedures of every kind from healing, exorcism, and divination to directions for calming the anger of masters and kings or for winning the heart of a woman, and including rites making it possible to enter into intimacy with the supreme god. Their discovery has an importance for Greco-Roman religion which not unjustly has been compared with the importance that the discovery of the Qumran texts has for Judaism or the Nag Hammadi texts for gnosticism.[5] These books date from the High Empire.[6] They are from the hands of learned scribes who sometimes had a real interest in textual scholarship.[7] Five or six of these books come from the library of an Egyptian specialist who was also versed in the Coptic language, who lived in Upper Egypt, and who had a genuine passion for magic and secret theology; also in his library are preserved books on magic written in Coptic, as well as a book of alchemy.[8] Although books like that were not secret, they were despised or feared. Greek and Roman authors sometimes mention them, but most of the time in a tone of disapproval and mistrust—we recall that the Ephesians, following the exhortations of Saint Paul, burned a great number of these books. Roman laws prohibited the possession of magical as well as of divinatory books (magic and divination, as we know, are related to each other).[9] The burning of books has never prevented them from being transmitted; there were curious persons always to be found who collected the magical books, as was the case of Ioannes Phoulon, a law student in Beirut toward the end of the fifth century; the description of his books with their "images of certain demons" and the wording of their foreign and barbarous names recalls the books as we know them.[10] Nevertheless, given the largely esoteric nature of ancient magic, to which most often one could have access only after undergoing initiatory rites, these books were no doubt transmitted in closed circles, from master to disciple, from father to son.[11] It is evident that under such conditions, in a tradition without scholarly control, the texts went through considerable alterations—additions as well as reductions, according to the collector's whim—because it was not a matter of sacred books that were unmodifiable or unadaptable; these texts were simply designed for practice with its changing requirements. In the rare cases in which the original owner of the copy that has come down to us went to the trouble of combining different versions of the same text, it is possible both to establish the fluctuations of tradition and even, as we shall see, to reconstruct some of its stages;[12] in other and equally rare cases, we can observe how a particular prescription was implemented for an actual rite and how its text was changed in the process.[13] Thus, these papyri constitute a gold mine of information on the thought and practice of Greco-Roman magic in the imperial era.

And not only in Egypt. Recently, Robert Ritner advocated a nearly exclusive derivation of the Greek Magical Papyri from Egyptian religion; even though this view confirms the (correct) thesis of G. W. Bowersock that Hellenization, in the Mediterranean East, means only to express indigenous concepts and traditions in Greek, not to transform traditions and concepts according a Greek mold, Ritner overstates his case.[14] It is true that Egyptian elements pervade these texts; a first superficial reading reveals the importance of the Egyptian divinities and their myths, and the most searching analysis has shown details of ideology and ritual that can be understood only in light of the Egyptian context. And the demotic spells differ from the Greek ones virtually only in their language.[15] However, one must insist on the wide distribution of these same magic rites outside of Egypt. There is a series of imprecations (defixiones) that allude to the god Seth, the primordial enemy of Isis, and that come from Rome as well as Cyprus or Athens;[16] here, Egyptian religion is part of the vaster fabric of Greco-Roman paganism. But the other, non-Egyptian elements of the papyri have a wider distribution as well; a formula from a spell in the papyri called "Sword of Dardanus" is attested in the German Rhine valley as well as in Beirut.[17] Rather than to look for a single source, we should note the varied origin of the constituent elements of these texts—Greek, Jewish, Assyrian, Babylonian, and even Sumerian—that make them evidence as exciting as it is complex for what is still readily called "late pagan syncretism."[18] In short, it would be much too narrow-minded and cautious to treat these books only as documents of Egyptian religion—nearly as narrow-minded as the pan-Hellenism of which our predecessors were largely guilty.[19]

The complexity of the tradition appears emblematically in the *Eighth Book of Moses*, reproduced by one of the Anastasi papyri, currently in Leyden (J 395), dating from the mid–fourth century A.D.[20] We know books I through V of Moses; however, we have no information about books VI or VII, and it is thought that these never existed. We are in a world in which the symbolism of numbers is important—after *Moses* VIII, only book X is attested, IX again is lacking. The significance of *Moses* X is obvious: according to the Pythagoreans, ten is the perfect number, for it is the sum of the elements of the "tetraktus."[21] The same holds true for eight: even though there is no early Pythagorean explanation; the number becomes important in Hellenistic Pythagoreanism and especially in Jewish and Christian number symbolism of the Imperial epoch. This symbolism of course fits in very well with the figure of Moses.[22]

The widespread opinion that Moses was a magician[23] we know from the *Acts of the Apostles:* "Thus was Moses instructed in all the wisdom of the Egyptians, and he was powerful in words and deeds,"[24] which amounts to saying that he practiced magic. The Hellenized Jewish circles from which the *Acts* come thus recognized Moses as a magician, and they gave this recognition a rather banal explanation: after living for a long time in Egypt, Moses was bound to be versed in the magicians' art.

But the idea is even more widespread than is commonly believed. Pliny the Elder, in his chapter on the history of magic, associates Moses with one school of magic.[25] Joseph Bidez and Franz Cumont suggested that the Plinian catalog of magi (of whom Moses was a part) might go back to the Peripatetic philosopher Hermippus, a pupil of Callimachus. In the pagan world, Moses the magician would thus have been known during the Hellenistic epoch; he is, in any case, vouched for as such toward the beginning of the Christian era.[26] In the final analysis, the notion of a magician Moses comes from the chapter of *Exodus* in which the famous magic competition is recounted between Moses and Aaron on the one hand, and on the other, the magi of the pharaoh.[27] An apocryphal Jewish text from the Hellenistic era states that the pharaoh's magi, also two in number, answered to the names of Iannes and Iambres; in Pliny's catalogues, Iannes figures as one of the founders of Jewish magic.[28]

Moses is thus described as a magician not only in the Jewish circles of Alexandria and Syria-Palestine but also in the Greco-Roman world.[29] There is consequently nothing surprising in what is found mentioned in the papyri where other Mosaic texts are represented, outside of *Moses* VIII; a magic formula is even known by which the magician claims to be Moses himself and to claim the privilege of having been the founder of Judaism.[30] *Moses* VIII contains only a single ritual that is treated at some length. However, the book is preserved in three versions to which the learned magician—the one who had had the book of Leyden written—added extracts drawn from other apocryphal books by Moses: an *Archangelike* (a rather enigmatic "archangelic" instruction manual), excerpts from the tenth book, and Moses's secret prayer to the moon. He also refers to a certain *Key to Moses* (to wit, *Moses* VIII), a commentary that gives allegorical interpretations, additional rites, and secret names that our text often makes use of.[31] This set suggests that we make a "genetic" analysis; it is clear that an original text, in the course of its transmission, was transformed, curtailed, and augmented to end up in these three distinct versions, but with an identical core. There are four fundamental stages in this transmission: (1) (a) the composition of the original book, followed, a short while later by (b) that of the commentary constituted by the *Key*; (2) the combination of the main text with the *Key* in such a way that this text alludes to some details contained in the *Key*; (3) the division of this unified tradition into three branches, A, B, and C, which are the basis of the texts of the papyrus of Leyden; (4) the bringing together of these three versions in the manuscript of Leyden. It is impossible to give a chronological approximation—even a hypothetical one—of this transmission; the only reasonably reliable date is the end of this chain given by the date of the Leyden manuscript, the middle of the fourth century.[32] The independent evolution of the three branches could have taken decades and even centuries. The considerable differences between the branches in no way constitute useful indices; although secret, such texts were transmitted from one magician to another without ever being corrected or improved by scholars, and each user was free to modify the text as he or she saw fit, it being neither a literary work to be treated with care nor a sacred book whose tradition had to be respected to the letter.

THE STUDY OF ANCIENT MAGIC

For many years scholarship on the religious history of antiquity, employing paradigms established long ago, very often produced sound but rarely exciting works. However, we now have been witnessing for a generation a growing revival of research in religion and mythology, the result of the change of paradigm brought about toward the end of the 1960s simultaneously by Angelo Brelich, Walter Burkert, and the team gathered around Jean-Pierre Vernant. Yet although, in this new context of research, rites aroused great interest, and, at least in theory, magic and religion ceased being opposed in the way that Frazer had done, ancient Greco-Roman magic has only very recently commanded attention in the world of scholarship. This astonishing lack of interest might have resulted from a distrust of all things magic as well as from the notorious difficulty of the magic texts themselves; and the growing interest in esoteric lore at the end of a millennium which has become tired of rationality helped to overcome this reluctance. Primary among the pioneers in this renewal of scholarly interest in magic are American scholars— first and foremost the authors of the English translation, valuable and judiciously annotated, of the Greek magic papyri, published by a team around Hans Dieter Betz in Chicago. Recently, John Gager translated and annotated important Greek and Latin defixiones, and Marvin Meyer and Richard Smith published the annotated translation of Coptic spells, making two more important corpora accessible to the nonspecialist.[33] In Europe, though, interest is much more limited. Although at the turn of the century Marcel Mauss had contributed decisively to the theory of magic, French scholarship remained reluctant; Jean-Pierre Vernant and his team had no interest whatsoever in magic; while outside Paris, Jean Annequin and Anne-Marie Tupet published valuable and sound books on magic that, however, still followed old theoretical paradigms, and the same is true for the recent book by André Bernard.[34] In Italy, Raffaella Garosi, a pupil of Angelo Brelich, developed the theoretical frameworks in a precocious study, which, however, could have no sequel because of

Garosi's tragic death.[35] It is the team around Reinhold Merkelbach in Cologne that does the most important work on magic on the continent, by publishing a series of translations and interpretations of magic texts,[36] whereas in other countries, individual scholars like Richard Gordon or Hendrik S. Versnel, following in the footsteps of Karl Preisendanz, produced some interesting papers.[37]

This state of affairs provides hope, suggesting that our own era will probably see the slow growth of interest similar to that aroused by magic in the past, during what could be called the heroic era of religious studies at the turn of the century, the interest that it met with and continues to meet with in anthropological research, French, German, and English. Diachronically, the renewed interest in magic in Christian culture must be added, whether in that of the Middle Ages, the Renaissance, or the contemporary era.[38]

In the scientific study of antiquity, interest in magic hit a kind of scientific peak before World War I. Resulting from that peak are large collections of texts—whether the *Defixionum Tabellae* of Auguste Audollent (1904) and the several publications by Richard Wünsch, especially his appendix to the *Inscriptiones Atticae* of 1897, or the publication of the *Papyri Graecae Magicae* by a team gathered around Karl Preisendanz. Although the first volume appeared only in 1928 and the third one (with the indices) fell victim to the bombing of Leipzig during World War II, this publication was in fact only an extension of the fortunate initiative of Albrecht Dieterich, whose death in 1908 interrupted the project.[39]

With the exception of the Frenchman Auguste Audollent, the German scholars were thus pioneers in the study of ancient magic; there were numerous reasons for this interest. It was first an interest in any ancient object, as modest as it might be, manifested by a philology that wished to be a science of antiquity in all its aspects. The inscriptions on lead, inept as they were, the remains of papyrus, and the bronze coins aroused as much curiosity as the great texts of Homer, Sophocles, or Virgil, or the imperial decrees inscribed on Delian marble or Roman bronze, and they were not analyzed any less zealously. Inaugurated by August Boeckh, this attitude was exemplified by Ulrich von Wilamowitz-Moellendorff and by his colleagues and friends. Concerning the magic papyri, Wilamowitz formulated this attitude in these now classic terms: "One day I heard a great scholar deplore the discovery of these papyri, which robbed antiquity of the distinguished luster of classicism. That is undeniably the effect that they produce, but I am delighted with it. For what I want is not to admire but to understand my Hellenes, in order to be able to judge them fairly."[40] "To understand the Greeks" through all the documents concerning their life, that was the aim of these scholars.

But there were more specific reasons underlying their attitude. After all, despite these declarations of intent, studying the magic papyri was so suspect in the eyes of a traditionalistic philology (as Wilamowitz reveals in the passage just cited) that in Heidelberg, Albert Dieterich felt obliged to conceal the object of his Summer seminar in 1905 on the magical papyri under the less provocative title of "Selection of Greek papyri."[41] Moreover, the position of Wilamowitz himself was not lacking in ambiguity with regard to the magic texts: in *Der Glaube der Hellenen*, he speaks in connection with the papyri of "savage and phantasmagorical superstition . . . that has nothing to do with religion." Albert Henrichs well brought to light the Christian, Protestant—and hence normative—sources of this conception of religion in Wilamowitz.[42] It was not the "Wilamowitzian" school of Berlin, but rather the circle gathered around Hermann Usener, that advanced the study of magic papyri and curse tablets, consisting of Albert Dieterich, Usener's student and son-in-law, and

Richard Wünsch, another of Usener's disciples, coeditor with Dieterich of the *Archiv für Religionswissenschaft* and the *Religionsgeschichtliche Versuche und Vorarbeiten;* Karl Preisendanz, the editor of the *Papyri Graecae Magicae*, was a student of Wünsch.[43] Usener's interest in magic was derived from his interest in the origins of religion; magic was part of popular religion, the religion of the masses, especially of the rural populations, the one close to the origins, to the primitive roots of religion—a conception of romantic origin, obviously, but one that has not totally disappeared from our cultural and scientific heritage.[44]

When still a student, Albrecht Dieterich published one of the great papyri of Leyden; he had noticed in the course of this work that the papyrus presented evidence not of primitive religion, but of religion of much later eras.[45] His interest also lay in the hope of discovering in the papyri the vestiges of an earlier state of religion: but it was not, in the manner of Usener, primitive religion, but rather elements of later Greek that he hoped could be reconstructed with the help of the magic texts. The most famous example of this salvage and reconstruction operation is the *Mithrasliturgie,* the text (according to Dieterich) of an initiatory ritual of the mysteries of Mithras, identified and isolated among the documents preserved by the great papyrus 574 of the Bibliothèque Nationale.[46] Thus, magic was not a source of interest for its own sake; the magic documents were simply sources concerning an earlier religion, of which they contained vestiges in a more or less disguised and degenerate form. Richard Reitzenstein, also a close associate of Usener, studied these texts for a different reason: he saw them primarily as evidence of syncretism, whose genesis and history he wished to reconstruct.[47]

But the vital impetus lay elsewhere. It was the works of Tylor and Frazer that provided the real debut to the studies of ancient magic. Frazer in particular attempted to mark out the evolution of the human mind from the era of magic to that of science, traversing the age of religion.[48] The German scholars around Usener had been concerned with magic well before Frazer. Their interest derived neither from Tylorian theory nor from the Frazerian project, but lay in the German romantic tradition, combined (in the case of Dieterich) with that of historicism. Frazer, in return, recognized his debts to Usener, as to the entire German scholarly tradition since the Grimm brothers (Jacob Grimm, the founding father of German folklore studies, had understood the golden bough of the Virgilian Aeneas as a mistletoe—Frazer took this over into his *Golden Bough*).[49] Finally, the two schools drew fairly close, and the Frazerian evolutionism, once it became dominant in the human sciences, exerted its influence on the succeeding generation—on Wünsch, on Ludwig Deubner, and on the man who was to become the specialist on ancient magic between the two world wars, the Norwegian Samson Eitrem.[50] Eitrem, who had set out as a specialist on literary papyri and who had followed the teachings of Diels and Wilamowitz, came to the study of magic through magic papyri (today the Papyri Osloenses), which he had purchased in Egypt shortly after World War I.[51] Eitrem pursued his work on ancient magic until his death in 1965, leaving uncompleted his long manuscript of a history of ancient magic.[52]

Thus, the primarily philological work of these scholars led to the discovery of new texts on papyrus, stone, or lead. On the other hand, philology was always rather hesitant in theoretical reflections; "speculations" were scarcely ventured beyond the unanimous agreement on the necessary separation of magic and religion on Frazerian lines. The consequence of this was vague and contradictory ideas on chronology. In an evolutionistic perspective, magic—being associated with rural ways of behavior and thinking that were obsolete in the era of the development of cities—was considered very old and even primitive; on the other hand, the magic known through the documents was rather late, and clearly constituted a degeneration from earlier, more noble traditions. At the level of categories, magic and religion were distinguished without undue concern for terminology and definitions. If a definition was required, the rather blurry one given by Frazer in the *Golden Bough* was adopted; as we know, he distinguished magic, religion, and science according to the agent's intention, rationality, and autonomy. Both magic and science were characterized by the autonomy of the agent vis-à-vis the world of natural and supernatural powers and by the empirical, realistic function that they take on and by which they mean to change the current facts of human existence. Magic is distinguished from science by its quite different rationality, obeying specific laws. Both magic and religion admit the existence of supernatural powers. Religion, though, is distinguished from magic by the absence of rationality and a practical goal—and it differs particularly in that the religious person humbly submits to supernatural powers, whereas the magician tries to bend these powers to his own will and interests; the "Christiano-centric" character of this definition of religion is clear.[53]

Theory remained practically stationary in the sciences of antique religion up to the 1960s.[54] The theoretical debate on magic took place elsewhere, among the ethnologists and the social anthropologists, with the classical scholars adopting more or less Frazerian positions. This book is not the place to analyze the long history of ethnological research on magic inaugurated by Tylor and Frazer; others have already done so.[55] Instead we shall apply ourselves to sketching the major lines of the debate and to attempting to delineate their consequences for the sciences of antiquity.

By adopting a near-scholastic way of proceeding, we can sort the ethnologists and the social anthropologists in this debate into two major camps: first, the great majority, those who, like

Frazer or Malinowski, looked into actual magic, magic in action; and second, those who looked primarily into ideology, into the accusations of magic, passive magic, like Marcel Mauss and, at least in part, E. E. Evans-Pritchard. These two fundamental positions produced completely different consequences. While the ideological way of proceeding started with indigenous categories, the interest in practical magic led to the much wider question of the interpretation of ritual, its functions, its semantics, and beyond to the (implicit or explicit) question whether a term such as *magic*, whether in its Frazerian threefold framework (the magic-religion-science opposition), or in a vaguer sense, makes any sense outside the European world. In this way, the debate of the ethnologists has become, in the final analysis, a debate about the understanding of foreign cultures and the hermeneutics of ritual.

We can once again distinguish two major lines in this debate. For English social anthropology since the time of Tylor, magic has been, as a science, a system that explains the natural world and that offers a means of checking and controlling phenomena. This intellectualist position, which was first formulated in an evolutionistic framework by Tylor and adapted by Frazer, acquired with time (and in contradiction to Frazer's positions) an increasingly functionalistic dimension; thus, Frazer's evolutionism very quickly collapsed in the presence of the work of his closest disciple, Bronislaw Malinowski. The firsthand experience of a so-called primitive culture, that of the Trobriand Islands, had led Malinowski to take an interest, not in the origins, but in the function of the phenomena of magic and religion. While preserving, with some modifications, the Frazerian triad of magic-religion-science, Malinowski contrasted magic with religion as emotional phenomena in opposition to rational science, and attributed to both magic and science (or rather, technology) pragmatic and empirical objectives and functions, with the difference that magic entered the lists where rational technology could not guarantee success. Thus, according to Malinowski, the Trobriands (to cite the now-classic case) did not resort to magic for fishing in the lagoon, but they did practice magic for the much riskier fishing on the high seas; this definition of magic as having a pragmatic function, in contrast to the nonempirical function of religion, has survived to the present day.[56]

Recently, the Trobriand material was scrutinized by Stanley J. Tambiah in light of another interpretive model, that of a "performative" kind.[57] This terminology comes from the vocabulary of Anglo-American linguistics, which distinguishes two types of utterance; whereas most verbs describe an act external to that of the utterance, there are "performative" verbs for which the act of utterance constitutes the very carrying out of the utterance: in saying "I swear," I am performing the oath. We shall take up this theory and its possible use for understanding Greco-Roman magic in the last chapter.

Since Frazer, magic has manifested itself mainly in its rituals; the entire discussion has turned on the distinction between magic and religious rites. None of the responses satisfied either the Frazerian distinction according to intention or that of Malinowski according to the function; Tambiah did not even attempt to consider a distinction between the two. While believing in the universality of the categories, Frazer's contemporaries had already denied the possibility of this distinction in the field of rituals,[58] and invented the term "magico-religious." Two generations later, instead of naively accepting magic and religion as universal terms, one began to catch sight of their European origin; the question remains whether these categories are still useful for the description of another culture. Some scholars, adopting a radical position, condemned the word *magic* as a "semantic trap."[59] Others, who were less extremist, proposed to retain the magic/religion distinction: for them, the debate hinged on the question of whether one ought to follow the terminological usage of a given culture or whether any intrinsic (or *emic*, according to a somewhat dated terminology) approach was impossible. Do we consider as magic only what the Greeks or Romans did (at the cost of possible inconsistencies), or do we use our own definition of magic and apply it to antiquity? This latter position, the only tenable one from the perspective of a rigorous epistemology, requires a definition of the hermeneutic tools as strict as it is artificial, because it might cut across all categories of an indigenous culture and leave us rather baffled about its way of looking at things.[60]

The other way of proceeding, the one that focuses on mental representations rather than rites, poses smaller problems. Already, Marcel Mauss, in the tracks of Durkheim, had at the time of the second edition of the *Golden Bough*, opposed to the individual intellectualism of Frazer, the conception of magic as belonging to the same collective representations as religious myths and rites. Thus, the interest no longer bore on what primitive peoples did, but on what their society thought of what they did.[61] After Malinowski, E. E. Evans-Pritchard took up this way of proceeding, much more resolutely than Mauss, while keeping the interest in functionalism. Evans-Pritchard investigated the function of the accusations of magic, or rather witchcraft, in a given society, that of the Nigerian Azande, following the indigenous terminology. Independent of the existence of sorcerers—who were even credited with quite unrealistic and empirically impossible features—according to Evans-Pritchard these accusations made it possible to give explanations that were accepted by the society, of the misfortunes and unhappiness that without them remained incomprehensible.[62] Magic thus proves an important means for understanding and interpreting the accidents in human existence. The folklorist Jeanne Favret-Saada has also shown the fruitfulness of this approach among contemporary peasants in the French Bocage.[63]

IN THE CLASSICAL WORLD, as we shall see, we have accusations of magic, but above all, in the papyri and curse tablets, detailed descriptions of certain magic rites. In theory, one could thus choose from a whole range of ethnological procedures. But there is a fundamental difference in relation to the ethnological facts: the very word *magic* derives from Greek and Latin. An indigenous terminology is thus available.

But these easy comparisons are deceptive. Viewed more closely, the terminology of classical scholarship and that of ethnology are not compatible. In the past, students of antiquity gave the term *magic* two antagonistic, though still related, meanings. On the one hand, a meaning was always referred to that was more or less close to the one that the word had in antiquity: *magic* meant everything that the Greeks and Romans could have designated under that heading. Now in making this use purely descriptive, it was forgotten that for the Greeks and the Romans, the term had always been normative. On the other hand, the term was taken up in the vaguely Frazerian, in any case evolutionistic, sense to designate, above all, phenomena from the prehistory of the Greek or Roman religion, and to speak of eras in which the ancients had not yet invented the word *magic*. The result was the vague chronology of which I have spoken, magic being situated both as a fact of prehistory and as a characteristic of late antiquity.

Clearly, such an ambiguity is inadmissible. There are only two possible attitudes: either a modern definition of the term is created and the ancient and Frazerian notions are resolutely cast aside, or the term *magic* is used in the sense that the ancients gave it, avoiding not only the Frazerian notions, but also all the other ethnological notions of the term. I shall choose the second way (although I am acquainted with the epistemological problems that it involves): this procedure will have the advantage of taking into account both the accusations of magic and the descriptions of magic rites, although it will imply the acceptance of some fluctuation in the terminology over the centuries. Instead of creating a rigid and artificial terminology, thus it will be necessary for us to consider and analyze the ancient use of the term *magic* as it constitutes an element of the indigenous discourse on the relationship between the human and the supernatural.[64] In this way, we shall avoid both the difficulties entailed by resorting to an artificial terminology and the excesses of the inveterate Frazerians, such as Kurt Latte or Herbert Rose, who ranked the Roman religion in the aggregate under the label *magic* because the Roman rites seemed to meet the Frazerian definition. Indeed, these rites often have pragmatic ends; they are not addressed to the one divinity (they are, Rose tells us, animistic), or they try to constrain the divinity rather than imploring it with confidence and humility. However, such an option implies the scrupulous analysis of the ancient terminology.

2

NAMING THE SORCERER

THE GREEK TERMINOLOGY

Words Referring to the Sorcerer

MAGIC (Greek *mageia,* Latin *magia*) is the art of the *magos, magus.* The term is attested to in Greek as early as the classical era and perhaps even a bit earlier.[1] Its origin is very clear: the word comes from the religious world of the Persians, in which the *magos* is a priest or, in any case, a specialist in religion.[2] It is Herodotus who first speaks to us of them: the *magoi,* who form a secret Persian tribe or society, are responsible for the royal sacrifices, funeral rites, and for the divination and interpretation of dreams; Xenophon describes them as "experts" "in everything concerning the gods."[3] In the *First Alcibiades,* Plato (or whoever wrote this dialogue) repeats this ethnographical definition when he speaks of the teachers of the young Persians: "The first one teaches the science of the *magoi,* owing to Zoroaster, son of Oromasdes: it is in fact the worship of the gods."[4] Much later, Apuleius was to use this passage to disprove the accusation of magic of which he was the object; Greeks and Romans could always recall

that *magi* were particularly pious Persian priests. Apollonius of
Tyana alone was to cast heavy doubts on their religious compe-
tence; nevertheless, the Platonic estimation of the *magi* survived
into modern times, not the least through the renown of Apuleius.[5] The Persians themselves could dispute the virtues of their
magi: in the inscription of Behishtun, Darius I denigrates the false
Smerdis as a *maguš*.[6]

But already for the Greeks of the fifth century B.C., the *magi*
could be something quite different from perfect wise men. If the
term *magos* is first attested in a fragment of Heraclitus of Ephesus,
it already had negative connotations at the end of the sixth
century, and for a subject of the Great King. Clement of
Alexandria thus reports: "Against whom are Heraclitus the Ephesian's prophecies addressed? The wanderers of the night: the
magi, the bacchantes, the maenads, the initiates—he threatens
all these men with tortures after death, he threatens them with
fire, for what men believe to be mystery initiations are impious
rites."[7] Scholars dispute the extension of Heraclitus' text; recent
editions tend to give the entire catalog of the false religious—
"*magi*, bacchantes, maenads, initiates"—to Heraclitus.[8] In any
case, the *magos* who is here lumped together with the faithful of
various ecstatic cults, notably Bacchic ones, cannot be a sorcerer
in the later current sense of the word, but rather one of those
itinerant priests whom Plato, in book 2 of the *Republic* (364b),
calls *agúrtēs* and *mántis*, "beggar priest" and "diviner," and whom
the Derveni papyrus defines as "a professional of rites"; if he is
a "wanderer of the night," the reason is that he is the specialist
of a whole series of private and secret rites.[9] Thus, I think that
a meaning of *magos* which is widely different from that of the
era of Clement guarantees Heraclitus' authorship; for an Ionian
of the end of the archaic era, the *magos* was put in the same
category as the itinerant experts of private cults, men on the

fringe of society, ridiculed by some, secretly feared by others, whose role in the archaic era has been described by Walter Burkert.[10]

In a very similar sense, the term *magos* is found in Sophocles, in *Oedipus Rex*. Oedipus, furious at Creon and at the diviner Tiresias, who he believes is Creon's tool, describes Tiresias as "this wizard (*magos*) hatcher of plots, this crafty beggar (*agúrtēs*), who has sight only when it comes to profit, but in his art is blind." An *agúrtēs* is an itinerant and beggar priest, and the *magos* ("wizard") is close to him.[11] The beggar priest is opposed to the diviner, who has an official status in a polis; the *magos* comes close to the beggar. A few lines later, Oedipus refers to Tiresias with the more official term *diviner, mántis*. Both terms, *diviner* and *beggar priest*, are combined in the passage already alluded to from Plato's *Republic*: "For their part, beggar priests and diviners come to the doors of rich men and persuade them that they have obtained from the gods, by sacrifices and incantations, the power to heal them by means of games and festivals, of some injustice committed by themselves or by their ancestors. And if one wishes to do harm to an enemy, they commit themselves for a small payment to harming a good man just like the wicked one by evocations and magic bonds, for, to hear them, they persuade the gods to place themselves at their service."[12]

This passage is of paramount importance because it sketches the portrait of a polyvalent expert combining initiations with private mysteries and "black" magic. This concern to "heal some consequences of an injustice" refers us to the preoccupations of the Orphic and Bacchic circles. It is said in a fragment of Orpheus cited by Olympiodorus, that the mental disorders are (as in Plato here) the result of the crimes of ancestors; what in Plato are initiations and purificatory rites with the power to free us from these disorders, are, in Orpheus, mystery rites (*orgia*, no doubt Bacchic ones); Plato's beggars and seers might have to do with Bacchic rituals as well.[13] When we remember the complex eschatology honored in these circles, matched with a system of punishments and rewards after death, the whole irony of the fragment from Heraclitus becomes clear: it threatens the diviners-initiators with the very same punishments from which they claim to free their customers.

On the other hand, these people are specialists at what we would call black magic, to wit, "evocations and magic bonds" with the goal of "doing harm to an enemy." What would indicate that they are specialist of those rites that we distinguish behind the hundreds of curse tablets found in Attica, in wells and cemeteries, since the end of the fifth century, and of those voodoo dolls, figurines of harmful magic, of which several were found in an archaeological context from the time of Plato?[14] Although, from a modern point of view, it is doubtless a matter of magic, Plato does not use the word *magos* in this passage of the *Republic*; the terminology is still open and fluid, and there is no "sorcerer" in the sense of a clearly defined specialist.

At the end of the fourth century, we meet the term in a context that gives sudden concretization to Plato's passage. A grave from the cemetery of Derveni (near Thessalonika) preserved a papyrus scroll—the famous but still not yet properly edited Derveni Papyrus—which contains not only an allegorical interpretation of a theogony by Orpheus, but also prescriptions about rituals. Here, we read about "incantations" (*epōidai*) of the *magoi* that are able to "placate *daimones* who could bring disorder. . . . Therefore, the *magoi* perform this sacrifice as if they would pay an amend"; and initiates (not those of Eleusis, but rather of Dionysus) "first sacrifice to the Eumenides, like the *magoi.*"[15] Not only does the unknown author connect the rites of the magi with those of the mystery cults (a topic which becomes fundamental with the Greco-Egyptian magical papyri),[16] but also he introduces the *magoi* as invokers of infernal powers, *daimones* whom he understands as the souls of the dead; the disorder that they bring manifests itself in illness and madness, which are healed by rituals of exorcism.

The other aspect of Plato's seers, miraculous magic, is mentioned already in Euripides, who connects it explicitly with the *magoi*. In the monody of the Phrygian in the *Orestes*, the slave mentions the disappearance of Helen, who, attacked by Hermione and Orestes, "disappeared all of a sudden . . . either from the effect of drugs or from the tricks of a wizard or carried off by the gods."[17] The occurrences of these "wizard's tricks" capable of making a person disappear are isolated in the fifth century; it is much later, among the sorcerers of the imperial era, that the ability to make oneself invisible or to make someone disappear was to play a certain role.[18]

Parallels to what another Euripidean messenger tells, this time about Iphigenia, are also attested to only much later; when preparing the sacrifice of her brother Orestes, "she howled and sang barbarian songs, like a magician." The "barbarian songs" of the magicians will concern us later; suffice it here to point out the irony when a native of Tauris ascribes "barbarian songs" to a Greek maiden.[19]

The *magos* is combined not only with beggars and seers, but also with the *goēs*. A *goēs* is a composite figure that combines ecstasy with ritual lament, healing, and divination. Plato connects his art with the activities of magi, seers, and initiators. Eros, he tells us in the *Symposium*, is the intermediary between the world of the gods and that of men, and that is why divination entirely belongs to him as well as "the art of the priests concerning sacrifices and initiations, just like incantations, prophecy in general, and magic *goēteia*."[20] Plato lists all the rites that make possible the passage between the human and the divine world, without taking account of the way in which society considered them. When Plato does take into account collective judgments, the *goēs* appears as ill-famed as the *magos*. Meno, in the Platonic dialogue that bears his name, reproaches Socrates for "bewitching him, drugging him and having totally cast a spell on him"— and he adds that Socrates did well in settling in Athens, for anywhere else, he would have run the risk of being arrested and accused of being a sorcerer.[21] Athens, unlike other cities, thus did not pass harsh legislation against "black" magic (a fact that could explain the number of Athenian curse tablets and magic figurines dating from that era). It was only much later, in the *Laws*, that in his ideal city, Plato proposed to introduce a harsh punishment for those "who, just like wild beasts, are not content to deny the existence of the gods or to believe them either negligent or corruptible, despise humans to the point of capturing the spirits of a good number of the living by claiming that they can raise the ghosts of the dead and promising to seduce even the gods, whom they bewitched by sacrifices, prayers, and incantations; who out of a love of money, make every effort to ruin individuals, whole families, and cities from top to bottom." These are the very actions that Plato in the *Republic* ascribed to the "beggars and seers": the seduction of the souls of the living or the dead (which amounts to claiming to cure the rich of the consequences of their own crimes and of those committed by their ancestors); and, finally, the exercise of an injurious magic thanks to the influence gained over the gods by means of rites parallel (at least in part) to the official worship, sacrifices, and prayers—and, more specifically through the magic rite of spells.[22]

Thus for Plato, these religious practices performed by marginal itinerant priests and outside the framework of the polis constitute so many punishable crimes. The reason is clear: the sorcerer constitutes a danger, just like the man who does not believe in the gods; like the latter, the sorcerer threatens the just relationship that normally unites humans and the gods. This threat involves the loss of the distinctively human qualities, the return of humankind to the savage state, prior to any civilization; being "like wild beasts" designates, in the theories of the development of the culture as they were formulated since Prodicus, the raw state of not-yet-civilized humankind.[23]

It is in Gorgias in his *Apology for Helen* that we first encounter the combination of *goēteia* ("wizardry") and of *mageia* ("sorcery"). Gorgias summons up the power of words: "For the ecstatic enchantments by words bring joy, chase away sadness; for, when the power of the enchantment unites with our soul by means of belief, it charms and persuades and transforms by the art of the wizard. Wizardry and magic are two techniques that both are the error of the soul and the illusion of opinion." "Wizardry and magic" are both arts of deception; the power of enchantment is based on illusion—the negative connotations are obvious, in that "sorcery" helps to devaluate the more neutral "wizardry." Gorgias could have said otherwise. His aim is to exculpate Helen, who was a victim of Paris's magical persuasion, against which humans are indeed defenseless. It is in this spirit that Gorgias likens the persuasive word of the charmer to the sorcerer's spell, even though his culture would have enabled him to make the distinction, if he had wanted to.[24]

First Results

The survey of the attestations of *magos*, its synonyms *agúrtēs* and *goēs* and the words derived from them, yields interesting results, which follow.

(1) The religious facts designated by this set of expressions are not identical with what we designate by the name magic. They cover both private mystery cults, with their initiation rites, and divination and injurious

("black") magic. All these phenomena are alike in not belonging to the collective religion of the Greek polis.

(2) All these practices could have negative connotations. The philosophers, with their spiritualized conception of the divine—Heraclitus with his critical distance towards traditional religion, Plato who identified divinity with the Good—despised magic and the rituals of the itinerant initiators. However, there were rich people—to wit, Athenians of the ruling class—who did have recourse to these practices in order to cope with critical situations; in the eyes of most Athenians, it was thus not a matter of contemptible religious behavior.

(3) In passing, it will have been noticed that the dichotomy between religion and magic, which is constitutive of the Frazerian approach, is already present in Heraclitus and in Plato. In the *Laws*, Plato distinguishes between magic and religion in that magic makes every effort to persuade the gods, whereas the truly religious behavior is to leave the gods a free choice, for they know better than we do what is good for us. We are already close to the idea that was to be repeated by Frazer, to wit, that magic forces the gods, whereas religion subjects itself to their power. Keith Thomas, in a rightly celebrated book, showed that the Frazerian categories had their roots in the English Protestantism of the seventeenth century;[25] but we can already see that these notions were even more deeply rooted in our own spiritual heritage.

The Persian Priests

Of all this vocabulary, only *mágos* and its family seem to be of recent origin. The word *agúrtēs* with its obvious etymology (it derives from *ageírein*, "to collect") is difficult to date; it could have originated in any epoch, and we cannot even guess at the epoch when the religious phenomenon that it designates originated. Another word with a Greek etymology, *góēs*, still bears traces of a more archaic function and still in accord with its etymology. The word derives from *góos*, the ritual lament; the *góēs* is connected with funerary rites, ecstasy, divination, and healing; if the *góēs* bears traces of shamanism, this belongs at best to prehistory. He certainly is a marginal figure, but still in the service of the society; in Aeschylus, we find him as the specialist who brings back the dead from their graves, a reversal of a function implied in his name.[26]

Despite this venerable past, the word *góēs* did not appear before the classical era. Another family, that of *phármakon*, is attested to much earlier. In the archaic vocabulary, the group is not reserved for what we would call magic, although Helen uses an Egyptian *phármakon* to chase away the sadness of Menelaus and Telemachus, and Circe transforms Odysseus's sailors into pigs with the help of a *phármakon*; and both the useful *móly* Hermes gives to Odysseus and the drug that undoes Circe's transformations are called *phármaka* as well.[27] In Homer, this same word refers to both the medicine with which the wounded are cared for and the poison that suddenly puts an end to life— Odysseus looks for a *phármakon* to poison his arrows; the suitors fear that Telemachus has gone to get a *phármakon* with which he could secretly kill them.[28] Almost as venerable is *epaoidḗ* (in classical and later Greek *epōdḗ*), which later will be confined to what we would call magic, but its one occurrence in Homer valorizes it positively. It is with an *epōidḗ* that his uncles stanch the hemorrhage when the young Odysseus was wounded in the leg by the wild boar; and the word preserved its medical meaning up to Plato, who juxtaposes, in an enumeration of remedies, "drugs, burns, cuts, spells."[29] It should be added that Plato also was familiar with the negative "magic" meaning of *epōidḗ*; in medicine, that is, the dichotomy between magic and science was still taking form in Plato's epoch.

Thus we witness, at the beginning of the fifth century, with the spread of these *mágos* and their group, the introduction of a new terminology, which was slowly to replace the traditional terminology. This change goes hand in hand with the constitution of what, in our cultural horizon, we call magic, as a special "region" among religious phenomena. This set of new terms was always to keep its original sense for the Greeks: *mageía* is always also the art of Persian priests. But during the fourth century, this art already lost all relation to the ethnographic facts reported by Herodotus. The definition of the *mageía* of Zoroaster as "worship of the gods," in the *First Alcibiades*, must have a polemical intention; in the name of an ethnography that means to be objective, the author is opposed to a tendency in which he sees a disparagement of the Persian religion. And in a fragment of the pseudo-Aristotelian dialogue *Magiká*, its anonymous author, no doubt from the Hellenistic era, asserts, in the same polemical vein, that "the *mágoi* do not know or practice sorcery."[30]

Magic as a practice of the Persian priests—which, in the Athens of the fifth century, did not mean only a non-Greek practice, but much more emphatically the practice of the enemies of the Hellenic people—fits into a well-known structure. Tylor already speaks of it in *Primitive Culture*, in which he draws up an impressive list of people who describe magi in the name of their detested (or dreaded) neighbors. The examples are numerous, down to the Swedes attributing witchcraft to the Finns, and the Finns accusing the Lapps; and since then, more examples have been brought to light, including some from the Ancient Near East.[31] In addition, Charles Stewart recently showed how in the confined space of contemporary rural Naxos, neighboring villages keep their distance by ascribing the practice of sorcery to each other.[32]

A Change of Paradigm

We have traced the evolution that led from the beginning of the classical era to the emergence of magic (or rather, of *mageía*) as an autonomous domain within religious practice. Two forces have contributed to this change of paradigm. The analysis of the passages from Plato made it possible to identify the first of these: the development of a philosophical theology. For traditional theology and cosmology, there existed an easy communication between man and the supernatural powers (the *daímones*): a human was capable of attaining the divine through the rites and could persuade the gods by means of prayers and sacrifices. Criticism appeared in the generation of Heraclitus, who fought, as we know, against the traditional practices—not only those of the initiates and the *mágoi*, but also against purification rites and Dionysiac rites, which he considered obscene.[33] Plato, at least the Plato of the *Laws*, is explicit, as we have seen: he ranks the sorcerer among those "who . . . deny the existence of the gods or believe them either negligent or corruptible"—an opinion that radically contradicts the Platonic conception of the divine as the supreme being, who cares about humankind in a perfect way and to whom they can only submit.

The other factor is science and, just like magic, it was beginning to take form as an autonomous domain of thought. A capital witness is the treatise *On the Sacred Disease* from the late fifth century B.C., whose author (anonymous, but close to Hippocratic thought) is vehemently opposed to the idea that epilepsy, the sacred disease, had supernatural origins: "In my opinion, those who first attributed a sacred character to this malady were like the magicians, purifiers, begging priests and charlatans of our own day, men who claim great piety and superior knowledge. Being at a loss and having no treatment that would help, they sheltered themselves behind the divine and called this illness sacred, in order to conceal their utter ignorance."[34] The enemies are once again the *mágoi*, who are radically devalorized: they are but charlatans.

The doctor's attack against the priests is carried out on two levels. The first one is immediately recognizable: it is the theological level. The doctor reproaches the priests for a false, feigned religiosity, implying that their recourse to the gods is merely a subterfuge to hide their failure. Further on, the polemic becomes even more clear: "As for me, I think that the body of man is not soiled by divinity, what is most corrupt by what is most pure. . . . It is thus divinity that cleans and purifies and sanctifies us from the greatest and the most impious of our faults."[35] The doctor opposes the theological conception of the purifier priests with his own conception, which is spiritualized in the sense that we have already noted in Plato.

But the anonymous doctor goes much further in his polemic, accusing the itinerant priests of deception: "By these sayings and devices, they claim superior knowledge and they deceive men by prescribing purificatory and cathartic rituals for them."[36] Therefore, these ritual cures are not a matter of true religion, of true worship (*eusebeíe*), but of a reprehensible aberration (*asebeíe*), a kind of atheism; let us recall Plato, whose formulation in the *Laws* is very comparable. The doctor knows surprising details about the claims of his opponents: "They profess to know how to bring down the moon, to eclipse the sun, to make storm and sunshine, rain and drought, the sea impassable and the earth barren"—in short, the claim to influence the laws of nature through their rituals.[37] But in doing this, the priests take as a matter of course powers that actually belong to the gods; thus, these priests claim to possess powers superior to those of the gods, in that they prided themselves on being able to employ such powers. That presumption of superiority reduces the gods to nothing, for the divine is defined by its absolute superiority with regard to humankind. "Therefore (these priests), seem to me to be impious and not to believe that there are gods."[38]

The attack is next pursued on a second level: the analysis of the illness. Here, the doctor does not use different rationality from that of the diviner: like the diviner, the doctor observes symptoms and infers the therapy from them. However, the doctor and the diviner start with different symptoms to arrive at different therapies. The purifiers look for signs that would enable them to recognize the divinity supposedly at the origin of the illness: if the patient bleats like a goat, the illness is sent by the Mother of the Gods; if the patient neighs like a horse, it is sent by Poseidon. All these steps are based on a knowledge of the laws of causality. The influence of the divinity is spotted through a symptom that refers to the sacred animal, and the therapy starts with the same facts. The person who has been attacked by the Mother will abstain from all the products of the goat, such as milk, cheese, and leather. To this, the doctor opposes his etiology, which, starting from the somatic functions and organs, is based on a chain of precise observations, from which the doctor also infers the therapy.[39]

What distinguishes the purifier from the doctor is not rationality, but cosmology, as Geoffrey Lloyd has demonstrated.[40] While for the priest, the disease is the result of a divine intervention, for the scientific doctor, all diseases have natural causes. Nature is a closed system, homogeneous and radically separate from the divine world. In this nature, the supernatural world, the gods and demons, never intervene. In the same way, on the theological level, humans are incapable of penetrating the divine world.

The purifiers and healers thus attacked must remain anonymous to us, even though the Derveni Papyrus gave new evidence about their rites. There is, however, a healer whom we know, a prominent one besides: Empedocles of Acragas in Sicily.[41] He professes to all the activities that the doctor attacked; in later tradition, not only is he a healer, but also he could influence the weather; and his pupil Gorgias watched him once practicing sorcery.[42] Empedocles himself gives promises to a pupil: "You shall learn all the *phármaka* there are for ills and defence against old age . . . And you shall stay the force of the unwearied winds which sweep over the earth and lay waste the fields with their blasts; and then, if you wish, you shall bring back breezes in requital. After dark rain you shall cause drought for men in due season and after summer drought cause air-inhabiting tree-nourishing streams. And you shall bring from Hades the strength of a dead man."[43]

We know already the ambivalent powers of *phármaka*, drugs; they are more than unguents or pills. Empedocles also claims the power to call back the dead from Hades; Plato's seers and beggars had made the same claim.[44] Yet it is especially the power over the forces of nature that Empedocles claims to possess, over weather, rain, and wind. The passage seems to find an echo in the description that the Hippocratic doctor gave of the claims of the purifiers; his opponents are not only the foreign and anonymous begging priests, but also the great charismatic men of late archaic Greece. Empedocles' claim to be "among you as an immortal god, no longer mortal" must have sounded, to Plato or the Hippocratic doctor, dangerously close to atheism.[45]

Thus, as late as the middle of the fifth century, we find at the Western border of the Greek world a man who combines healing, weather magic, and the calling up of dead souls: contemporaries might have called him a *góēs*. Surprisingly enough, Empedocles adds to this philosophy—therefore, his name survived. The people of his own world would not have separated the different elements combined in such a figure, nor would they have valued them negatively—to them, he was "honoured among all, as it is fitting, adorned with ribbons and with flowering wreaths."[46] Such high esteem would change within a generation: Empedocles' pupil is Gorgias, one of the sophists.

Thus there is, at the origin of the emergence of magic as a highly circumscribed domain in Greek religion, a turning point composed of two events in the history of Greek thought. First there occurred the advent of the philosophical theology based on a radicalization of the traditional theology, in the sense of a purification and spiritualization; then came the birth of a natural science based on the conception of nature as a closed and homogeneous system. In the final analysis, this twofold radicalization resulted in the separation between the world of nature (including humankind) and the world of the gods, a separation much stricter and more clear-cut than in the traditional religion of the cities. The philosophers and the doctors thus appear as opponents of the traditional healers, purifiers and specialists for marginal rituals. In this debate, *magos*—"Persian priest"—became a polemical term of disparagement.

We thus discern in the development of Greek religion the separation of an original unity—religion—into two opposing domains—magic and religion—where "magic," *mageía*, is not identical with what we call magic, but encompasses a whole series of noncivic religious forms: Bacchic mysteries, ecstatic private cults, purifications, and malevolent sorcery. Although this might sound like another version of nineteenth-century evolutionism, there is a crucial difference: the evolutionists hypothesized such a differentiation from magic to religion, in a hoary past, at the end of "animism." "The issue came to a head when man believed in gods; magic and religion were thereafter differentiated"—to cite but one voice, the influential one of Martin P. Nilsson.[47] There was differentiation—but in a fully historical epoch.

This differentiation at first did not concern the polis; originally it was a debate among specialists at the margin of society. After all, in the final analysis, philosophers and doctors are no less marginal and less itinerant than are the purifiers and begging priests. These philosophers and these doctors have their own associations, as we know; and the theology of the philosophers is not the civic theology with whose cults it is often enough at odds. The cities can be opposed to magic, as Plato's *Meno* proves: but they oppose it not for religious motives (as Plato's opposition does), but because the consequences of malevolent sorcery conflict with the civic code. The only early legislation against sorcery comes from the city of Teos, from the so-called *Dirae Teorum*: the city curses whoever harms a citizen or the entire polis through *phármaka dēlētēria*, injurious practices; this is not impiety, but murder.[48] The marginality of the opposition explains the paradox that Plato fights against magic, whereas his peers use it.

I HAVE ALREADY noted that the magic/religion contrast and the tendency to distinguish them according to the kind of relations that they have to the supernatural world, which were restored to honor by the Frazerian triad, were already prefigured in Plato. We now see that the second contrast, that between magic and science, was also prefigured in ancient medical thought. In the author of the treatise on the sacred illness, as in Frazer, the sorcerer and the doctor have a shared rationality—they are distinguished from each other only in that the sorcerer starts with false premises. The Hippocratic doctor already clearly insisted on the fact that the sorcerers claim to force and constrain the gods—another essential feature of Frazer's system. If there were a need to demonstrate the ethnocentric nature of the Frazerian classification, one would have absolute proof of it here.

THE ROMAN WORLD

Sorcery and Magic in the Republican Era

The situation in Rome seems comparable to what has just been described for Greece—yet, at the same time, it is rather different.[49] The most striking parallelism is that in Rome as in Greece, the terms *magus* and *magia* appeared only late, at the moment when conscious reflection on magic had developed within the Roman culture. The divergences resulted first from the fact that in Rome the practices of sorcery had always been fought by the civil authorities and, therefore, the accusation of magic was much more serious than in Greece; after that, and especially in Rome, we see the interlacing of a series of Greek influences.

Let us begin with the first attestations of the words *magus* and *magia*, which were obviously borrowed from the Greek. These terms are found, around the middle of the first century B.C., in Catullus and Cicero. In both authors, the *magus* is placed in relation to Persia. For Cicero, the *magi* are nothing other than the official priests of Persia. In his dialogue *De legibus* from the later fifties of the century, Cicero uses the word for the first time: Xerxes, he says, burned the sanctuaries of the Greeks at the behest of the *magi*. The later attestations are consistent: in *De divinatione*, written in the spring of 44, Cicero writes that the *magi* interpreted the dreams of Cyrus and that they would initiate each successive king into their art. At the first occurrence of the word in this dialogue, he tries a definition—the *magi* are a group of "wise men and scholars among the Persians."[50] The definition is necessary because Cicero is introducing an unusual word, an ethnographic technical term drawn from his Greek sources.

The small booklet of poems by Catullus is about contemporary to Cicero's *De Legibus*. The learned poet uses the same ethnographic term in one of his epigrams:

> *Nascatur magus ex Gelli matrisque nefando*
> *coniugio et discat Persicum aruspicium.*
> *Nam magus ex matre et gnato gignatur oportet,*
> *si vera est Persarum impia religio,*
> *gratus ut accepto veneretur carmine divos*
> *omentum in flamma pingue liquefaciens.*[51]

A magus should be born from the abominable union of Gellius with his mother, and learn he should the divinatory art of
the Persians! For a magus must be born from the mother and
the son, if there is some truth in the impious religion of the
Persians, so that he will adore the gods with welcome song, when
he makes the fat entrails of the victims melt over the flame.

Anne-Marie Tupet does not treat this text in her (otherwise
exhaustive) corpus of poetic passages on magic in Latin: and
rightly so, since once again, here it is a matter of the Persian
magi, specialists in divination. The invective is rather cold and,
above all, very learned. Catullus makes use of a literary ethnographic detail of Greek origin: the incest of the Persian *magi* is
well attested to since the historian Xanthus of Lydia in the later
fifth century. The detail that Catullus introduces—a genuine
magus must be the fruit of this incest—is isolated. In a way, the
learnedness takes away the bite of the invective (if, that is,
Gellius did not happen to be a *haruspex*); the scorn directed
toward "the impious religion of the Persians" serves to defame
Gellius—it is enough that the Persians are impious for the insult
to strike home.[52]

The next generation of poets, the second neoteric generation,
makes us pose the problem in a different way. In the young
Virgil, the poet of the eighth *Eclogue*, the adjective *magicus* refers,
for the first time in known Latin texts, to magic rites. The second
part of this eclogue begins with precise ritual instructions:

effer aquam, et molli cinge haec altaria vitta,
verbenaque adole pinguis et mascula tura,
coniugis ut magicis sanos avertere sacris
experiar sensus: nihil hic nisi carmina desunt.[53]

Bring water, surround this altar with a narrow band of soft cloth, burn some fat verbenas and male frankincense, for me to try, by magic rites, to lead astray my lover's reason; the only thing lacking here is incantations.

In this passage, Virgil is echoing the second *Idyll* of Theocritus, *The Sorceresses* (*Pharmakeútriai*), one of the masterpieces of Alexandrian poetry: the learned Roman poet introduces not Roman practice, but Greek literature. Not even the burning of *verbenae* has to be Roman, despite the Latin term; such rites have their place in Greek religious practice as well.[54]

Greek magic seems to fascinate the poets of late Republican Rome as well as their Alexandrian models. In his speech before the Roman governor, Apuleius quotes some lines of the learned poet Laevius, the precursor of the neoterics. He too describes the preparations for a magic rite:

philtra omnia undique eruunt:
antipathes illud quaeritur,
trochisci, iunges, taeniae,
radiculae, herbae, surculi,
saurae inlices bicodulae,
hinnientium dulcedines.[55]

They dig up all the love potions from all over; one looks for the famous *antipathes*, for wheels, iunges, ribbons, roots, herbs, tender growths, the attractions of the two-tailed lizard, the charms of whinnying animals.

Without wishing to go into the details of this magic process—it is a matter of erotic magic, obviously, as the mention of love potions already proves, but also that of the iynx and the *hip-pomanes* (the erotic stimulants gained from the sweat of mares: therefore "the charms of whinnying animals")—the fundamentally Greek character of this list must be insisted on. Laevius brilliantly builds a poem with a long list of Greek technical terms. Besides the rather banal *phíltra*, the "love-charms," we find *antípathes*, the "antidote," the *íunges* and the *trókhiskoi*, magic objects rather similar and very often confounded in the Greek sources; finally, there are *tainíai* and *saûrai*, "ribbons" and "salamanders" for which he could have used proper Latin verbs as well. The iynx, of course, is peculiarly important in Theocritus' second *Idyll*, as is the *saûra*, the salamander.[56] When the literary critics postulated a Laevian adaptation of Theocritus' second *Idyll*, they rather point out the general sphere that influenced Laevius, that is, Alexandrian poetry with its interest in strange and marginal things. In any case, we deal with a poetic alexandrianism, with literature and not necessarily with Roman realities, as in Virgil's eclogue.

In the language of the Romans of the republican era, *magus* and *magia* thus did not refer to magic. The words began their career as ethnographic terms in the prose of Cicero, and then as learned Hellenistic expression in the poetry of the early years of Augustus and referred, at least in Virgil, to the exotic rites already beloved of the Alexandrians. Must it thus be concluded that even in that era, the collective thinking of the Romans refused to isolate a domain specific to magic?

We would be led to think so, judging from a surprising passage of Cicero. In his invective against Vatinius, he attacks his opponent as follows: "You are in the habit of calling yourself a Pythagorean and of covering up your vile and barbarous manners with the name of a great scholar. Tell me, I beseech you, you who have taken to unknown and impious rites, who are in the habit of evoking souls from hells, of soothing infernal deities with the entrails of children, what perversion of the mind, what madness, led you to scorn the auspices?"[57] The rites are obvious for those familiar with Greek literature: it is a matter of the most ghastly magic, of necromancy and human sacrifices; the accusation of having immolated children for purposes of divination was later to be repeated, and the Roman laws of the imperial era provided for sanctions against the sorcerers' human sacrifices.[58] It is surprising, therefore, that Cicero does not integrate these rites in an accusation of magic (nothing would have been simpler and more effective if that had been possible for him). Instead, Cicero constructs two pairs of contrasts, between the wisdom of Pythagoras and the savage customs of Vatinius on the one hand, and on the other, between innocent rites and those *inaudita ac nefaria sacra* performed by Vatinius, that is, between an inoffensive religious culture and its reversal by Vatinius. Both pairs of oppositions contrast Vatinius and civilization—the former pair opposes Greek philosophy, the apogee of civilization, and barbarous uncivilized behavior by an argument that is inscribed in the categories of commonplace Greek erudition shared by Cicero's audience, the senators; the second pair contrasts true piety with sheer nefariousness. In both cases, Cicero makes use of nonjuridical categories; it seems that there existed neither in sacred law, nor in civil law, a notion corresponding to his accusation. At the end of the passage quoted, suddenly Roman categories appear, and the accusations become really threatening: Cicero now accuses Vatinius of having, as a magistrate, "scorned the auspices."

All this is even more surprising when we learn that a generation later, the Roman authorities reacted to accusations which cannot be very different from what Cicero tells about Vatinius. During his second aedileship in 33 B.C., Agrippa had "astrologers and wizards" driven out from Rome, and in 28 B.C., Augustus deported a Greek, Anaxilaus of Larissa, from Rome and Italy.

While in the first instance, we have no way to learn the Latin terminology then used (our source is the Greek Cassius Dio), the second case is reported by Jerome, in his *Chronicle* (in terms that are unfortunately too laconic): "Anaxilaus of Larissa, a Pythagorean and *magus*, was deported by Augustus from the city and from Italy." There now appears the formerly missing word *magus*—was it introduced by a later historian, or is it the very term of the Augustan senatorial decree?[59]

Laws of the Twelve Tables

But we must be more precise. Republican Latin already had terms for referring to magic. Several writers report some terms of law of the Twelve Tables aimed at what we would now call black magic. It is Seneca who gives the longest excerpt from it: *Et apud nos in XII tabulis cavetur "NE QVIS ALIENOS FRVCTVS EXCAN-TASSIT."* ("In Rome also, the law of the Twelve Tables gives a warning: 'Nobody shall, by spells, take away the harvest of a neighbor.'") Pliny the Elder completes it by mentioning another law coming from the same collection: *Quid? non et legum ipsarum in XII tabulis verba sunt: QVI FRVGES EXCANTASSIT et alibi: QVI MALVM CARMEN INCANTASSIT . . .* "What? do we not read these words in the very laws of the Twelve Tables: 'Person who has by spells taken off the harvests of a neighbor,' and elsewhere 'Person who has uttered an incantation.'"[60]

Thus, it is *carmen*, with the precision of *malum carmen*, that refers to the malevolent, harmful charm; it is *incantare* that refers to the action of harming someone with *mala carmina*; finally—and most surprisingly—it is *excantare*, to make a neighbor's harvest magically disappear, an operation that has a surprising, but logical, object: to transport it from the neighbor's field to one's own. That is what the young sorceress relates in the eighth *Eclogue* of Virgil (*atque satas alio vidi traducere messis*) and which Servius comments on by quoting a reference to another law of the

Twelve Tables: *TRADVCERE MESSES: magicis quibusdam artibus hoc fiebat, unde est in XII tabulis NEVE ALIENAM SEGETEM PELLEXERIS:* TO TRANSPORT THE CROPS: this was done by magic, that is why we read in the law of the Twelve Tables "Do not put a curse on the crops of others." Virgil, we see now, may supplement his Greek rituals with genuine Roman ones.[61]

It needs to be stressed that the law does not punish magic as such, but punishes the violation of the right to property in order to cause harm to others or to enrich oneself at their expense. It is not the (magic) act that is punished but the offense against property.[62] In an agrarian society, damage to fields and harvests can rather quickly call into question the status of the landowner and thus harm the social equilibrium.

These clauses of the Twelve Tables do not imply that magic as a specific and delimited practice does not exist in early Rome; they mean that its limits do not match up with either our own or those we have just found in classical Greece. The Romans evidently believed in the powerful efficacy of certain vocal rites, the *carmina:* one could *incantare* or *excantare*. But we do not know whether the negative value of these terms is peculiar to them or whether it comes from the context; only in the case of the noun *carmen*, we find a contextual distinction between the *malum carmen* and the other, neutral or beneficent *carmina*. The same law of the Twelve Tables also uses *carmen* in the neutral sense of verbal composition, according to Cicero: *Si quis occantavisset sive carmen condidisset, quod infamiam faceret flagitiumve alteri* . . . "If any person had sung or composed against another person a song such as was causing slander or insult to another . . ."[63] As defamatory songs, these *carmina* also have a destructive force, for they are capable of compromising an individual's social position and even of ruining it, which can have an effect more devastating than the destruction of the person's harvests. Once again, though, we note that the categories of the Romans do not correspond more to our own (we distinguish between incantation and song) than to those of the Greeks, who could certainly distinguish the ōidē from the epōidē.

A Healing Rite

Besides *carmina mala*, there exist the beneficent *carmina*. It is interesting to glance at an example—a *carmen auxiliare*, to use the expression of Pliny the Elder, against dislocations. It is Cato, in his treatise on agriculture, who records it:

> *luxum si quod est, hac cantione sanum fiet:*
> *harundinem prende tibi viridem p(edes) iiii aut v longam, mediam diffinde, et duo homines teneant ad coxendices. incipe cantare: [in alio s(ic) f(ertur): MOETAS UAETA DARIES DARDARIES ASIADARIES UNA PETES usque dum coeant.] MOTAS UAETA DARIES DARDARES ASTATARIES DISSUNAPITER usque dum coeant. ferrum insuper iactato.*
> *ubi coierint et altera alteram tetigerint, id manu prehende et dextra sinistra praecide; ad luxum aut ad fracturam alliga; sanum fiet. et tamen cotidie cantato. [in alio s(ic) f(ertur) vel luxato vel hoc modo HUAT HAUAT HUAT ISTA PISTA SISTA DANNABO DANNAUSTRA] et luxato vel hoc modo HUAT HAUT HAUT "ISTASIS TARSIS ARDANNABOU DANNAUSTRA."*

If a dislocation occurs, it will be healed by this incantation: take a green reed four or five feet long, split it in two through the middle and let two men hold it against their hips; begin the incantation (another manuscript reads: *moetas . . . petes* up to where the halves meet) *moetas . . . dissunapiter* up to where the two halves meet. Wave a piece of iron over it. After the two halves meet and are in contact, take the reed in hand and cut the end to the right and to the left; fasten it by a ligature over the dislocation or fracture; it will heal. Nevertheless, do the incantation every day (another manuscript reads: either for the dislocation or in

this way: *huat . . . dannaustra*) and for the dislocation or in this
way: *huat . . . dannaustra.*[64]

The text is difficult in all respects. The textual tradition of the
two *carmina* present nearly insurmountable problems, and I shall
not go into the technicalities of textual criticism—at any rate,
the *carmina* were handed down in two different, but equally
ancient, versions, as the scribe of our archetype noted. In addition, we find, among modern scholars, another and much more
characteristic hesitation. While some understood the text as the
simple and direct description of a medical operation, others
viewed it as a recipe for obtaining a magical cure. It is appropriate to look at this rite more closely.

Cato calls the entire rite *cantio*, "a singing," Pliny a *carmen
auxiliare*, "a helpful song"; what defines the rite is its being sung,
although the vocal rite is part of a more extensive ritual—this
trait has its parallels elsewhere.[65] The structure of the ritual is
easily understood. There are preparatory acts: one takes a rather
long (four or five feet) reed and splits it (lengthwise, a rather
tricky operation); two servants press the halves against the hips
of the outstretched patient. Then the rite proper begins. Slowly
the servants bring the two halves together, while the master-
doctor sings the text; a piece of iron is put on the patient's limb.
When the two halves of the reed are joined, they are shortened
to the right and to the left (the halves had been passed above
the ailing person), and then the whole is attached to the affected
limb.

Viewed in this way, the *cantio* is for us pure magic: we cannot
see any medical purpose in it, and commentators tend to speak
of homeopathic magic. This, however, is very problematic. For
Cato and his contemporaries (and, it seems, for Pliny as well),
it is not magic, but medicine, an efficacious treatment for a
dislocation or fracture—an accident against which the ancient

medicine is even more powerless than our own, especially in the case of a fracture of the neck of the femur, where the limbs cannot be set in splints. In principle, one must immobilize the limb and leave the rest to nature, which is what Cato advocates after the rite. The ritual itself, understood as a symbolic act, uses a very flexible green reed, supposed to represent the desired reunification of the fractured limb. The ritualistic symbolism uses an analogy to represent (in the eyes of the ailing person and of the helpers) the process of healing desired. The ritual has a theatrical and also a collective aspect; it unfolds, I think, in front of three categories of persons, the ailing person, the healers, and the (family) community.

A more delicate problem is posed by the *carmina* that go together with the gestural rite. In the form preserved, they appear as an unintelligible babbling, and the fact that a scribe, or rather an editor, of late antiquity noted two traditions, between which he did not wish or know how to choose, clearly shows that the ancients did not have a better understanding of them. Modern commentators note also that this can be likened to a whole series of verbal rites described in the magic papyri, whose formulas mean nothing to us.

But we must not rely too much on this. The magical formulas of the papyri are not mere arbitrary and staggering splutterings. The more we study them, the more we understand that they derive from eastern, Persian, Acadian, Aramaic, and Coptic names. The very phenomenon is found in other magic cultures, in which magical formulas often rely on older languages—in Christian magic, it is often enough Latin, Greek, or Hebrew. Moreover, many formulas show intentional deformations, inversions, assonances, rhymes, wordplay: often, there were playful minds at work.[66] The parallel with the papyri is thus misleading. On the other hand, some scholars have attempted to reconstruct comprehensible Latin from Cato's text; this process seems highly problematical, and it is not worth the effort to get lost in the labyrinth of these reconstructions.

The important thing is that in Cato, we find a rite that has all the features of what we would call "magic," but that was not seen as such by Cato or Pliny. What for the indigenous actors defined magic was not a specific ritual form, not the *carmen*, but the *carmen malum*: the intention—whether harmful or not—of the agent.

Veneficium and Veneficus

It remains to examine another term, the key word of the Roman legislation, *veneficus* (with its derivative *veneficium*). In 81 B.C., Sulla voted the *lex Cornelia de sicariis et veneficis*, which henceforth served as the fundamental law for any legal action against magic. As was already the case for the Twelve Tables, the law does not condemn magic as such. What Sulla was aiming at were crimes threatening the lives of citizens, whether by armed attacks (*sicarii*) or by ways in fact more subtle and less visible (*venefici*); in both cases, the terms included kindred ways of killing.

Cicero speaks of *veneficiis et cantionibus*, sorcery and incantation, as means of harmful magic; and Plautus's Amphitruo accuses Jupiter of being a *veneficus Thessalus*, a Thessalian sorcerer, who disturbed the minds of his slaves. In Greek, this would have read *góēs Théttalos*: *veneficium*, like *goēteía*, means witchcraft of any kind, not merely poisoning and the application of drugs. *Venenum*, the basic word, has thus a wider meaning than the Greek word *phármakon*, which in turn it can translate. In Plautus, once again, Medea rejuvenates Pelias "by her drugs and poisons"—in the Greek Medea story, the use of herbs is of paramount importance.[67] The *Lex Cornelia* looks for more precision and speaks of *venena mala*; a commentator concluded (and it is necessary to follow him) that obviously other *venena* were known: "drugs for healing" (*venena ad sanandum*) and "drugs for love" (*venena amatoria*), whose usage, surprisingly, was not prohibited. Another commentator on the same law mentions a senatus consultum of unspecified date in which the term *sacrificia mala* referred to magic rites; as with the *mala carmina* of the Twelve Tables, magic is still defined by the malevolent intention, not by specific forms of ritual.[68] It should be added that Cato always refers to prayers by the term *bonae preces*: there must have been others as well.

Let us return to *veneficium*. The word refers first, it seems, to an action that brings on sudden death, either by the effective administration of a poison or by some other clandestine means; it is no mere chance that the *lex Cornelia* also dealt with arson, of which in the imperial epoch, people readily suspected sorcerers (or other marginals, like Christians). Death by poisoning and death by "black" magic are thus but a single category contrasted with death by violence. One of the imperial experts who commented on the law understood the dichotomy as one between *factum* (murder) and *dolus* (poison or sorcery).[69] We must remember that before the development of chemical analyses, the administration of poisons was as hard to establish as the practice of magic. In both cases, the only recourse of the accusers was the appeal to witnesses, who of course had to be more or less reliable. It must not be forgotten that an unexpected death damaged the social structure much more drastically than death from old age or long, drawn-out illness. The damage had to be repaired as quickly (and as visibly) as possible—in the case of violence (*factum*), by the punishment of the *sicarius*, and in the case of nonviolent death (*dolus*), by the identification of the causes of the death and the possible punishment of the *veneficus*. We glimpse a state of things well known to ethnologists: in traditional cultures, every sudden death is liable to be interpreted as the result of magic acts.

The problem appears in a particularly clear way through an affair of which Livy speaks, although with caution and a certain skepticism. In 331 B.C., the city was unsettled by the sudden death, under similar conditions, of a series of dignitaries (*primores civitatis*); Livy insists on an epidemic, but says some of his sources interpreted things differently: a maidservant was said to have revealed to the magistrates that some matrons poisoned their husbands after preparing the poisons themselves. Consequently, the women were called into court; but instead of appearing before the magistrates, they all preferred to drink their *venena* and to die of them. Whether the story is true or false, what matters here is that the Roman tradition (the annalistic tradition of the second century B.C., and not any old oral tradition) held that it was plausible that such extraordinary deaths—the unexpected death of a number of dignitaries, likely to threaten the functioning of the Roman order—could have unnatural causes. The suicide of the matrons by the poison that they intended for the dignitaries—thus, a verifiable death—reestablishes the order of things, to the extent that it constitutes the symbolic counterpart of the *veneficium* aimed at the leading citizens.[70]

It is time to summarize a complex argument. Our analysis of the terminology from republican Rome has shown three things. First, *carmen* and its derivatives, already attested in the Twelve Tables, could refer to a magic act such as the seizure of harvests (in violation of the right to property), but could also refer to salutary medical practices: the distinction depends on the intention behind these acts. Then, it became clear that *veneficium* and *veneficus* had been at first (and were still in the era of Sulla) special terms reserved for an inexplicable death in contrast to violent deaths; it was only later that these words came to refer to any evil spell. And, finally, the terms *magus* and *magia* belonged to the learned language, that of Cicero and of the neoterics and had nothing to do with magic (we will have occasion to qualify this assertion); it was perhaps under Augustus, in the affair of

Anaxilaus of Larissa, that *magus* was attested to for the first time in the sense of "sorcerer."

Missing in archaic and republican Rome is a figure we met in Greek sources, the *góēs-agúrtēs-mágos*, the itinerant specialist who practices divination, initiation, healing, and magic. Certainly, itinerant priests were not unknown in Rome, either, but they seem to have specialized in divination. Cato forbids his steward to receive at home a haruspex, an augur, a diviner, a Chaldean astrologer, not for religious reasons, but in order to avoid needless expenses, as in the same paragraph, he forbids his steward to have a *parasitus*, one of those costly house-guests known primarily from comedy.[71] The Romans did not confound these specialists with sorcerers; only in the poetic universe of Virgil's eighth *Eclogue*, a Chaldean practices erotic magic as well. Only once, outside poetry, does one have the impression of being in Grecian country. In 186 B.C., the Roman authorities took measures against Bacchic mysteries; it became a famous affair. According to Livy, our main source, the mysteries (in which *venena* played a certain role) had been imported by a *sacrificulus ac vates*—an *agúrtēs kaì mántis*, in the terms of Plato. But we should not press this: Livy seems to use a ready-made expression, while deleterious magic, important in Plato, is absent from the Roman account.[72]

History of Magic in Pliny the Elder

About a century after Cicero, the situation completely changed; witness the brief history of magic that Pliny the Elder puts at the beginning of book 30 of his *Natural History*. From its beginning, he vehemently accuses the *magicae vanitates*, the "vain beliefs in magic." It is more or less the terminology of the Greeks: *magicus* is a polemical term, as in Heraclitus or Sophocles; magic is *fraudulentissima artium*, "the most deceitful of all the arts."[73] It is worth the trouble to take a closer look at these chapters of Pliny, because we shall see that he develops a conception widely different from that of Republican Rome. Although the text is fueled by different sources, primarily Greek (Pliny quotes a whole series of authors), the overall view expresses Pliny's own time and own personality.

Pliny begins by describing the origin of the *magicae vanitates* in two very distinct steps. In the first step, he outlines how magic came into being. It was born of the combination of three *artes*, medicine, religion, and astrology (XXX, 1); and it is medicine that is found at the origin of magic. That fact, however, does not mean that Pliny considers the practices of the kind attested to by Cato as being at the origin of magic; rather often in his work, he speaks of them without any pejorative connotation. Pliny distinguishes between two ways of healing—*medicina*, true medicine, and *magia*, the false and arrogant medicine—and he defines the latter as a medicine that claims to be higher and better anchored in the divine (*altiorem sanctioremque medicinam*). The tone is close to that of the author of the treatise *On the sacred disease*, thundering against the itinerant priests who claim to know more than the others and who make a display of religiosity in order to hide their ignorance. Only, it is characteristic for Pliny that in other parts of his work he recommends *magorum remedia*, in case all other remedies should fail.[74] Thus, magic originates from that part of healing which only pretended to be real medicine;[75] Pliny does not describe a historical evolution, but rather projects the prejudices of his own time and class upon history (not so much different from what Frazer did).

As a second element, *magia*-medicine appropriated the power of *religio* "to which even today the human race remains most blind." What the term *religio* is aimed at here goes beyond the limits of what religion is for us (the term "religion" is modern, anyway).[76] Rather, it is religious fervor, an excessive religiosity—

called also *superstitio*—used by magic to achieve its own ends; often enough, the magician uses religious means, where other people would act more pragmatically. Finally, there is astrology, *artes mathematicas*, referring to the well-attested divinatory function of magic: Pliny insists on this aspect.

These three components formed magic in the Persia of Zoroaster, where up to Pliny's own day it has reigned as undisputed master (XXX, 2). Starting with Persia, Pliny traces its growth in time, plainly impressed by its lengthy past (six thousand years before the death of Plato) and the tenacity of such a tradition, which is not conveyed either by writings or by the institutionalized and stable school: "At first glance it is surprising that these memories and this art have survived for such a long period in the absence of any writing in this period and beyond, without the tradition being maintained by well-known and persistent intermediaries" (XXX, 4).

Magic thus has a fundamental unity that was preserved throughout its diffusion over the centuries—from Persia to the Greeks, to the Carians of Telmessus, to the Jews and the Cypriots, then to the people of Italy, to the Gauls, and to the Britons. In this vast panorama, magic includes Circe, Proteus, and even the sirens of Homer, as well as the Thessalian witches who draw down the moon. It includes that knowledge that Pythagoras, Empedocles, Democritus, and Plato went to seek in Persia, a knowledge that Democritus discussed even in writings. Moreover, magic also includes the legislation of the Twelve Tables, human sacrifices, and the art of the Druids, prohibited by Tiberius but surviving and flourishing at the end of the world, among the *Britanni,* a circumstance that inspires this patriotic commentary by Pliny: "And we cannot sufficiently assess our debt to the Romans for having abolished these monstrosities in which to kill a man was a religious act and to eat him was also a very salubrious practice" (XXX 13).

In the overall picture drawn by Pliny, magic assumes a certain number of fundamental features. First of all, it is something foreign and non-Roman; of Persian origin, it is from the outside that it arrived in Italy where, moreover, it no longer plays a large role: "It is also certain that magic has left traces among the Italian countries," notes Pliny, but none of the examples he gives is recent (XXX, 12). On the other hand, Pliny does not share the twofold attitude that he finds in some of his predecessors. The Greek philosophers who allowed themselves to be charmed by magic are denounced just as harshly as Nero, who had himself initiated by the *magi*. The philosophers, from Pythagoras to Democritus, are the victims of a "mad desire for knowledge"— their travels were not visits of their own free will, but rather exiles into a barbarous world; Pliny expresses as much astonishment at the behavior of these philosophers as he does irony with regard to Nero's attitude. Finally, in Pliny's eyes, of those two functions that magic claims to take over, medicine and divination, the central function is that of divination; that is why he likens to it the diviner Proteus and the Telmessians, whose fame for divination he stresses;[77] human sacrifices also must have a divinatory function.[78] Nero himself was impelled toward magic by curiosity; Pliny relates the anecdotes about Nero to the typology established by Osthanes, who made magic a category of divination and according to which the different divinatory procedures—from lecanomancy, divination with the help of a reflecting water-bowl, to necromancy, divination with the help of a deceased person's ghost—are related to magic (XXX, 14).

There is something surprising in Pliny's position. The two functions that magic fulfills (or seems to fulfill: after all, it is deceptive)—healing and divination—do not correspond either to what we have just examined for the republican era, in which neither healing nor divination was part of *carmina mala*, or to the

Greek facts of the fifth or fourth century, in which *mageía* included magic as well as private initiations in order to allay fears of the next world. Nor do these functions correspond to magic in the imperial epoch according to the image that we get from the papyri and inscriptions. Certainly, healing and especially divination of all kinds are important here, but the black magic of the *defixiones* and the erotic practices are more predominant. Even if the special status of erotic magic is taken into account, to be spared, like weather magic, by the sanction of the Roman laws, the absence of black magic—so important in Plato's eyes and so easy to attack—surprises.[79]

Pliny does not always pass over these practices in silence. In book XXX, 3, he refers his reader to the Twelve Tables and "to what I discussed in the preceding volume." In reality, this reference is to book XXVIII, where he speaks of the Twelve Tables and of a whole series of maleficent practices: the ritual binding by maleficent prayers; the *incantamenta amatoria*, imitated by Theocritus, Catullus, and Virgil; the magical destruction of jars in the potter's kiln; the *carmina* of the Marsi against snakes; and even the ritual *evocatio* and the measures against it, including the secret name of Rome.[80] Thus, we find a certain tension between books XXVIII and XXX, but it must be stressed that only in the latter book does Pliny use an unambiguous terminology, whereas, in the case of the *evocatio* of book XXVIII, he makes reference, certainly free of negative connotations, to the discipline of the *pontifices*.[81]

Our surprise grows when we take a look at the accusations of magic under the Julio-Claudian dynasty, which Tacitus recalls and of which, after others, Raffaella Garosi drew up an inventory.[82] Of the ten accusations in which magic plays a role, there are three for which the nature of the magic is not specified (*magicae superstitiones, magorum sacra*), two that belong to magic divination, and five—thus half—that concern malevolent magic.

This latter type of magic was practiced either in private (the case of Numantina—a fine example of intraconjugal magic—who "caused, by incantations and poisons, the insanity of her husband"), or against the public sphere (as with Servilia, daughter of Barea Soranus, who was accused of "having spent money for magical rites," presumably in a classic case of judicial *defixio*, spells against Nero who was conducting a trial against Soranus).[83] Although injurious magic was in full swing during the era in which Pliny the Elder lived, he almost completely leaves it out of his account of magic in book XXX of his *Natural History.*

On the other hand, the association of magic and astrology, which has a central place in Pliny's theory—and which is rather surprising when we remember the solely ritual function of Greek magic, in healing, binding, and initiation—refers to a real preoccupation of the era. Here again the trials attest to it. In two cases, the consultation of the Chaldeans is accompanied by magic rites. Lollia Paulina was accused of having sought from astrologers information about Claudius's life expectation, in connection with his wedding. In the other case, which is the first in chronological order and which concerns Drusus Libo, the interest in astrology was mixed with necromancy and the wish to revolt against the emperor; its consequence was the expulsion of the Chaldeans and the *magi.*[84]

Once again, the definitions are not those that we would expect, and the terms are far from being clear-cut. First, there is everything covered by the term *veneficium*, to wit, the violation of a person's integrity by secret means, a charge that figures next to open armed violence in the *lex Cornelia de sicariis and veneficis.* Pliny is not sure whether it is truly a matter of real *magia*, and Tacitus constantly speaks of *veneficium* without making use of a more modern (and less ambiguous for us) terminology. Later, the jurists decided to integrate with the delinquency of *veneficium* the *magia* in its non-Roman aspect of a technique (*ars*) practiced by specialists and contained in books. At the beginning of the third century A.D., the jurist Paul informs us that the law also punished the possession of magic books and the accomplices in magic practices.[85] This clear position fits into the movement that was to lead the term *magia* from the sense of "divination" to that of "harmful practices." In the middle of the fourth century A.D., this movement ended in a new change of terminology; although the official term remained *magus*, the word in common use had become *maleficus*, "he who does evil."[86] This changed terminology did not affect the theory where divination always stayed an important part of magic—so much so that in the influential encyclopedia of Isidore of Seville, magic nearly coincides with divination; given the importance that Isidore's books had, this definition lived on until the high middle ages.[87]

On the other hand, there is that set of medical and astrological practices that Pliny calls magic. This magic is a science, *scientia* or *ars*, as Pliny clearly states, a science that possesses a scholarly tradition, with a host of books and foreign specialists. At the beginning of the empire, at least, there existed no particular legislation against these specialists;[88] nevertheless, they were deported from Italy every time that a private individual made use of their art for the purpose of meddling in the affairs of the state—whether it was a matter of knowing whether one's political ambitions were successful or of informing oneself of the destiny of the prince.

It can be stated differently. In fact, the knowledge of the *magi* was supposed to be limited normally to the private sphere—to divination concerning the destiny of the individual, whatever the person's importance—and also, as Pliny clearly indicates, to the "magical" treatment of illnesses. In these cases, no one intervened, and every person was free to talk with the *magi* as one would have done with the Greek philosophers. That is the reason why the medical side of the *magia* is never mentioned by Tacitus, and why there is no accusation on the lone charge of *magia*. It was only when by means of *magia* one tried to obtain information concerning public affairs, that things changed. The reason is that the state had a monopoly on divination that no private individual could touch. Therefore, in the two cases that are cited by Tacitus and that do not concern black magic, we see the accusation of consulting *magi* combined with the accusation of high treason: it was not enough to accuse someone of consulting the *magi*.[89]

Historical Evolution in Rome

The Roman conception of "magic" developed in two stages. In the first stage, under the republic, the Romans distinguished between practices that attacked the integrity of persons or their property by ritual means (*malum carmen, in-, excantare, malum venenum, veneficium*) and other practices without malevolent intention, although rather similar in appearance. The word *magia* does not occur, and nothing suggests that the Romans considered these practices foreign—with the exception of some stories about the snake charming Marsi that do not concern us here.[90]

In the second, Julio-Claudian stage, everything changed. The crime of *veneficium* continued to exist, and it became important through interpretation of the Lex Cornelia, although it was not yet systematically associated with *magia*. This term, on the other hand, combines medicine and astrology, and its divinatory function is essential; it is without any doubt a foreign thing, as the Greek terminology indicates. While Pliny reconstructs the history and routes of its distribution, the senate never hesitated to deport the foreign specialists, the carriers of this art, from Italy.

Such are the facts.[91] Explaining them is more difficult. The most important event seems to be that the Hellenized Roman elite took over the Greek term for magic, with which this elite partly associated the old beliefs in *veneficium* and the recipes of the traditional medicine, and especially the new divinatory technique of astrology. This new astrology had to be a much more sophisticated art than that of the Chaldeans who presented themselves at the door of Cato's steward. It met the new demands of an individualized elite that was cut off from its traditions and thereby from its old system of divination (as Cicero attests).[92]

Certainly, this is a matter of assertions rather than proofs, the latter being hard to produce. However, a certain number of cases reveal this amalgam of Roman traditions with the new, Hellenized thought in the elite milieus of the ending republic.

The first is a case of literary stratification. We have already spoken of the *excantationes*, the seized and transported harvests mentioned in the Twelve Tables: a violation of property rights that neither Pliny nor the texts of the laws describe as magic. We also mentioned the neoteric poets who used the Greek term *magia* with a learned connotation, unrelated to the Roman realities. Only the incantation Virgil depicts, in his eighth eclogue, is more complex. At the beginning, he gives as the aim of the erotic incantation "to try by magic rites to turn aside my lover's reason" (*coniugis ut magicis sanos avertere sacris experiar sensus*, l. 66); then, the sorceress indicates where the substances she uses come from—her herbs and her "poisons picked in the Pontus," the country of that archwitch Medea, and given by Moeris in person, who had found them highly effective:

> *his ego saepe lupum fieri et se condere silvis*
> *Moerim, saepe animas imis exciri sepulcris*
> *atque satas alio vidi traducere messis.*[93]

I saw Moeris, thanks to them, often change into a wolf and go deep into the woods, often raise the souls of the dead from the bottom of graves and transport the crops on foot to another field.

Lycanthropy and necromancy are topics of Greek literature (Herodotus already mentions the lycanthropy of the *mágoi*).[94] The conveyance of crops is a Roman theme from the reality of the law-courts, as the Twelve Tables show with which Servius connects it. Virgil's combining both topics shows that in his mind, the old *carmina* of the Twelve Tables and Greek magic were somehow connected.

There is, on the other hand, the *lex Cornelia*, which appeared at a precise moment in Roman history. We can imagine the necessity, at the end of the decade marked by the civil war between Marius and Sulla, of a legislation suppressing armed violence. Less do we see the necessity for punishing the *venefici*— or had this sort of crime become common and suspicions of poisoning and magic more frequent? That situation is what a certain number of indicators suggest—rather few of them, it is true. First, there is the frequency of the *defixiones* found on Roman soil. In the still-indispensable catalog compiled by Audollent, there is no Latin *defixio* from the urbs prior to the end of the republic—though given that the private inscriptions of the republican era are not very numerous, and that we know several *defixiones* from late Archaic southern Italy, we must not rely on it too much.[95] In any case, two generations later, Pliny the Elder judges the risk of being a victim of a binding spell to be very real.[96] More revealing is the attitude of Cicero, the witness to the first accusation of ritual binding in Rome. In *Brutus* he remembers an affair of the year 79 B.C., which concerned C. Scribonius Curio: "One day when in a very important private case I had pleaded for Titinia, a client of Cotta, Curio's turn having come to speak against me on behalf of Servius Naevius, he completely forgot everything he had to say; he said the blame was due to the incantations and spells of Titinia."[97] This is a nearly classic case of judicial magic, many times attested to by the leaden tablets from Attica and elsewhere, and where the adversary binds the tongue of his enemy so that the latter is no longer able to plead in court. We know of another spectacular case, this time told for the purpose, not to accuse, but to praise the divinity responsible for it: when some enemies of the Delian priest of Sarapis had brought him to court, the god tied their tongues—and the accused went free.[98] Cicero hints that he considered the accusation as a poor pretext for his colleague whose poor memory was notorious. It remains true that to be believable, a lie must necessarily be anchored in reality and must correspond to some widespread belief that is neither too absurd nor too marginal. It is obvious, therefore, that in Cicero's lifetime, at least some members of the ruling class believed in magic. It is impossible to say when this fear and this belief became widespread, but it suggests that the clause against *veneficium* in the *lex Cornelia* also met a need.

The third clue is the least certain, but the most important, if the hypothesis proves correct. In book II of the *Laws*, Cicero discusses (among other subjects) religious legislation. One law draws our attention; it concerns the secret rites: *nocturna mulierum sacrificia ne sunto praeter olla quae pro populo fient. neve quem initianto nisi ut adsolet Cereri Graeco sacro.* (Let there be no sacrifices at night by women with the exception of those made for the people, and let them not initiate anyone with the exception of the traditional initiations for Ceres, according to the Greek rite.)[99] Nocturnal sacrifices performed by women are surprising and somewhat unclear. The text suggests mysteries; the presence of only women in any case rules out those of Dionysus and of Isis—what private rites remain as target for the prohibition imagined by Cicero? Would it not be necessary to think of the magic sacrifices—nearly always nocturnal, and often a concern of women (at least in the fears expressed by men)? Whatever the case is, later, in connection with the interpretation of the *lex Cornelia*, the lawyer Paul mentions the same prohibition in a context of injurious magic, and the emperors Valentinian and Valens forbid "impious prayers, magic rites and sacrifices to the dead during night-time."[100] The Ciceronian law thus already testified to this anxiety, which one would be tempted to relate to the *lex Cornelia*. Cicero, moreover, also points to one basis for the legislative prohibition; it is the people and the senate that have the monopoly on strange rites, and they want to control the ritual behavior of the marginal group of women.

3

PORTRAIT OF THE MAGICIAN,
SEEN FROM THE OUTSIDE

WHO IS THE MAGICIAN, that figure as changing as the content of his art, in turn diviner, priest, doctor, charlatan, philosopher, or charismatic "godlike man"? What did the magician do in ancient societies? More than eighty years ago, in his fundamental essay on magic, Marcel Mauss formulated a general rule: "It is . . . public opinion that creates the magician and the influences he has. The individuals to whom the practice of magic is attributed already have . . . a distinct condition within the society that treats them as magicians."[1] If this is true, it is necessary to ask what opinion the Greeks and Romans had of the magician. How did they recognize and define the magician, and how did they distinguish this figure from other fairly similar but less detested figures? In an attempt to analyze the person as seen from the outside, we can focus on two magic trials, one that took place in Rome under the republic, and the other that occurred in Africa, in the middle of the second century of the empire.

We recall the law of the Twelve Tables and the threats that it expresses against all those who "by their songs (or charms) would take away the harvest of a neighbor." We know of only a single trial in which this law played a role. Pliny the Elder speaks of it, following Calpurnius Piso, the annalist of the second half of the second century B.C.[2]

The story appears simple. One man regularly obtained a harvest much larger than that of his neighbors. Thus, people began to envy him and even to hate him (*in invidia erat magna:* the Latin gives both senses). One day this man finds himself accused of having appropriated the harvest of others by unlawful practices. Pliny's wording of the charge—*fruges alienas perliceret veneficiis*—rather faithfully reproduces the text of the law of the Twelve Tables in the version of Servius, with the exception of the term *veneficia*, which is too recent.[3] But the text is worth taking a closer look at.

Pliny's account does not come from book XXX, his history of magic, but from a context concerned with the virtues of the ancestral Roman farmers; his interest here is not sorcery, but *mores maiorum,* the agricultural virtue of the ancient farmers whom the Romans were proud of having once been. This is how he tells the story:

> I cannot resist reporting an example taken from antiquity, which can show that the custom was of presenting before the people even affairs concerning agriculture and how the men of that time defended themselves. C. Furius Cresimus, a freedman, reaped from a small field harvests much more abundant than his neighbors with vast properties; so he was much envied and suspected of having attracted the harvests of others by evil spells. Summoned for this reason before Spurius Albinus, the curulian edil,

and afraid of being convicted by the voting of the *tribus*, he brought all his farming equipment to the forum and all his slaves, sturdy and, as Piso says, very well-groomed and well-dressed people, well-made tools, heavy pickaxes, weighty plowshares, well-fed cattle. Then he said, "These are my evil spells, citizens, and I cannot show you or bring to the forum my nights of work, my watches, and my sweat." So he was unanimously acquitted.

Pliny explicitly names two participants in the trial, the town councillor, Spurius Albinus, and the otherwise unknown hero, C. Furius Cresimus. It has been proposed to identify the town councillor with Spurius Postumius Albinus, consul in 186 B.C. and praetor three years earlier, thus placing the event in the first decade of the second century B.C. The identification has been disputed, but nothing prevents dating this affair to the first half of the second century B.C. Pliny stresses the low social standing of C. Furius Cresimus: he is a freedman, literally *e servitute liberatus*, a man freed from slavery (a curiously high-flown and nontechnical expression). He must be of eastern origin, since he bears a common Greek name, Chresimos, which became his cognomen upon gaining his emancipation. His adversaries are clearly rich people, of a much higher social condition; we are thus in the presence of a considerable social distance, a situation more likely than any other to produce conflicts.

The conflict breaks out at the moment when year after year (Pliny suggests a certain duration), the harvest of Cresimus's small farm does not tally with his social standing, a situation that, given the competition between unequal rivals, constitutes a reversal of the original gap; the poor man, the freedman, threatens to become rich, even richer than the others, thereby endangering the social structures. At this point, others react. The marginal one, who does not seem to abide by the rules of the game, is accused of *incantamenta*, because his so-threatening success can be due only to unlawful means. Confronted with the risk of a social turnabout, the others in turn respond by another reversal: they change the farmer into a sorcerer.

This accusation must not be taken lightly. We do not know exactly what penalty was risked by the person judged guilty of an *incantamentum.* This person would certainly have been cast out of the society, as was (much later) stipulated in the *lex Cornelia,* either by exile or by death.[4] Cresimus thus prepares himself the best he can. The trial takes place in the forum, and Pliny stresses the public nature as well as the participation of the *tribus,* the "tribe" to which Cresimus belonged. There is thus a confrontation between Cresimus and the whole of the society, represented by the tribal association, while the magistrate serves as mediator. Cresimus succeeds in convincing his group that his success resulted not from magic but from the good quality of his work.

What kind of arguments did he use in his defense? Pliny says it with a certain pomposity: Cresimus presents himself as a more industrious farmer than the others. He knew how to prove that he, too, the former eastern slave, had those virtues of which the Romans were so proud, and that he had more of them than the others had. Hence, a new gap opens, thus reversing once again the social relation between the freedman and the rich citizens; it is the former slave from the east who appears to be a truly perfect Roman. The reaction on the part of the tribus is immediate and unanimous; his fellow citizens acknowledge his explanations and are willing to redintegrate him. In addition, he acquires such a renown that Pliny still remembers him as a fine example of ancient virtues.

A person who was accused of magic was thus one on the margins of society, who, through his or her actions, set off a process that seemed to threaten the social structures; that person's success provoked a crisis within the group. The goal of the trial for magic is to resolve the crisis, either by permanently casting out the one who threatened the social structures or by definitively integrating that person. In either case, the social structures will be reaffirmed and order reestablished. Through this trial for magic and this game of shifts, someone from the outside—provided the person gains a trial—is firmly and definitely integrated into the society; from the fringes, that person was settled inside.

AN AFRICAN DRAMA: THE TRIAL OF APULEIUS AT SABRATHA

Between 156 and 158 A.D., Apuleius, a young orator and Platonic philosopher, born in an imperial Africa rich in talented men, had to appear before the proconsul Claudius Maximus, who then governed the African province and held his court of law in Sabratha. Apuleius pleaded as lawyer for his wife, Pudentilla. In the course of this trial, his adversaries reproached him for being a magician. In the face of the enormity of this reproof, Apuleius dared them to accuse him formally. They did so, and Apuleius became the defendant in a trial for magic. Five or six days after the first accusation, still in Sabratha, the trial of Apuleius took place, in which he defended himself, obviously with success. His defense has come down to us through his writings—in his *Apologia sive de magia*.[5]

Here lies the first problem that faces the historian. What we have is a literary text published after the trial. Nothing suggests the amount of alteration that the original defense may have undergone; we must rely on that text, which is in any case carefully worked out and full of learned information. Such an elaboration may be surprising, especially when we realize that the original defense must have been written in barely a few days, with the possible help of a private library. The same kind of problem is posed for the speeches of Cicero. We sometimes know how much time and work lie between the actual speech of Cicero and its subsequent publication. The case of Apuleius, the sophist, is no better; it is unlikely that he did not rework the wording of his speech. Worse yet is that for the speeches of Cicero, we often have other sources, whereas for everything concerning the details of the African trial, Apuleius remains our sole witness. But we have no other choice than to rely cautiously on this text.

The accusation is clear and simple: (1) Apuleius is accused of *magica maleficia,* and (2) his adversary insists on the *crimen magiae;* Apuleius will repeat the word *magia* many times. Although here he does not use the more technical term *veneficium* (which, however, appears further on, in chapter 78), it is, without a doubt, the *lex Cornelia de sicariis et veneficis* that is at issue. Apuleius's situation must have been beset with danger. In 199 A.D., the prefect of Egypt threatened with capital punishment those who indulged in divination, magic or otherwise, and the jurist Paul— if he is indeed the author of the *Sentences*—attests to the existence of this charge at the start of the third century A.D.[6] Nevertheless, it seems clear that Apuleius sought the trial in order to be cleared of the suspicion of being a magician; rumors must have spread for a time in Oea, a situation which, in such a small town, could not fail to be embarrassing or even dangerous.

Apuleius's defense allows a glimpse of how his adversaries had formulated the charge: Apuleius was accused of erotic magic. The chief testimony is a passage from a letter written in Greek (in that corner of Africa, people were at the least bilingual) by Pudentilla, a letter in which she ironically echoes the accusations made by her son against Apuleius: "Thus it happened that all of a sudden, Apuleius became a magician, and I was bewitched by him and I am in love."[7] The letter had been written before the marriage of Pudentilla and Apuleius; these accusations and rumors had been abroad for some time.

To get a good understanding of the accusation, we need to reproduce the background of this affair in its setting, that of a small provincial town.

Apuleius, a native of Madaurus (the Algerian Mdaourouch, in the region of Constantine), had studied at the Athenian Academy. If we are to believe an allusion slipped into the *Metamorphoses*, his teacher was Sextus, the nephew of Plutarch. Apuleius's own works all reveal this Platonic education, in which, however, are mixed certain Aristotelian elements.[8] He is proud of this lineage and held the title of *philosophus Platonicus*, as is attested on the sole inscription in his honor that has been preserved for us.[9]

After his studies and some journeys, Apuleius returned to Africa. During one trip to Alexandria, he visited some friends in the little town of Oea. When he fell ill there, a friend from his years in Athens, Sicinius Pontianus, looked after him, invited him into his home, and healed him. This thoughtfulness, it seems, was not altogether lacking in ulterior motives. Pontianus had a widowed mother, whose age is discussed in the defense without exact numbers being indicated (but she cannot have been more than forty). Pontianus had the idea of marrying her to his friend. At first Apuleius refused, but he stayed on in the house as a tutor to a younger brother, Sicinius Pudens; and inevitably, a friendship developed between this still-young widow, Aemilia Pudentilla, and the young philosopher. They studied together (which is not without interest for the intellectual history of Roman women), and finally the marriage was decided on.

Now the villains come onstage. Aemilia Pudentilla was not only intelligent and attractive, but also very rich—a matter of some four million sesterces. After the death of her husband, the father-in-law, Sicinius Amicus, who wished Pudentilla's fortune to stay in the family, had proposed another of his sons, Sicinius

Clarus, as a new husband. Pudentilla had successfully opposed this attempt, as she was opposed to all the advances of the town's leading citizens, and above all to the advances of the third Sicinius brother, Aemilianus. Of this brother, prototype of the villain, Apuleius has left a dark and repellent portrait. In the midst of these small-town quarrels and intrigue, the philosopher comes onstage, worldly but ill, who takes hold of the widow and, above all, the fortune.

Rumors of *magica maleficia* begin at the moment that the marriage is planned. Pontianus himself seems to have believed the rumors; but according to Apuleius, it is without any doubt a matter of sinister machinations set in motion by Sicinius Aemilianus, aided by a certain Herrenius Rufinus, Pontianus's father-in-law, who was, of course, as motivated by those millions as was his son-in-law.

This story deserves attention. As in the case of C. Furius Cresimus, the underlying issue here is a challenge to the social structure; and again, we find rivalry, with rather unequal competitors. On the one hand, there are the members of the family of the Sicinii, well-established in the area and no doubt prosperous; on the other hand, there is the foreign philosopher, a marginal figure—both as a foreigner and as a philosopher—whom his adversaries blamed for his poverty at the same time that they accused him of homosexuality, another marginal trait in this society. Here again, this rival walked off with the victory and the prize (the millions, not to speak of the woman); thus, the society and its categories are in danger. In accusing him of magic, Apuleius's adversaries tried to explain this reversal of fortunes. We must take seriously their beliefs, which Pontianus himself, though trained in Platonistic philosophy, held. Mainly, by laying the charge of magic, the adversaries were trying to incite the very closed society of this town to get rid of an element that threatened the established structures; the situation was not without its dangers. The aggressiveness of all persons concerned still speaks to us from Apuleius's account of how Herennius Rufinus had, for the first time, accused him of magic: "This trafficker of his wife was swollen with such anger, in such a blazing rage, that he uttered against the purest and most chaste of women . . . talk worthy of his own bedroom . . . calling her a prostitute, me, a magician and sorcerer (and this in the presence of many persons, whom I shall name, if you wish); he would kill me with his own hands."[10] Rufinus makes use of a quasi-technical description (*magus et veneficus*), which calls to mind the *lex Cornelia*, and he also makes his accusation *pluribus audientibus*: the affair concerns not just the two men. The final threat—to kill Apuleius with Rufinus's own hands—sounds as if he wished to anticipate the capital punishment laid down by the *lex Cornelia*.

Unlike the freedman Cresimus, the philosopher Apuleius did not try to integrate or reintegrate himself into the town's society. This fact is shown by the rhetorical strategy of his *Apologia*. Apuleius right away explains that he considers his plea not a private defense, but rather a defense of philosophy. He announces in his second sentence, "I am pleased with it, I declare it, at having, before a judge such as you, the opportunity and the good fortune of justifying philosophy to laymen and of exculpating me myself."[11] And, later on, "I defend not only my own cause, but that of philosophy."[12] Next, he tries in the first chapters to establish that he is a philosopher by skillfully repeating the start of the charge: "You thus a little while ago heard how this accusation began: 'We accuse before you a philosopher, good-looking and—abominable crime!—of an equal eloquence in Greek and in Latin.' It is, if I am not mistaken, with these very words that Tannonius Pudens began his indictment against me."[13] Then, in the course of this defense, several times he clearly contrasts magic and philosophy.

This strategy requires that he clearly mark himself off from his adversaries. He implies that they are *imperiti*, uninitiated laymen; that their lawyers are not eloquent, but *stulti*; and that Aemilianus himself is only a rustic with no education, a considerable exaggeration, for Apuleius leaks the information that Aemilianus himself pleaded in Rome on the forum. He intimates that Pontianus's father-in-law is a debauched old man and that the mother-in-law is an old prostitute . . .

Correspondingly, all along his defense, Apuleius tries to link himself with the proconsul Claudius Maximus. The proconsul, who has had a philosophical education, knows his Plato ("The very words of that divine man are still in my memory: let me recall them to you, Maximus"), his Aristotle ("You denounce as a crime in me what Maximus and I admire in Aristotle"); he has read the philosophers of old, and he is in possession of their wisdom: in short, he is, like Apuleius, a philosopher.[14] From the reference to his *austera secta*, it has been inferred that he was a Stoic; we know of a Stoic named Claudius Maximus: he was Marcus Aurelius's philosophy teacher, and there exists, among scholars, a certain tendency to identify the philosopher with the proconsul, who was also governor of the Upper Pannonia between 150 and 154 A.D.[15]

Moreover, Apuleius goes to a lot of trouble not to appear a beggar philosopher, but rather a good citizen. After a long digression on philosophical poverty, in which he glorifies the sack and the cloak typical of the philosopher, he stresses that he comes from a well-to-do family, that his father and he himself, after his father's death, were *duoviri principis*, priests in the imperial cult of their hometown, a dignity open only to the local elite. He manifestly does not wish to appear to be one of those itinerant philosophers of cynical extraction who, in his epoch, were not too well thought of.[16]

For Apuleius, the problem, obviously, is not the fellow citizens of the little town of Oea. His goal is not that of integrating himself into the provincial society, but of establishing himself as a member of that elite of the itinerant intellectuals of the imperial society, which was not too different from the elite— also itinerant and nearly as intellectual—of the senatorial admin- istrators of the Empire.[17] His concern is not merely a matter of private aspirations of the cosmopolitan Apuleius; the facts of the juridical system of the High Empire leave him no other choice. It is significant that the trial is not conducted in the agora of Oea, amidst the citizens, but before the proconsul in another town some sixty miles away. Although a certain number of citizens of Oea attend the trial, it is not the affair of their community, and they cannot influence its unfolding; the trial is entirely in the hands of the proconsul and his *consilium*. The society that threatened to make Apuleius a sorcerer has no occasion to take an active part in the proceedings. This new asymmetry gives rise to obvious dangers; how can a position be regained in a group that tried to resolve the imbalance by trying to resort to expulsion but that does not have the power either to reestablish a new balance or to resolve the crisis by its own means? Neither Oea nor Apuleius did manage to resolve the difficulty, for we find him some years later with his wife, well established as an orator in Carthage.

Apuleius's defense, which is rich in information, enlightens us not just about his private affairs. It is a crucial text for under- standing the image of the sorcerer in his society and for per- ceiving the very clear distinctions among the magician, the philosopher, and the doctor assumed by this defense—presum- ably against a society that tended to blur these distinctions.[18]

To find and analyze the features of magic activity as Apuleius's fellow citizens represent it, we must examine the whole of the accusation as Apuleius presents it to us.

After a long introduction (which barely touches on the prob- lem of magic), Apuleius finally reaches those details that he long ago promised to clear up: "That said, consistent with my plan, I go on to examine all the insanities uttered by Aemilianus here present. And first, you have noticed it, what was raised at the beginning as being the most likely to confirm the suspicion of magic, is that I paid the fishermen to procure me certain species of fish."[19] Apuleius does not deny this accusation but, on the contrary, amplifies it: all his friends, all his slaves received the order to bring him any fish—alive or dead—that seemed to them out of the ordinary. But the explanation that he gives is very innocent: Apuleius was writing a treatise on fishes and their procreation. As a decisive proof, he has some passages from the treatise read before the court.

Now his adversaries had been more precise. They had mentioned three species of fish—the *lepos marinus* (the "sea hare"), a poisonous fish, and two kinds of fish whose names echo the words for the male and female sexual organs. Apuleius pokes fun at the obvious difficulty of the lawyers, who have to pronounce these touchy words (it is one of those passages that suggest that the construction of Norbert Elias would at the very least need to be modified to take account of ancient societies): in his society, a free and easy way of using sexual terms was a sign of culture. Adam Abt, in his detailed commentary on the magic part of the *Apologia*, proved that the two Latin names proposed by Apuleius, *veretillum et virginal*, not attested to elsewhere, can repeat the Greek words *bálanos* ("gland") and *kteís* ("comb"), which have an obvious sexual connotation (obvious in the case of "gland," whereas "comb" in Greek also denotes the female organ), but have no parallels in the world of magicians.

What is more important to us than these vagaries is to understand how these African bourgeois imagined the function of magic, especially when Apuleius claims (and we have no way to contradict him) that it was in fact not just those specific fishes that he was seeking.

Concerning the *lepos marinus*, which actually is not a fish, but a large marine slug, it suffices to know that it is very poisonous. The person who uses it must therefore be a *veneficus* and consequently becomes guilty according to the *lex Cornelia*. The ancients told terrifying tales about this animal: Pliny the Elder ranks the *lepos* from the Indian Ocean with the *araneus* and the *pastinaca* (the stingray) among the most poisonous marine animals; a single contact with it caused immediate vomiting. In his *Life of Apollonius of Tyana*, Philostratus reports that the young prince Titus died of the poison made from a *lepos* and administered by Domitian—a death predicted by Apollonius, who had warned him "against death from the sea." Philostratus adds that Nero too had often rid himself of his enemies thanks to the *lepos* served in a course of seafood.[20]

One detail proves that the accusers really suspected a *veneficium*. It is only in the case of the *lepos* that they insist on the fact that Apuleius cut up the fish—an insistence that offends Apuleius, who was in the habit of cutting up fish for the purpose, of course, of making anatomical examinations.[21] For the accusers, however, cutting up any old fish was not the same thing as cutting up the sea hare; in their minds the latter was cut up only in order to collect the poison.

Regarding the two "sexual" fish, Apuleius is very clear on the motivation for these choices. To his accusers, the verbal association would suggest the use of these fish for erotic magic, which the philosopher finds stupid: "What indeed could be sillier than to conclude, from a relationship between words, qualities of the same order as between things?"[22] But this is a philosophical polemic rather than an account of the truth. We indeed know enough about plants, animals, or even stones to which popular medicine or magic attributed a property derived from their name, although it is sometimes hard to decide whether the name preceded or followed the usage. It is enough to cite the example, taken from Pliny, of the reseda or mignonette, whose etymology is discussed by linguists, but whose name was popularly connected with the verb *resedare*, "to soothe an illness." This purpose gave rise to a beautiful rite: "In the vicinity of Rimini, a plant is known which they call reseda. It clears up abscesses and all inflammations. Those who use it add these words: 'Reseda, be the sedative of illnesses. Do you know, do you know what chicken [perhaps, or: what sprout] planted its roots here? That it has no head or feet.' Three times they repeat this formula and three times they spit on the ground."[23] It is a fine testimony on the force of oral rites; the cure would not work if one ate the reseda without adding the words. Repetition and wordplay *(reseda, reseda morbos)* differentiate the spell from ordinary spoken language. The triple repetition of the rite is characteristic (and commonplace): a single repetition may be due to chance rather than to the desire for the repetition; since four times is already too many, we are left with three.

Let us return to Apuleius. There is another problem yet to be solved. Although Abt mustered a dozen examples of similar wordplay, that does not prove that we are dealing with magic. The conviction that the names of things are related to their nature is deeply inscribed in Greco-Roman thought; we are acquainted with the debate, begun by the Sophists, on the relationship between words and substances. By inferring erotic magic solely from the fact that the philosopher was interested in fish with an erotic name (which is already a hypothesis on their part, one contradicted by Apuleius), his adversaries were following a mental habit that was widespread in antiquity and which is not peculiar to magic nor to the domain of popular medicine that we associate with it.

The problem of the origin of words, incidentally, is important to the subject under discussion here, magic. A surprising text proves that fact. In his long treatise against the pagan philosopher Celsus, the Christian apologist Origen attacks Celsus's assertion that the specific name of a divinity is absolutely without importance, because the same god could have different names according to the language spoken by the god's worshipers; this is a perfectly Greek, Herodotean conception. On this basis, Origen works out a general discussion on the problem of the divine name, and then on the problem of the origin of words. He compares three theories, that of Aristotle (for whom words, fixed by usage, had a purely accidental relation to things); the opposite theory of the Stoics (according to whom the first humans had, in the first words, consciously imitated the nature of things with their voices); and the intermediate theory, that of Epicurus, for whom the first men reacted to things more or less accidentally but all in the same way—languages were thus born both by convention and in a natural way. Origen chooses the Stoic solution—at least for "those efficacious names of which certain ones are in use among the sages of Egypt, the more learned among the magi of Persia, and the Brahmins or Samanaeans among the philosophers of India." He thus accepts the idea that some words are more powerful than others, words of Persian, Egyptian, or Indian origin. But Origen is not lecturing on eastern languages; instead, he is aiming at a well-known domain: magic with its strings of exotic words. These words are not inventions, but rather contain a profound rationality, so that "what is called magic is not, as the disciples of Epicurus and Aristotle think, an entirely incoherent practice but, as is proved by experts in this art, a coherent system of which few persons understand the principles."[24]

Apuleius has a different opinion. Before counting up the names of interesting Greek fish—a long series of learned and rare words—he jabs again at his adversaries: "Now listen carefully: you are going to shout that I am reciting a list of magic words drawn from Egyptian or Babylonian rites."[25]

In conclusion, from his interest in rare fish, an innocent and purely philosophical interest, after all, his opponents thus inferred practices of *veneficium* and erotic magic, relying on beliefs and opinions that were widespread in their epoch. In doing so, they had interpreted the philosopher's actions according to categories that were certainly different from his own, but which nonetheless were available in their time and society.

The same findings hold as to the other points of the accusation. The second argument was that a young boy and a woman fell into a trance, in the presence of Apuleius. In the case of the boy, Apuleius blames his adversaries for not having a precise knowledge of magic divination. Their account of the circumstances—incantations performed without witnesses, in a secret place with a small altar, a lamp, and in the presence of only a few close friends—had been correct; nevertheless, they were not sufficiently precise: "For the fable to be complete it would have been necessary to add that the same boy had revealed many things to come. For here is where we learn what creates the practical interest of the incantations: I mean the predictions and the oracles." And immediately, Apuleius reveals the source of his knowledge about these things, which is an account by the philosopher (*sic!*) Varro of an event that happened in Tralles during the wars against Mithridates and of a meeting organized by the Roman Pythagorean Nigidius Figulus, a story that also involved the younger Cato. Apuleius has no direct experience of such magical rites, but he is in a position to refer to some perfectly respectable Roman philosophers. Less respectably perhaps, he could also have cited a perfect parallel from the magical papyri.[26]

Once more, as in the case of the fish, Apuleius contrasts magic and science: the two victims were epileptic. Apuleius concentrates his scientific argument on the second case, that of a woman who had come to see him and who had an epileptic fit when visiting him. In this case, the proof was easily provided; Apuleius had obtained the testimony of the doctor who treated her and who himself had sent her to the philosopher for a second professional opinion. By means of a long quotation from Plato's *Timaeus*, Apuleius manages once again to prove that philosophers too were perfectly capable of giving an etiology of the illness.

Since the treatise *On the Sacred Disease*, the problem posed by epilepsy has been well-known. The writer-doctor of the Hippocratic treatise rejected the idea of a divine cause, which understood the illness as demonic possession; this demonic view justified the intervention of itinerant priests in the role of exorcists. A few centuries later, Plotinus, in his attack on magicians, invokes the same arguments.[27] The case of Apuleius is more complex. The accusers indeed do not seem to have known that young Thallus was epileptic. What seemed significant to them was that the presence of the philosopher had been enough to provoke the trance, in the course of a suggestive ritualistic setting, to which Apuleius later adds the sacrifice of a rooster or a chicken, *gallinas hostias*. He was even capable of giving a technical name to this ritual: he "initiated (the child) by an incantation."[28] The term *initiare*, "to initiate," is, however, a bit vague. In the magic context, the corresponding Greek verb, *mueísthai*, is most often encountered in connection with divinatory rites; the rooster sacrifice is even vaguer, but is also found in divinatory rites.[29] The story thus seems coherent.

The ritual evoked is, moreover, relatively commonplace. It is a nocturnal rite solemnized by a very small group. The magical rite is again defined in contrast to the common civic rite, because civic sacrifices take place during the day, with the participation of all the citizens, whereas the magicians use the night for their sinister rites—Heraclitus already called them "wizards who wander in the night."[30] This rite is conceived as a sacrifice, but with a rather uncommon victim: the rooster or hen hardly figures in the civic ritual. In Greece, it is the marginal healer Asclepius who receives the rooster, and this animal is sacrificed to the powers invoked in the rites of the papyri and *defixiones*.[31] Our Africans thus have a fairly precise knowledge of the nature of a magical sacrifice, although Apuleius is right to stress that the ritual or initiation as they described it would not have made sense.

The case of the woman, whose illness was well-known, seems less clear. Apuleius committed himself to taking care of her, but during the treatment she fainted—in the eyes of the accusers, she fell victim to a spell.[32] This whole affair has a whiff of exorcism, and this suspicion is strengthened by the rather naive argument advanced by Apuleius: "My adversaries either must establish that I am a magician and a maker of evil spells to find a cure for the illnesses . . ." as if the exorcist were an unknown in his society.[33] But once again the picture presented is vague. We learn nothing about the demonological or theological superstructure necessarily implied by the exorcism. There is neither a precise reference to the complex ritualistic processes of the exorcism nor one to the rite used to identify the superhuman power, to make contact with it, and to drive it out.[34]

Apuleius's society was well acquainted with exorcism. Even apart from the testimonies provided by the Gospels or the Acts of the Apostles, for example, concerning the exorcism of a woman in Thessalonika, on the periphery of Greece itself, a sufficient number of pagan texts exist, from short recipes contained in the magic papyri to longish accounts reported in the literary texts.[35] In his *Philopseudes* (*The Friend of Lies*)—a satirical text that, however, contains much valuable information on the ideology and the practice of magic—Lucian describes the technique of "singing out" (*exáidein*) a demon from those "who make a demon" (toùs daimonoûntas), who, that is, are possessed by a demon. His interlocutor even saw an exorcist in action, a Syrian from Palestine, capable of making direct contact with the demon and of having the latter replying—in Greek or in a barbaric language, according to his country of origin; speech contact (communio loquendi, to cite Apuleius) was indispensable in exorcism, for it is the force of the word that expels the demon. The exorcist made him swear, and, if he resisted, the exorcist threatened him, after which one could even see the demon go up in black smoke.[36]

In the case of Thallus, Apuleius is well aware that his argumentation is not entirely convincing—but do we have to assume that he cheats? His adversaries having spoken of an exorcism, would he himself intentionally distort this accusation? This possibility is unconvincing. Not only was Claudius Maximus well-informed, but also he could always interrogate more witnesses; moreover, in the presence of the other party, such a crude maneuver had no chance of leading to something. It is therefore preferable to assume that what Apuleius says represents the accusation and to conclude that his accusers did not have a precise knowledge of what a magus could do. They must have supposed him capable of making a subject go into a trance without any divinatory intention, capable of curing someone possessed without any resort to the demonological apparatus. Clearly, the philosopher is better informed than are his accusers.

We come to the third point of the accusation, according to which Apuleius possessed some instrumenta magiae, wrapped up in a cloth and preserved in the library "next to the household gods in the home of Pontianus."[37] There is nothing out of the ordinary about that, and Apuleius had an easy game. He did not hide instruments of magic, but ritual objects referring to the different mystery cults in which he had been initiated. However, the opinion that the magician possessed secret objects was very widespread. We shall come across a very complete set of similar *sacra* when it is a matter of rites.

The fourth point is that in a house, the philosopher and a friend of his performed some nocturnal rites, *nocturna sacra*. This time again, everything is vague. The only indications left by these rites were traces of smoke on the wall (traces of torches or of sacrificial fire?) and some feathers from a bird, the animal sacrificed on the occasion of these rites. These traces seem sufficient to evoke magic. It is a nocturnal thing (Thallus already went through his initiation during the night), and its rituals are solemnized only in small groups (see Thallus); the animals sacrificed are not those of the civic ritual, or more precisely, not only those of the civic ritual. It is thus that in the papyri, in which ewes and pigs are only rarely mentioned, a certain number of birds, in addition to ibises and sparrowhawks, Egyptian animals, are in return well attested to even though they are practically absent from civic ritual, which is communal and takes part during the day. It seems that the presence of a certain number of deviant features sufficed to conjure up the vision of magical rites in the mind of Apuleius's fellow citizens.[38]

The fifth point is much more precise. Apuleius, it goes, secretly made a statuette in the form of a skeleton, sculpted in rare and precious wood, a statuette that he used for his magic rites. He venerated it in costly rites (*impendio*) and gave it the Greek name of *basileús*, king.[39]

It is unimportant that Apuleius was able to prove that this accusation was false, that he did indeed possess a statuette of precious ebony, and that it was just a Hermes, sculpted by a well-known craftsman of the town. Apuleius had commissioned it to be made from common boxwood; without his knowledge, Pontianus had instead supplied the sculptor with the much more precious ebony, in order to surprise his friend. What does matter is the belief of the others: a magician used *in magica maleficia*, for his magic rites, a superhuman power represented by a statuette and associated with the world of the dead. Still, one should not forget that, according to the magical papyri, ebony was the perfect wood for a magical statuette of Hermes; Apuleius's long (and somewhat contorted) explanations rather make one wonder whether he might have known this.[40]

Moreover, any private devotion attached to such a domestic image could, in the Roman world, lead to an incrimination of *superstitio*, of excessive religious fervor. Suetonius tells about Nero, who fervently adored the statue of a girl as his personal tutelary spirit "like a most powerful divinity." Nero had been given the image by an unknown admirer on the same day that a conspiration against his life had been uncovered; thus, he hoped that it would reveal future perils as well.[41]

Scholarly efforts were made to identify this "King," without a convincing result.[42] There actually exist divinities called "King" in the magic papyri, but they are not infernal beings. Nevertheless, the papyri provide certain indications. In all cases, the "King" is a powerful demon whom the magician obtains as his *parhedros*, a superhuman helper and assistant. In a prayer taken from one of the Berlin papyri, the magician, after some preparatory rites, finally invokes the one who must become his assistant: "Come to me, King, I call you, god of gods (in another text, king of kings), powerful, infinite, immaculate, inexplicable, Aion fixed forever, remain unmoving by my side, starting today and for all of my life."[43] The name *King* refers not to a subordinate demon but to the supreme power that the magician hopes to obtain as his all-powerful assistant. We are in a world in which the "kings"—the pharaohs, the Hellenistic kings, and the Roman emperors—were accepted as holders of an almost unlimited power (the word *king* was ambiguous only in the language of Rome itself, which was marked by its republican memories).

Thus, in the opinion of his adversaries, the magician Apuleius had access to immense, but ill-omened, powers, which come, as the skeleton proves, from the world of the dead. This detail, once again, is unusual. Indeed, the literary and iconographical documentation on the *parhedroi* never mentions skeletons; nor do the powers attested to *parhedroi*, demonic helpers, in the papyri come from the world of the dead. On the other hand, the known images of skeletons have nothing to do with magic; they belong to domestic luxury.[44] The association of the magician with the infernal world is found elsewhere, in the literary texts that inform about necromancy, and in the universe of the curse tablets. To judge from the frequency of binding-spells, it is by them that the ancient person most often came in contact with magic. We note, here again, that Apuleius's fellow citizen had no precise idea of what a magician was.

Moreover, Apuleius himself was well aware of these popular notions about magic and magicians. In a passage where he refutes the unjustified accusation of magic, he gives a list of the behaviors that could be interpreted as typically magic, although they are, in fact, innocent enough and even religious—inscribing a wish on the thigh of a statue, offering a silent prayer in a temple or not praying there at all, making an offering, making a sacrifice, picking up a sacred branch.[45] Not everything, in this list, is as innocent as Apuleius would have us believe. Certainly, the leaving of votive gifts, the performance of a sacrifice, and the use of herbs (*verbenae*) are part of the everyday civic and private religious practices. The other acts are more dubious. The ancient human was in the habit of praying aloud; the silent prayer, which was the exception, was barely distinguished from the absence of prayer.[46] Furthermore, such a prayer was danger- ous, and there is no lack of testimonies that the recitation of a silent prayer set off an accusation of magic. In the framework of the civic and communal religion, speech addressed directly and without societal control to the gods was not well thought of. This perception is not confined to pagan antiquity; in seventeenth century England, a Latin prayer could also be a sign of a sorcerer ("charmer"), no doubt because it is a prayer that is unintelligible to the group.[47] The same goes for the wish inscribed on the leg of a votive or cult statue as a means of direct access to the divinity who resides in the image. This belief was very widespread. Seneca suggests that it was customary to bribe the keeper of the temple to have access to the statue and whisper wishes in its ear; this combines silent prayer and physical contact with the statue.[48] According to Lucian, people were in the habit of pasting onto the statue of the healing heroes either tablets containing prayers or coins as the recompensation for the healing. Here again, one sought physical contact in order to communicate one's problems better.[49] It is not unimportant that here it is a matter of heroes and consequently of a being who was human, and of whom the statue still remains more or less in the image of the figure endowed with power. We do not have an example of *defixiones* pasted or inscribed on such statues, but some might have existed. We shall in any case see that many *defixiones* come from sanctuaries of divinities such as Demeter.[50]

These observations are confirmed by another passage in which Apuleius produces a proper definition of magic. After proposing a philosophical definition that repeats the one given in Plato's *First Alcibiades*, Apuleius concludes that magic is thus not opposed to religion, but, on the contrary, is the purest expression of it. Then, he attacks another definition, *more vulgari:* "What if, however, my opponents as common people judge that the *magus* is in fact he who, by keeping up verbal communication with the immortal gods, has the power to bring about everything he wishes by the mysterious force of certain incantations. . . ?"[51] With more emphasis than his accusers, Apuleius underscores two things: the theological superstructure of ancient magic, and the magician's autonomy in relation to the gods. The magician speaks directly to the gods, and he has direct access to them; that relationship is what determines the force of his spells, which are not ordinary words, but words packed with divine power. These gods, on the other hand, and this contradicts all the beliefs of ancient humans, do not impose limits on the will of the magician. It is not the gods who define the space of human power, but the magician acts according to his or her goodwill with regard to both humans and the gods.

The second definition contrasted philosophers and the crowd, the common person. Apuleius immediately repeats this dichotomy: the ignorant people (imperiti) have always accused the philosophers who devote themselves to the study of nature—although then the accusation is not one of magic, but one of irreligiosity and atheism. What, then, is the difference between philosophy and magic in Apuleius's society?

There is a dichotomy immediately perceptible just about everywhere in the Apologia. For Apuleius, the contrast between philosophy and magic reflects the contrast between education and ignorance, or more precisely, between urban education and rustic ignorance. It is thus a matter of social distance, in that the same facts are interpreted differently according to the speaker's social position.

This way of seeing things is characteristic for the literary tradition. From the moment Theocritus represented his sorceresses, in the second Idyll, as "petites-bourgeoises," this distance is well attested and established in literature, and its transformation by Virgil into an Arcadian setting hardly affects it. The social reality is, however, more complex. Up to the end of antiquity, we certainly still find the old women of dubious reputation who perform erotic or healing rites.[52] On the other hand, even in the simplest case of binding spells, many names on the tablets of *defixiones* belong to the upper classes, and even to the elite.[53] It was the "doors of the rich" that the seers and beggars of Plato visited.[54] The Romans Vatinius, Nigidius Figulus, or C. Scribonius Curio (according to the story told by Cicero) belong to the late-republican elite; the accusations of magic known from Tacitus concern people belonging to the same elite of early Imperial Rome. It was not just the death of Germanicus that was surrounded with rumors of magic for which his colleague Piso was held responsible; in Julio-Claudian times, magic seems to have been an established weapon in the political struggle.[55] In the later empire, Libanius was not the only orator to fall victim of a binding spell—or to be blamed for magical aggression; under Constantine, the powerful Christian Ablabius accused his rival, the pagan philosopher Sopatrus, of magical rites, and then caused his downfall; two centuries later, another philosopher, Boethius, died as a victim of a similar accusation.[56] It is not hard to understand why this elite looked for protection against magical attacks—witness a series of splendid medals, used as amulets in Rome in about 400 A.D.[57] Even students—the future elite—dabbled in magic, as the scandal at the then famous Law School of fifth century Beirut demonstrates.[58] It is but reasonable that the Imperial lawgivers differentiated, when deciding about penalties for magic, between members of the upper class and the *humiliores*.[59]

It thus seems that in no era were things as simple as people like Apuleius would have it. But the idea that magic was characteristic of the lower classes survived to the end of antiquity. Transformed into the opposition between natural and demoniac magic, the idea lived on through the Middle Ages and the Renaissance;[60] in the eighteenth century, it became an ethnographical concept that, integrated into the evolutionistic construction of Tylor and Fraser, survives in scientific thought as in the distinction that the common language makes between magic and sorcery. We only begin to glimpse the problems posed by such a "two-tiered" model.[61]

Certainly, in contrasting the magician and the philosopher, Apuleius, it has been said, played on a theme that had been known from the time of Heraclitus and Plato. But here again, differences must be stressed. Apuleius is not opposed to magic as such, neither in the name of a philosophical theology, as Plato had done, nor in the name of science, as did the author of the treatise *On the Sacred Disease*. In fact, Apuleius establishes different distinctions from those used by the *imperiti*. This difference is perfectly clear in the passage following the introductory chapters, in which he once again dissociates himself from the crowd and effects a more precise distinction between *irreligiosi* and *magi*. Among the philosophers, the *irreligiosi* are those who do not (or nearly not) believe in the gods as active agents in the world, who explain the functioning of this world by appealing to purely mechanical laws, as do the Atomists, always an easy target for the accusation of atheism. The so-called *magi*, that is, the theological philosophers, not only explain the functioning of nature and the world by the intervention of the gods (*providentia*, which does not necessarily imply a rigid *heimarmene* after the Stoic model), but also wish to know, through an excess of curiosity, how the divine administration of the world functions.[62] The *imperiti*, on the contrary, accept neither the lack nor the excess of religiosity, but only the happy medium. This circumstance corresponds to what has already been noted; in the eyes of the crowd, *magia* presents itself as the excessive search for contact with the gods.

Apuleius does not accept these distinctions. The philosophical search for the divine is not magic, just as philosophical research on nature is not atheism. His accusers, however, were not entirely consistent; in the case of the fish, Aristotelian research on nature will bring forward an accusation not of atheism, but of magic. Therefore, Apuleius's fellow citizen distinguished only between the happy medium and the lack of balance. Religion is the happy medium, any lack of balance is viewed as magic.

In the same discussion of fish, Apuleius had introduced another idea: ". . . and if it was certain remedies that I sought to get from fish?"[63] Following this, he refutes the malevolent interpretation of the story of the *lepos*, which leads him to contrast the philosopher, the doctor, and the sorcerer: ". . . is, to your mind, knowing some remedies, and seeking to obtain some, the doing of a magician, and not rather that of a doctor—nay, of a philosopher, who will not use them to earn money but to help other humans. The doctors of old were even well acquainted with charms as remedies for wounds: that is what Homer teaches us, our surest authority in matters of antiquity . . ." There follows the story of Odysseus taking part in the hunt for the wild boar.[64]

There is thus a twofold contrast. The first is the one between the doctor and the philosopher, both in search of natural remedies, but the one as a professional who must live from his art, and the other as a disinterested benefactor of suffering humanity (a contrast that was repeated in the case of the epileptic woman in which the philosopher is presented as the true scholar). The second contrast is between the doctor and the sorcerer, who are differentiated by their intentions, an idea with which we are well acquainted.

We measure the intellectual distance between this passage and the conceptions of the Hippocratic author of the treatise on the sacred illness. Hippocratic medicine rejected *mageía* as an inadequate technique that sought healing by referring to an erroneous cosmology. Apuleius is not so radical. In his eyes, it is possible that the philosopher, the doctor, and the sorcerer start with the same cosmology. The distinction is made in terms of intentions, which can be good or bad, and within these two more or less honorable categories.

The case of Apuleius is thus a fine example of the general rule formulated by Marcel Mauss. Although Apuleius is not a magician, the society makes him into one. In his opinion, this confusion between the philosopher and the sorcerer has two causes. On the one hand, it is the curiosity of the naturalistic philosopher that lends itself to erroneous interpretations, according to which the cutting up of a fish looks like the preparation of a *veneficium*, whereas the diagnosis of a case of epilepsy is understood as an exorcism. On the other hand, it is the curiosity of the theological philosopher, whose private religion is more intense than the norm tolerates, that gives rise to other malevolent interpretations. Both a statuette of a god, adored as a personal divinity, and ritual objects coming from mysteries in which the philosopher was initiated are considered as signs of that too-close intimacy, of the *communitas loquendi cum deis*, which constitutes, in people's eyes, the most characteristic sign of the sorcerer.[65]

In short, the sociological analysis derived from Mauss, who saw not only the sorcerer as a marginal figure, but rather the marginal person as a possible sorcerer ("any abnormal social condition prepares for the practice of magic"), becomes, in the society of Apuleius, a religious analysis: "Any abnormal interest in the sacred can lead to the suspicion of magic."[66]

HOW TO BECOME A MAGICIAN:
THE RITES OF INITIATION

IN THE PRECEDING PAGES, we gradually approached the figure of the magician, starting with the study of the different names taken by this personage in the Greco-Roman culture—from *góēs* to *maleficus*, with *mágos/magus* as its center. With C. Furius Cresimus and Apuleius, we encountered two men wrongly declared sorcerers by their society. After the case of these unintentional magicians, we must now examine the case of those who became magicians by their own accord; who were they, and how did they become magicians?

AN EGYPTIAN PROLOGUE

According to the opinion of the ancients, we must seek these magicians in Egypt.[1] "When we were sailing up the Nile, there was among us a man from Memphis, one of the sacred scribes, an extraordinary scholar who knew everything that Egypt could teach him. He told us that he had spent twenty-three years in the secret chambers under the earth, where Isis had taught him how to become a magician." Thus begins the well-known story of the apprentice sorcerer, immortalized by both the poem of Goethe and the music of Paul Dukas.[2] In the eyes of Lucian, who tells this story in a tone of satire, it is not easy to become a sorcerer. The initiation, which lasts a long time, includes doctrines as well as rites. Pankrates (that is the name of Lucian's extraordinary sorcerer) must remain secluded for twenty-three years underground, close by Isis herself.[3] It seems even more difficult to become a magician than to become a druid, a role that, to believe Julius Caesar, required an apprenticeship of twenty years.[4] In another and somewhat dubious account, the apocryphal autobiography of Cyprian, a former orator who became bishop (d. 258 A.D.), the time is shorter; Cyprian had lived only ten years with the priests of Memphis in order to become a magician.[5]

The *adúta*, those secret and subterranean chambers, call to mind what was slanderingly told about Christ. It was thus affirmed that he was a magician and that he had performed his miracles through hidden techniques; supposedly he had learned these techniques in the secret chambers of Egyptian temples, along with the names of powerful "angels" (*angeli*) and certain secret doctrines.[6] This is a very precise accusation. The "secret chambers of Egypt" not only echo Lucian but also belong to a more or less technical vocabulary to designate the interior of the temple, especially the Egyptian temple. Cassius Dio narrates that Septimius Severus, when visiting Egypt in 199 A.D., took "from practically all the secret chambers" every book that he believed to contain some secret, mysterious teaching;[7] a magical papyrus knows that the true name of a divinity "has been inscribed on the sacred stele in the *adúton* at Hermoupolis where your birth is."[8] And the "angels," another technical term, do not refer to the Judaeo-Christian angels; they are demonic beings who served as assistants to the initiated magicians and whose names had to be known to the person who wished to make use of their services.[9] The pagans who called the Christ a magician knew what they were talking about and could confirm their accusation by drawing on Christ's biography: had he not, in his youth, spent some years in Egypt?[10]

Egypt, moreover, does not constitute the only reference for these stories. Some Greek facts are close as well—although it would be rash to identify either Greece or Egypt as their sole source. Herodotus tells us that Zalmoxis, the former slave of Pythagoras, was hidden in an underground chamber to prove to his fellow Scythian citizens that there existed a life after death. This story follows the one told about Pythagoras himself, who is reported to have hidden for a time in a small subterranean chamber and to return from it as if he were returning from the dead; he was well-informed, however, about everything that had happened on earth, for he had obtained this knowledge from the Mother, a figure curiously parallel to Isis, who plays the role of teacher for Lucian. At the origin of these stories, there was long suspected a rite of Scythian or Pythagorean initiation, in the latter case into mysteries of the Great Mother Cybele or Demeter.[11] Similar rites are known at the oracular sites. In Clarus, the priest entered, at the end of a labyrinthine pathway, a subterranean chamber to obtain the oracle's answer. At the oracle of Trophonius in Boeotia, each visitor performed a ritual journey into the netherworld before obtaining the answer of the oracular hero.[12] A higher knowledge always results from the subterranean meeting with a superhuman being. Another catabasis is reconstructed in the mysteries of the Dactyls, in the course of which the initiate "descended into the *megaron*" (another subterranean chamber) to meet some infernal beings and thus acquired knowledge that would help the initiate to confront the powers of the netherworld.[13] To become a magician requires rituals that are very widespread. The story told by Lucian is certainly an invention, being, after all, taken from *The Lover of Lies (Philopseudes)*, but it is grounded in precise information about contemporary beliefs and rituals.[14] It thus must be concluded from it that the magician, being a religious specialist, had to undergo an initiation like all religious specialists in various cultures, from the Siberian shaman to the Christian monk.[15] It must also be concluded that there existed, at the level of the ritual, affinities between the mystery cults and magic. It is these two paths that will be explored in this chapter.

MAGIC AS A GIFT OF THE GODS

Let us take up the story of Pankrates, the great magician, for it contains other reasons of interest.

Pankrates was instructed by Isis herself. The supreme knowledge of the magician is a gift of the gods, and this affirmation is not rare in the world of magicians. Thesallus of Tralles, a doctor of the Neronian era, wished to know whether Egyptian magic still existed. After long investigations, it is Imouthes in person, the god of magic in its center, Heliopolis, who was going to instruct him—at least, if we believe this story from an autobiographical account that is certainly apocryphal.[16] An anonymous magician, the author of a recipe preserved in the Mimaut Papyrus at the Louvre Museum, prides himself in these terms: "There is no procedure more effective than this one; it was tested and approved by Manethon, to whom it was given as a gift by Osiris the Great."[17]

But the idea is much older than the fourth century A.D., from which the papyrus Mimaut dates, and it is not only Egyptian: its first attestation is Greek, in the poet Pindar. According to him, it was Aphrodite who taught Jason erotic incantations and the use of the *iynx*, the magic tool used in this type of magic and sometimes depicted in the hands of an Eros in Greek earrings (after all, female jewelry has its own erotic aims).[18] Certainly, that is not sufficient to make Jason a sorcerer; no Greek hero is a sorcerer,[19] and Pindar clearly and not without a certain irony suggests that the crafty Medea fell herself victim to another, stronger magic coming from Aphrodite. Despite these reservations, this myth still contains some surprises. To begin with, we note that it is the divinity who gives men magic, and Pindar stressed that by this means, Aphrodite founded an institution. "She gave the iynx to men for the first time and taught Jason the prayers." The passage uses the language of cultural theory, of the stories about the origin of culture or at least of a particular feature of ancient culture. It is Aphrodite who introduced, as a kind of "first finder" (prōtos heuretēs), the ritual usage of that curious instrument that is the iynx as well as the vocal rite that accompanies it.[20]

On a more general level, Jason's journey to the land of the Colchians is structured like a myth of initiation. He departs from ordinary geography to reach the limits of the contemporary geographical horizon or even to go beyond this limit. He travels with a group of young men, a kind of age class; he will return as the future king in the company of his queen.[21] In this initiatory framework, the encounter with a goddess and the acquisition of some specialized knowledge are not surprising.

The theme thus seems rather old, and it has an early attestation in Greece. In the eyes of the Greeks of the archaic age, the special knowledge that is magic, the knowledge of its tools, its rites, and of its effective prayers, belongs to the gods, and it is they who make a gift of it to man. The way of acquiring it involves a ritual initiation. (To recall our discussion in Chapter 2, nothing points to a differentiation, in this age, between religion and magic.)

The same conception is attested to in Plato's remarks about the beggar priestess and the seers in the *Republic*. These people, he says, convince their clients "that they possess a faculty of healing, obtained from the gods by means of sacrifices and incantations."[22] So, then, what are these "sacrifices and incantations," which provided these wizards with special powers obtained from the gods, if not rites of initiation?

This search for a knowledge that derived directly from the gods became much more common in the imperial era, and it was not limited to magicians. Their desire for an esoteric and powerful knowledge was shared by others, such as neo-Platonic philosophers, gnostics, and charismatics of all sorts; all of them sought that *communio loquendi cum dis* of which Apuleius speaks. The neo-Platonists sought direct contact with the supreme divinity through ecstasy and theurgy, the white magic of philosophers.[23] The charismatics claimed superhuman powers (or were attributed with them by their society), such as the enigmatic Apollonius of Tyana, known through the fictionalized biography written by the sophist Philostratus. Apollonius, who was elected by Asclepius of Aegae in Cilicia, spent three years in his youth in its sanctuary, in direct contact (by means of dreams) with the divinity of the place. He pursued his training through a period of voluntary silence, a sort of renunciation of verbal communication with the world and humans, which did not prevent him from performing extraordinary deeds, like the quelling of a revolt in Aspendus. Finally, to improve his knowledge, he spent four months as a disciple of the Indian Brahmins. Although a large part of the information that Philostratus, who himself wrote between 216 and 220 A.D., gives us about Apollonius, who lived between Tiberius and the Flavians, is of doubtful value, his *Life* must contain a historical core. It is probable that the information on the years he spent in Aegae came from earlier sources, sources of the second century at the latest, when this sanctuary was acquiring international renown and when it had every interest in making use of the stay of this charismatic neo-Pythagorean for purposes of propaganda.[24] Whatever their historical value, these stories about Apollonius at Aegae already provide a glimpse of a figure gifted with extraordinary religious power, in quest of a purer spirituality than that offered by the civic worship.

The case of Apollonius—as well as that of certain gnostic and hermetic sages—attests to the same kinship between magic and excessive religious fervor that we have already noted in Apuleius. Apollonius, as well as the gnostics and hermetics, aspired to divine revelation by ritual means, which could lead to the accusation of magic. That is what happened not only to Apollonius (at least according to Philostratus) but also to Marcion, founder of the gnostic sect of the Marcionites. Irenaeus, his Christian detractor, accuses him, in his treatise *Against Heresies,* of a whole series of magic practices—possession of demonic assistants, erotic magic, exorcism.[25]

This kinship between magic and gnosticisms is based, however, on much more precise facts; it was Richard Reitzenstein who demonstrated this for the magical papyri, our essential source.[26] The following story, which could be described as an "initiatory myth," provides a fine demonstration. Magic, we shall see, takes several paths to reach superhuman powers. The most effective and most widespread means is to learn the secret name of a higher divinity. The person who knew this name had the power to call on the divinity for assistance, but could also threaten the lesser beings. In several spells in the papyri, the magician claims that the supreme god had revealed his secret name to him, and the magician uses the religious formula that is especially known from the cult of Isis: "I am he whom . . ."[27] In a papyrus—now preserved in Leyden—the magician invokes the divinity with these words: "I am he whom you met at the foot of the sacred mountain and to whom you gave a knowledge of your greatest name." Implicitly, the magician perhaps assumes the role of Moses, as he explicitly does in another text from the papyri: "I am Moses your prophet to whom you transmitted your mysteries celebrated in Israel." Moses going to the sacred mountain appears also on an amulet with a remarkable variation, as its inscription shows: "Amulet of Moses when he went on the mountain to receive the [entirely enigmatic] *kasty*."[28] The same myth is found in the hermeticists. In the eighth hermetic treatise, Tat, the son of Hermes, brings about a revelation by reminding his father of an old promise that he had made to his son: "When I was your supplicant, when we came down from the sacred mountain talking together, I asked you questions on the doctrine of regeneration, the only doctrine of which I am ignorant; and you promised to reveal it to me." We find the same theme, as Morton Smith recalls it to us, in the story of Christ's transfiguration.[29] But a person's encounter with a divine power that reveals to the person a supreme knowledge is a motif known to all Hellenists. It is indeed at the foot of the Helicon that the Muses reveal both the truth and the lie to Hesiod, the poor shepherd of Ascrae, as he himself tells in the prologue of the *Theogony*.[30] We are thus dealing with a theme that is attested to in all the ancient Middle East and that magic and hermetism took up into their own mythmaking.

MAGIC AND MYSTERY CULTS

Cyprian, if we are to believe his apocryphal autobiography, not only underwent a magic initiation among the priests of Memphis but also was initiated in a whole series of mystery cults in Greece and elsewhere. The text gives a rather amusing list of these cults in which we find the mysteries of Ceres in Eleusis; those of Artemis Tauropolus in Sparta (an obvious confusion of the cruel but famous Spartan Artemis Orthia with the other and even crueler Artemis Tauropolus, who was adored among the Taurians as well as at Halai Araphenides in Attica); of Hera in Argos; and of Cybele in Phrygia and in the Troad.[31] It is obvious that the author has only a very vague idea of Greek pagan religion, an idea coming from a hasty reading of earlier texts. Nevertheless, the list is interesting: it shows that the epoch saw a close relationship between magic and mysteries. It will be recalled that Apuleius refuted the accusation of magic by invoking his many initiations into mystery cults, whose secret tokens were interpreted by his adversaries as so many magic instruments. But it is especially the magic papyri that at different levels show this association.[32]

The first level is that of vocabulary. The individual magic ritual is often called *mustḗrion*, "the secret thing," even *theîon mustḗrion*, "the godly secret thing"; even more often, one simply speaks of *teletḗ*, "rite."[33] Magic in general, as the combination and linked series of different rites, is called *tà mustḗria* or *hai teletaí*, "mysteries"—although *teletḗ* referred, in the Greek of the fifth century B.C., to any ritual whatever; in the imperial epoch, its meaning is more restricted and reserved for secret, mysterious rites.[34] The *mustḗrion*—a singular not attested before Hellenistic Greek—also designates magical objects or tools, like a ring or ointment. A magic ring of special power is even called "a great secret thing," *megalomustḗrion*.[35] The magician's colleagues are called "fellow initiates," *súnmustai*; ordinary people are the "uninitiated ones," *amustēriastoí*; and a magician of superb knowledge becomes "he who introduces to the mysteries," *mustagōgós*.[36]

It could be—and has been—thought that this terminology is not that of the magicians, but that of the mystery rites that the magicians had adapted to their purpose; they kept a terminology that, however, had lost its proper meaning and was of no importance for understanding the ritual. Many scholars firmly believe that there are such adaptations of earlier, nonmagic rituals. A case in point is the so-called "Mithras Liturgy" in the great papyrus book of the Bibliothèque Nationale, a ritual scenario that Albrecht Dieterich had isolated and put into relation to the mysteries of Mithras. A number of scholars doubted such a reconstruction, and Reinhold Merkelbach prefers to interpret it rather as an Egyptian initiatory rite—at any rate, in this text the magician is called an "initiate," and his colleague a "fellow-initiate."[37] But the theory of a mechanical adaptation is too radical, anyway. Even if the magicians should have adapted entire ritual scenarios from their sources, nothing allows us to surmise that the mystery terminology was alien to the world of the magicians, that it was only a relic of an earlier state. The authors of the magic papyri were not stupid enough just to combine materials from different sources without eliminating contradictions and dissonances. And there are unambiguous cases in which the terminology of the mysteries is consciously applied to the magic rites. The magician, without any doubt, considered himself the adept of a mystery cult, who underwent a ritual, an experience very close to that of the well-known mystery cults. In the text that, according to Betz, came from an initiation into the cult of the Dactyls, the magician affirms having been initiated into their cult—an affirmation that has an obvious goal in the magic ritual, which is to insist in one's initiation, in front of the infernal beings whom the magician encounters, on the means to claim special protection from one's familiarity with the powers governing the infernal world.[38] Centuries earlier, in a Euripidean tragedy, Heracles explained to his father why he was able to brave the dangers of the beyond in order to fetch up Cerberus: "I have been initiated in Eleusis."[39] Moreover, the devotees of Bacchic mysteries, who carried with them into their graves the famous "Orphic" gold leaves, had learned during initiation what they should say when the guardians or the rulers of the nether world intercepted them; this knowledge, made permanent on the leaves, constituted proof of their initiation and assured their bliss after death.[40] To the magicians, it was not just the mysteries of the Greeks that counted. One of them addressed himself to the supreme god in these terms: "I am your prophet Moses, to whom you conveyed your mysteries celebrated by the Israelites": not only does he claim to know these mysteries, but also he proves his intimacy with a powerful god, whose power stands at the magician's disposition too.[41]

Yet if magic and mysteries have such close links, what, then, are their common features? There are at least three of them, I think: magic and mysteries involve secrecy, they seek direct contact with the divine, and they are reached by means of a complex ritual of initiation.

The divulging of what happened during the mystery rites was strictly forbidden—although it was not everywhere that one paid with one's life for any disclosure, even involuntary, as one did in Eleusis. The same prohibition is attested to for the magic rites and for objects connected with them (we are reminded of Apuleius's problem with his secret tokens). The papyri very often require secrecy, although not always in such excited words as in the case of a magical consecration of a ring, a "supreme and divine action," called Ouphôr and used by one Urbicus: "This is the true rite . . . So keep it in a secret place as a great mystery. Hide it, hide it!"[42]

To believe the magicians, the secret character of their art also came from its Egyptian origin; the documents were written in a writing that could be read by only a few rare scholars. Thus, in one of the papyri in Leyden, the somewhat pompous author of a collection of magic recipes presents the text as follows: "Interpretation which the temple scribes employed, from the holy writings, in translation. Because of the curiosity of the masses, the scribes inscribed the names of the herbs and other things they had made use of, on the statues of the gods, so that the masses, since they do not take precautions, might not practice magic, being prevented by the consequence of their misunderstandings. But we have collected the explanations from many copies, all of them secret."[43]

This text illuminates the mentality of the magicians of the time. In the course of the imperial era, the knowledge had been lost that made it possible to read the hieroglyphs (engraved, among other things—or, in our text, exclusively—on Egyptian statues).[44] The enigmatic signs became a secret writing, seeming to contain a powerful knowledge, but one of very difficult access. The knowledge of these secrets distinguished the true magus from the masses (aptly enough, the Christians suspected any study of the hieroglyphs as magic)[45]—in an opposition rather close to that of Apuleius separating the *philosophi* from the *imperiti*, the philosophers from the common folk. Again, there is the reproach of excessive curiosity, only this time attributed not by the *imperiti* to the magicians and philosophers, but reversed and addressed to the crowd. The consequence of secrecy is the necessity of initiation and training; prolonged practice was needed to be able to read and translate these writings and to become a specialist in the language of magic, one who could construct a text on the basis of several models.[46]

The second characteristic shared by magic and the mysteries is the quest for direct contact with the sphere of the divine. We must take a closer look at the concrete forms that this *communio loquendi cum dis* could take in the world of the magicians. Once again, it is the papyri that provide the most valuable clues.

For the magician, this contact is indispensable if the magician wishes to perform his ritual (the *praxis*, to use the technical term). In order to achieve the goal of the rite, to end the quest for love, knowledge, or power, the magician needs the help of the gods, of a divine or demonic assistant, and to get it, must know the secrets of the supreme god. In this quest, the magician distinguishes himself or herself from the adepts of Gnosticism, hermetism, or neoplatonism less through the religious forms that are used than through the aim of his or her actions.[47] The magician rarely seeks knowledge for its own sake, usually pursues a more practical goal, and has a material need to satisfy— though (to blur the all too clear-cut distinction again) it is not entirely unheard of that a magician seeks only community with the gods, as, on the other hand, theurgy could have its very utilitarian aims as well.[48]

It is even more difficult to grasp the difference between the traditional initiate and the magicians. Again, it is not so much a matter of forms: ecstasy is well-known among magicians, as it is among the followers of Bacchus; however, unlike the initiates of an ecstatic cult, the magicians usually do not seek the experience of the divine as the final goal, but rather are looking for information and prophesy.[49] Still, to blur the differences again, the mystery cults always had a utilitarian side as well, for they were supposed to improve the human condition, in this life as well as in the next. Already in the middle of the seventh century B.C., the *Homeric Hymn to Demeter*, a fundamental document on the Eleusinian mysteries, promises to send "Plutus [divine Wealth] to the hearth of the great house" of those who have been initiated . . . "and, in the dark world of the dead, their fate will be different," for the familiarity with the infernal divinities guarantees them a better destiny. And at the other extreme of the chronological chain, well after the middle of the second century A.D., Apuleius, in his *Metamorphoses*, tells not only how Lucius underwent initiation into the mysteries of Isis but also how the goddess helped her initiate in his efforts to construct an existence as a lawyer in Rome.[50] All that does not differ so much from what the sorcerers seek, if only in that they show no interest concerning eschatology, the fate of the soul and the individual after death.

There is a still more important difference at another level. The experience of the mystery cults is a communal one, and one of the reasons for the success of these cults in the Hellenistic and imperial eras was their social function. The associations of initiates could offer a group identity, and, on a more practical level, communal services to individuals who were increasingly cut off from their traditional groups.[51] The hypothesis has even been expressed that the mysteries of Mithras were created for the middle-level civil servants of the imperial government and of the army to offer them a stable point during the moves throughout the provinces of the empire necessitated by their career. In this perspective, the mithraea almost identical everywhere appear like a chain of Hilton hotels.[52] However that may be, it is significant that an itinerant intellectual such as Apuleius was initiated "in most of the rites of Greece"; reality cannot have been very different from what happened to Lucius, the hero of Apuleius's *Metamorphoses*; Lucius found, at Corinthian Cenchreae as well as in Rome, Isiac communities that immediately accepted him and helped him both materially and spiritually.[53]

Here again we must introduce light and shade. There existed a communal spirit among the magicians; cooperation and a sense of solidarity are not unknown, as is shown by the term "fellow initiate" mentioned before; and long magic initiation periods in an Egyptian temple took place not in isolation, but in a community. One must, however, be careful not to confuse fiction and reality, and here the papyri are once again of great help to us. These texts, although in their current state they appear to be a rather heterogeneous mass reaching us in a state of unequal transmission, give us an inkling of their much more uniform and coherent predecessors. In them we find incantations, rites, and books that claim to have been transmitted from father to son or daughter, from magician to king.[54] We note, moreover, that the letter is the dominant literary form in the papyri, as is attested to by the conclusion of a recipe: "Here, my child, is the sacred book that brings good luck, the Monad, which no one could interpret or carry out before. Be well, my child." "Be well," *khaîre*, the equivalent of the *vale* in Latin letters, is the usual formula for good-bye in Greek letters.[55]

Nevertheless, the majority of the papyri do not testify to this communal spirit. Indeed, most of the texts give the impression of being meant for an isolated individual who will make use of them for the individual's own personal ends. The bid to refer oneself to a "fellow initiate" or to collaborate with a mystagogue is rare and exceptional; and even in this case, we notice signs of distrust, that to which at least this text testifies, clearly showing that there existed different degrees of collaboration: "If you wish to use a fellow initiate, so that he alone may hear with you the things spoken, let him remain pure with you for seven days, and let him abstain from meat and a bath. And even when you are alone and you carry out the things communicated by the god, you speak as in a prophetic ecstasy. But if you wish to show him, then judge whether he is truly worthy as a man, treating him as if you were yourself judged in the ritual of immortalization, *apothanatismós*, and whisper to him the first prayer that begins as follows: 'First origin of my origin ΑΕΗΙΟΤΩ.' And say the rest as an initiate, over his head, in a whisper, so that he may not hear, as you are anointing his face with the secret. This ritual immortalization takes place three times a year."[56]

This passage marks the end of the "Mithras Liturgy," a ritual meant to induce the appearance of a god and his prophecy before the magician in trance; it is called "immortalization," because the practitioner leaves his mortal nature to converse with the god. The text contrasts two ways of collaborating with a colleague. In the first instance, the magician may invite a colleague to listen with the magician to what the god will prophesy; the colleague has only a more or less passive role, but nonetheless, needs the same purifications as the magician. In the second instance, the "fellow initiate" may also be shown the rites ("to show," *deîxai*, is also a technical term for introducing performers into mystery rituals), and it goes without saying that the conditions are then much stricter. Some reservations remain, however; the most important prayer must be said *sotto voce*, so that the other does not hear it: the fellow initiate is effectively initiated and capable of seeing the apparition (the reason for anointing the eyes) but lacks the ultimate knowledge necessary for performing the ritual. Thus, there remains an indisputable hierarchy.

It is in the ritual of magical initiation that the similarities and differences between magic and mysteries are the most clear-cut. The magicians as well as the initiates, neoplatonists, or hermeticists all took an interest in the extraordinary experience that the initiation could provide. Apuleius (in the eleventh book of the *Metamorphoses*) is our best witness for the mystery cults; his text reveals the fascination that he felt for the rituals and the experiences that resulted from them. We come across the same fascination in the magical papyri. The initiation ritual often leads the magician (and the modern reader) well beyond ordinary experience, which confirms our reservations against a commonplace and utilitarian interpretation of these rites. The rites can assume strange forms: "Crown yourself with black ivy when the sun is in the middle of the sky, at the fifth hour; and while looking upward, lie down naked on the linen [which had been spread out on the roof of the house] and have your eyes covered with a black band. Have yourself wrapped like a corpse, close your eyes, and—still turned to the sun—begin these words."[57]

Such a rite can have surprising results: "After you have said this three times, there will be this sign of divine encounter (but you, armed by having this magical soul, be not alarmed): a sea falcon flies down and strikes you on the body with its wings, signifying this: that you should arise. But as for you, rise up and clothe yourself with white garments . . ."[58] (Only a spoilsport will ask how many times the falcon appeared this way.)

The structure of this ritual resembles any rite of initiation, as will be shown later. As always, however, it is the differences that are the most interesting, and one of them seems to be fundamental. In the mystery cults, a single initiation (or, in some rare cults, a series of well-hierarchized rituals) sufficed to change the status of the initiate definitively, and to promote the person from the outside into the group of initiates.[59] In magic, things are more complicated; we are dealing with two very distinct types of initiation. On the one hand, we find in our documentation (that is, in both the papyri and the literary texts) a single ritual that definitively transforms a layperson into a magician. We have seen this situation in the case of Lucian's Pancrates and in the rumors concerning Christ, but also in Plato's account of the itinerant seers or in the story of Nero, initiated into magic by a real magus, Tiridates of Armenia, "with magic banquets." Comparable rituals were used, in the ancient world, to initiate priests or other religious specialists.[60] But we also find in the papyri a whole gamut of rituals that transform the status of a person who is already a magician to promote the person to a higher level of power. In this case as well, we are dealing with initiatory rites, rituals performed in order to change the status of a human. Among this second group, there are two kinds that seem particularly important. The first kind makes it possible to obtain a *párhedros*, an "assistant"; the second contains the *sústasis* ("rite of encounter"), the rituals for presenting the magician to a god. Both types of rites introduce the sorcerer to the domain of the divinity.

The *sústasis* can be illuminated thanks to a rather brief ritual that belongs to a complex and much more extensive ritual, at least in the first version of what is called the *Eighth Book of Moses*.

The book contains only that single prolonged ritual scenario whose intention is to bring about the visit of a divinity who is able to provide revelations about the future. In its preparatory stage, the version A, the longest and most elaborate, interpolates (according to the commentary of the *Key*) another ritual to aid in the preparatory rite; it is the "Introduction to the Gods of the Hours of the Day"—to benefit from their help means to be helped at every moment of the day by a specific divinity, which facilitates the main ritual task.[61] Every contact with a divinity is dangerous and risky, because the god might by angry or an evil demon might use the god's form in order to deceive the magician.[62]

The ritual instructions use the language of the mysteries. They begin with an introductory remark (l. 32): "You will be made their initiate as follows . . ."; and it ends with this confirmation (l. 38): "You will then have been made their initiate." It thus is indeed a typical initiatory progression, during which the candidate is transported by the ritual from an earlier state to a new and permanent state expressed here in the transition from the future (*telesthései*) to a perfect tense (future anterior *tetelesménos ései*): the help of the gods in the mysteries in which the magician will have been initiated and will enjoy as a personal protection, will be assured and definitive for that person.

The ritual itself is very simple. At the new moon, the future initiate forms three statuettes of fine flour, one fitted with the head of a bull, the next with the head of a goat, and the third with the head of a ram, all three represented on the zodiac, holding Egyptian whips. The initiate fumigates these statuettes with incense, and then eats them while reciting the prayer and the "constraining formula" contained in the *Key*, but not detailed in our text. Version B adds (which could have been guessed) that the *Key* also contained the names of the "Gods of the Hours of the Day," which are unknown to us.[63]

The period of the new moon, the interval between the month past and the month to come, is an auspicious period for all magic acts. It is also the moment when the Greeks exposed the meals of Hecate at the crossroads, these crossroads being themselves intervals between spaces.[64] It is thus a rather commonplace date. The three statuettes presumably represented the "Gods of the Hours of the Day," which explains their position on the zodiac. The fact that they are only three in number suggests that these gods operated in four groups of three gods each. The whips— explicitly described as Egyptian—as well as the animal heads, testify to the Egyptian origin of these statuettes. It will be noted, however, that though the ram and the bull are well-known sacred animals in Egypt, the goat is not—it might just be a Greek element.[65] The ritual program itself, with the fabrication of the objects, their sacralization by fumigation, and their total appropriation by ingestion at the same time as the invocation of the god concerned, recall the structure of a mystery rite. Both initiations, in mystery cults as well as in our magical ritual, take up the canonical structure of a rite of passage according to the analysis of van Gennep, with its progression from separation to marginality and back to integration; the ritual considered so far performs separation as a way to marginality where (in mystery cults as well as here) the human performer meets his gods.[66]

But the initiation to the minor divinities that are the "Gods of the Hours" brings only limited benefits. It is much more advantageous to obtain a *párhedros*, a superhuman or even divine assistant: Plotinus impressed an Egyptian colleague with his personal spirit "not being from among the demons, but a god."[67] It is the parhedros who makes it possible for the sorcerer to perform what a human cannot do alone, especially divination and obtaining dreams. Precision about the function of such a parhedros comes from the accusation brought forward by Irenaeus against the gnostic Marcion: "He even has an assistant demon, thanks to whom he takes on the appearance of prophesying himself and makes the women prophesy whom he judges worthy of partaking of his Grace."[68] It is the prophecy by possession that is in question here. Thanks to the power that the sorcerer has over demons, the sorcerer not only is an exorcist but can also command the demons to enter into his or her own body or that of others.

One of the magic papyri preserved in Berlin provides us with an even longer list of what a parhedros might be used for, such as to help bring on dreams, to couple women and men (i.e., erotic incantations), to kill enemies, to open closed doors and to free people in chains, to stop the attacks of demons and wild animals, to break the teeth of snakes, to put dogs to sleep. The parhedros might also bring forth water, wine, bread, oil, vinegar, and anything else one wants to eat (with the exception of fish and pork, not eaten in Egypt). The parhedros even helps to acquire demons in fine livery and, when one wishes, to organize a banquet in "rooms with ceilings of gold and walls of marble" ("which," the cautious writer adds, "you will judge partly real, and partly only illusory").[69]

This remarkable passage finds its closest parallel in a somewhat unexpected text. Celsus, the bellicose pagan, makes Christ a magician also, but a rather entertaining one: "He—Origen writes, meaning Celsus—likens Christ's miracles to the works of the sorcerers, who promise to perform rather surprising things, and to the achievements of the Egyptians. For a few oboli the latter sell their venerable knowledge on the public square, drive out demons from men, cure illness with a breath of air, evoke the souls of heroes, bring forth rich meals, tables filled with delicacies and food of all kinds that in reality do not exist, and make move as living what is not really so but appears so to the imagination."[70]

Egyptian magicians, it seems, are not devoid of pleasurable

aspects. After all, they had to earn their living by professional miracle-working, in fairs and public squares. In the papyri, we sometimes find instructions meant for shows such as teaching how to ride on a crocodile or how to free a person chained in a locked room: "Having put a man in chains, you will lock him up in a room, and remaining outside, say the formula six or seven times; then, for the door to open, say the formula . . ."[71] What is striking in this portrait of everyday magic is not simply that it does not resort to the help of a demoniac parhedros (as the papyrus suggested) for its extravagant feats; it is rather the fact that this magic of the fair contains things that we would consider much more serious: healing, necromancy, and exorcism. But it is our categories again that are at odds with the ancients—many contemporaries of Christ accepted these facts as facts, not illusions. Even the Roman officer who kept guard over Perpetua and her fellow martyrs was afraid that they might disappear from jail, with the help "of some magical incantations."[72] Healing through a mere breath of air is found, moreover, in the instruction for an exorcism in the magic papyrus in the Bibliothèque Nationale.[73]

Obviously, for the magician, it is essential to obtain a parhedros; one does not become a true *magus* without such an assistant. To acquire one is thus also a kind of initiatory rite. The papyri supply us with a series of examples—a most characteristic one is taken from the same papyrus in Berlin.

A demon comes as an assistant: he will reveal everything to you, he will live, eat, and sleep with you.
(1) Take two of your fingernails and all the hairs from your head. Take a Circaean falcon and deify it [drown it] in the milk of a black cow, after you have mixed Attic honey with the milk. And once you have deified it, wrap it with an undyed [that is, pure] piece of cloth and place beside it your fingernails and your hairs; take some royal papyrus, write what follows on it in ink of myrrh,

and set it in the same manner along with the fingernails and the hairs, then smear it with uncut frankincense and old wine.

(1a) Here is what you will write on the paper: A EE HHH IIII OOOOO ΥΥΥΥΥ ΩΩΩΩΩΩΩ. But write it arranged in two figures.

(2)(a) Take the milk with the honey and drink it before the sun rises, and something divine will be in your heart. Take the falcon, set it up in a temple made of juniper wood, and having crowned this same temple, make an offering of non-animal food, and have on hand some old wine.

(b) Before going to bed, make a prayer before this same bird after you have offered it a sacrifice as you usually do and say this spell: A EE HHH IIII OOOOO ΥΥΥΥΥ ΩΩΩΩΩΩΩ, come to my place, good farmer, good demon . . . Come to my place, o holy Orion, you who dwell in the north, who cause the currents of the Nile to roll down and mingle with the sea, transforming them with life as does the sperm of man in sexual union, you who built the world on an indestructible foundation, who are young in the morning and old in the evening, you who journey through the subterranean pole and who rise, breathing fire, you who have parted the seas in the first month, who ejaculate your sperm into the sacred figtree of Hermupolis. This is your authoritative name: ARBATH ABAOTH BAKCHABRE.

(c) But when you are dismissed, be shoeless and walk backward, and set yourself to the enjoyment of the food and dinner and the prescribed food offering, coming face to face as companion to the god. This rite demands total purity; hide, hide the procedure and abstain from intercourse with a woman for seven days.[74]

This rite (of which I shall not explain all the ramifications) proceeds in two main phases: the preparation and the execution. The first phase includes the preparation of the rite's ingredients: one drowns the falcon in the milk, makes a mummy of it, and sets down next to it pieces of one's own fingernails and hairs as well as a choice papyrus on which a short formula is inscribed, and then one coats the whole with a mixture of incense and wine.

The execution of the actual rite begins shortly before sunrise. Here again two phases are distinguished:

(a) A preparatory rite of introduction: the magician drinks the mixture of milk and honey in which he has drowned the falcon; he sets the mummy down in a small sanctuary, crowns it, and prepares a meal.

(b) The rite proper is the sacrifice to the deified falcon, accompanied by a long prayer, that constitutes the central evocation.

(c) When the god has appeared (that is, when the rite has reached its goal), the god and the magician eat together like colleagues.

(d) To end the rite, the magician withdraws in bare feet, walking backward.

The order of the ritual sequences in the last part of the rite is not very clear. I have tried to clear it up by separating enjoying the meal and walking backward. The final prohibitions (the requirement of maximal purity and sexual abstinence) are elements that do not concern the time following the rite, but rather the preparatory period to which this kind of ritual purity normally belongs, not only in magic, but in all rituals putting the human in contact with the divine (as do the mystery rites); it is a rite of commonplace separation in the sequence of the rites of passage.

Another commonplace rite is that of eating and drinking. In our scenario, we see two variants. First the magician drinks a special milk, which transforms him, making him divine: "Something divine will be in your heart," which points to an ecstatic experience. This rite—performed shortly before sunrise—marks the transition to the marginal space in which the magician will encounter the god. The ingredients contribute to it: milk and honey are liquids used in marginal rites; the color black is also a marginal color; and the milk from a black cow is often mentioned in magic, and some comparable beverages are found elsewhere.[75] A single example, taken from a papyrus, will also help us to understand why one drinks the milk in which a sacred animal has been drowned, in this case the sacred falcon of Horus. In the three versions of *Moses* VIII, the magician writes the most important charm on the two sides of a tablet of sodium carbonate, and then he erases the text of one side by licking it, while he washes the other side with milk from a black cow; then he mixes this milk with some pure wine and drinks the whole, after which he makes a prayer, and the god appears.[76] Here again, the ritual act of drinking marks the transition that immediately precedes the entry into marginality. In this rite of passage, the milk and the pure wine express one more time the reversal characteristic of the marginal phase. But there is more: by licking or drinking the central incantation, the magician appropriates this cardinal text. This concept is widespread in Near Eastern thinking. In Egyptian rituals, one often either licks a sacred text or drinks a liquid in which a text has been dissolved. And in a popular tale from the Ptolemaic era, the hero ingests a secret book of the god Thoth, which he so much sought, and, in doing this, appropriates all the powerful knowledge contained in the book.[77] We will also recall the prophetic initiation of Ezekiel, during which God forces him to eat a book.[78] We also find some modern parallels to this rather unappetizing ritual (we are reminded that sodium carbonate is used to make soap) and to its ideology. In northern Italy during the fifteenth century, at the decisive moment of the initiation of a witch, the candidate drinks a beverage made of the excrement of a giant toad, hair, and ashes. In the confession of a Bernese sorcerer of the same epoch, a similar drink (unforgivably, the recipe is not spelled out) had the result that the candidate "felt in my heart the image of our art and the principal rites of our school."[79]

These parallels help give a better understanding of the role of the falcon that was deified in the milk. The central prayer is a mixture of various allusions to Egyptian mythology, based on the cult of the sun. The god "who is young in the morning and old in the evening, who passes the subterranean pole and who gets up breathing fire" is, of course, the sun god. He "who separated the seas in the first month" is again the sun, Rê, who was born of the chaotic primordial waters; and he "who ejaculates his sperm into the sacred figtree of Hermopolis" is again he, creating by masturbation the gods of Hermopolis. It is thus indeed a form of the sun god with whom the magician wishes to join forces.[80] But the falcon is also a form of the same god, both sacred animal and symbol of the god. By drinking the milk in which a falcon was drowned, a person thus appropriates the life of this sacred animal; it is the reason for which, after drinking, one will have "something divine" in the heart. In the same way that Ezekiel appropriates the divinatory power by eating the book or that the Bernese sorcerer appropriates his art by drinking a magic beverage, the Greco-Egyptian sorcerer appropriates a part of the divine essence, which makes it possible for him to leave human existence to meet the god. In these rites, eating and drinking are acts of immediate and perfectly comprehensible appropriation of an essence. In their structure, these rites mark the entrance into the space of the other; in their ideology, they mark the entrance into the world of the god.

This brings us to the second rite in which the meal is consumed. This meal taken in common with the god (face to face) represents the *communio*, the overall equality between man and god. The meal is made up of "non-animal" vegetarian food and old wine. There is nothing exceptional about the wine (apart from the quality), and if it is pure wine, which is very possible, it is not specified. The vegetarian food is quite characteristic of that world in which this sort of diet is constitutive of that renunciation of the human norm sought by charismatics like Apollonius. Death, associated with meat, which is the result of a violent death, is incompatible with the divine. An anecdote told by Porphyry in his *Life of Plotinus* is revealing. The philosopher introduces an Egyptian priest to his divine personal assistant. But in the excitement of this experience, one of his friends, a spectator of the scene, accidentally strangles the little bird that he is holding, and the demon disappears because he cannot bear the presence of death.[81]

One last aspect is unambiguously Egyptian. The falcon is, it has been said, a symbol of the god and his sacred animal. As a sacred animal, it could not be killed, and such "murders" could give rise to mutinies in Greco-Roman Egypt.[82] However, killing a sacred animal also takes on a symbolic function in the structure of the rite; by killing the animal, the sorcerer cuts himself off from the laws meant for human beings. The murder of the sacred animal then becomes a rite of separation, comparable to those ritual murders spoken of in the secret societies. In the thinking of Egypt, killing a sacred animal had always been a sign of extreme impiety. Such was the case of Cambyses or Antiochus Epiphanes, who killed the bull Apis, or in the much crueler story, told by Manetho, of the coalition of the Hyksos and the Jews who forced the priests to kill and eat their sacred animals.[83]

In the structure of our rite, in which we would expect to find the tripartite structure of the rite of passage, the rites of integration seem poorly in evidence. In many cases, it is the common meal that reintroduces the participants to ordinary life, even though in our ritual, this meal with the divinity is the main event of the phase of marginality. We have, however, those curious instructions concerning the behavior of the magician at the moment when he may leave: the magician must walk backward barefoot. Walking backward is found as a final rite in a whole series of ritual scenarios for magic.[84] Normally, the rites of integration express the new status: walking backward could be the sign that the magician has definitively left the human norm, and going barefoot can have the same function. After all, it is also characteristic of the charismatics like Apollonius.

This rite made use of some elements of the Egyptian sun mythology, yet the *parhedros* was named Horos-Agathos Daimon. A god, of course, is more powerful than a *parhedros;* one can obtain even the Sun God himself in this role. The great papyrus of the Bibliothèque Nationale contains a ritual instruction, addressed to king Psammetichus by a certain Nephotes. Its purpose is to obtain powerful divinatory abilities: "When you have tried it, you will be amazed at the miraculous nature of this operation."[85] The operation includes two very distinct parts: the actual divinatory rite, which must be repeated each time one wants to consult the god about the future (lines 222–285), and the prior rite, which is named *Sustasis to Helios,* a rite that was performed once and that definitively transforms the performer: "Come back as lord of divine nature after performing this rite."[86]

Its form is as simple as it is odd. At sunrise, the future magician goes up to the highest part of his house and unfolds a sheet of pure white linen. At noon, the magician crowns himself with black ivy, undresses, and stretches out on the sheet, with eyes "covered with an all-black band" and wrapped up like a corpse; with eyes still closed but turned to the sun, the magician recites a long prayer to the god Typhon. At the end, a sea falcon will appear and touch the recumbent body with its wings. This is the central act. After that, the magician rises, dresses all in white, makes a fumigation with incense, thanks the god, and comes down from the roof.

The prayer enlightens us about the meaning that the rite had for the indigenous participants. The magician played the role of an associate of Seth-Typhon, killed by his enemies Isis and Horus. And in our text, Seth-Typhon is a form of the Sun God. The god is fooled, and in the form of a bird, he comes to aid his endangered associate.

This is the ideology, the mythological superstructure. Underlying it, however, we recognize a well-known ritual structure. The magician seeks the point farthest in space from his everyday dwelling. As the magician seeks contact with the Sun, it is the vertical direction that matters, and thus the magician must go up onto the roof, which is the highest point of the house. The magician performs the ritual in a pure space, as in other rituals one seeks the inside of a temple or a place "on the banks of the Nile, not yet touched by a man's foot."[87] Our ritual creates this space by unfolding the sheet of pure material. In this sacred space, the magician undresses, then in the end puts on other clothes, new and white. The initiatory function represented by such changes of clothes is well-known. In this same space, the magician undergoes ritual death and resurrection. The magician is wrapped up like a mummy and crowned with black ivy, the plant of Osiris, that infernal Dionysus, Lord of the Dead. The resurrection follows, resulting from contact with the divine, thanks to the wing of the falcon. Restored to life, the magician is transformed into a superhuman Lord "just like the gods." This is a most instructive example of the initiatory symbolism of death and rebirth, whose curious absence has been noted in the Greco-Roman mystery cults.[88]

By way of conclusion, I would like to stress a few points. A rite of initiation is also a kind of self-definition, and this is also true for magicians. The most prominent feature of this self-definition is the search for the divine. Apuleius's fellow citizens, it seems, had not been completely wrong to suspect of a magician someone who went in for the divine more zealously than was either usual or necessary.

The rites of initiation analyzed in this chapter follow a well-defined ritual structure and contain well-known ideologies—be it van Gennep's tripartition, the ideology of death and resurrection, or the function of a change of status. This fact is not that surprising, but it should be stressed that this does not mean that these rites have a venerable antiquity. The use of the terminology of the mystery rites and the fact that a certain number of rites peculiar to mystery cults crop up in the middle of magic, make us rather suspect that mystery rites could have had a decisive influence on the formation of magical rites. To prove this hunch, however, would be quite another matter.

Magic thus fits into a set of well-known facts about the religion of the imperial era, and one final remark will confirm it. The essential goal of the potential magician is to acquire a *parhedros*, that demoniacal or divine companion who helps and protects the magician for life. But the search for such a powerful helper is not the prerogative of magicians. The philosophers too had their companions, as is shown by Plotinus and his Egyptian rival; Socrates' *daimonion*, which became a focus of later platonic interest, was viewed as a precursor of this conception.[89] Moreover, this quest for companions and individual protectors intensified in later antiquity until, finally, the Christian saints became the most effective and sought-after *parhedroi*.[90]

5

CURSE TABLETS AND
VOODOO DOLLS

THE MAGICIANS whom we met in the preceding chapters, those people who were driven by an excessive desire for contact with the divine and who took their meals face-to-face with a god, hardly correspond to received ideas about sorcerers. Other activities, widespread and often discussed, are much closer to these ideas, notably the rites of binding (*defixiones*), which are attested to over a very long period of time and which became the very emblem of black magic.

The ritual binding in antiquity has been well investigated, much more so than have other domains of ancient magic, mainly because of the existence of texts.[1] These texts, primarily written on tablets of lead, have sparked the interest of archaeologists and epigraphers. On that account there exist two collections of documents, old but indispensable. First is the one put together by Richard Wünsch in 1897, to conclude the publication of the Attic inscriptions of the *Inscriptiones Graecae*.[2] A few years later, in his thesis, Auguste Audollent collected all the texts, Greek and Latin, that were not included in Wünsch's publication.[3] We are familiar with the progress made in epigraphy and archaeology since the beginning of this century. A very large number of new tablets have come to light, but only a considerably smaller number have been decently published. The texts are poorly written, often on badly preserved sheets of lead and in sometimes puzzling Greek or Latin, and thus they are difficult to read, to translate, and to understand in their religious and social setting; consequently, they have not proved very attractive to scholars. Still, the collection of texts with translations and comments presented by John Gager is a great step in the right direction and opens this strange world to social historians and historians of religion; all the more urgent is the need for new and comprehensive editions. The catalog published in 1985 by David Jordan has shown the vastness of the territory yet to be cultivated.[4]

LITERARY SOURCES

The practice of ritual binding is not invisible in literary texts. The first instance of binding has been detected in Aeschylus' reference to the "binding hymn" of the Eumenides;[5] in Cicero's lifetime, Curio could, to excuse his spectacular lapses of memory, accuse his adversary Titinia of having bound his tongue; Pliny the Elder judges binding spells nearly omnipresent in his era; and for the era from Tiberius to Nero, Tacitus reports a whole series of accusations of *devotio*, as do later authors, pagans and Christians alike.[6]

But it is once again Plato who gives us the first detailed information. In the passage of the *Republic* on the itinerant seers, he makes them promise to harm the enemies "by incantations and binding spells."[7] He comes back to it in the *Laws*, where he not only describes the respective rituals—sorcery, *pharmakeía* with the help of incantations and binding spells, and with "waxen images" that were put under doors and on graves—and specifies the legal sanctions against them, but also offers a proper psychological theory of injurious magic.[8] At about the same era, the orator Dinarchus spoke of magical binding, if we are to believe the lexica.[9] The practice thus is well-attested in the fourth century B.C.

However, the goal of these practices, as Plato defines it, "to harm one's enemies," remains vague. A papyrus from the imperial epoch, now in the British Museum, is more detailed: "I bind NN to some particular end: that he be unable to speak, that he does not contradict, that he can neither look at nor speak against me, that he be subject to me as long as this ring is buried. I bind his reason and mind, his thoughts, his actions, so that he be impotent against all men. And if it concerns a woman: let this woman be unable to marry some particular man."[10]

The usual objective of ritual binding is, thus, to subject another human being to one's will, to make the person unable to act according to his or her own wishes. The papyrus presupposes that someone specifies this as a function of whatever is the case, erotic or otherwise. Following this casuistry, Audollent had classified the texts as a function of their practical purposes, which makes five rather clearly delimited groups. They are as follows, in Audollent's Latin terminology:[11]

(1) the *defixiones iudicariae* ("judicial spells"), in which one attempts to do harm to one's adversaries at a trial. Although these spells most often come from Athens and from the fifth and fourth centuries B.C., there are examples in all eras and from all regions;[12]

(2) the *defixiones amatoriae* ("erotic spells"), which have the aim of causing reciprocal and wild love in a beloved person. A literary subject as early as Sophocles in the *Trachiniae*, this erotic magic is also very widespread;[13]

(3) the *defixiones agonisticae* ("agonistic spells"), in the context of the amphitheater or other spectacles, and which are especially well attested to in the imperial era;[14]

(4) the *defixiones* against slanderers and thieves; there is an impressive series of them from the sanctuary of Demeter at Cnidos, but also evidence from other places and eras;[15]

(5) the *defixiones* against economic competitors, attested to from the fourth century B.C. up to the imperial era (in the magic papyri).

Magical binding is, above all, a rite. To understand it better, the first thing to do is reflect on the ancient terminology: behind the facts of language appear the facts of ritual.

CATEGORIES AND FORMULAS

Plato and Dinarchus both use the words "to bind" (*katadeîsthai*) and "binding (spell)," *katadesmós*. This was common usage, as is shown by the inscriptions; in the Attic material from the fifth and fourth centuries B.C., *katadeîn* is the dominant verb. Literally, it means "to bind (or to tie) down," which leads to the meaning of "to bind (or to tie) fast, immobilize," with a meaning of the preverb *kata-* as in *katékhein*, "to hold low, hold immobile." This semantics fits in most cases, and it is confirmed by an etymological wordplay: "I tie Euandros in ties of lead . . . Euandros the actor." Correspondingly, breaking the spell is expressed in the vocabulary of unbinding of what has been bound: "I bind down and shall never unbind."[16]

But, in the world of the magicians, the use of the term "down below" is not always innocent. Consider this other text, both long and frightful, which is inscribed on a tiny sheet of lead and dates from the beginning of the fourth century B.C.:[17]

(A)(1) I bind down Theagenes, his tongue and his soul and the words he uses; (2) I also bind down the hands and feet of Pyrrhias, the cook, his tongue, his soul, his words; (3) I also bind down the wife of Pyrrhias, her tongue and her soul; (4/5) I also bind down the cook Kerkion and the cook Dokimos, their tongues, their souls and the words they use; (6) I also bind down Kineas, his tongue, his soul, and the words with which he helps Theagenes; (7) I also bind down the tongue of Pherekles, his soul, and his testimony in favor of Theagenes; (8) I also bind down the tongue of Seuthes, his soul, and the words he uses, just like his feet, his hands, his eyes, and his mouth; (9) I also bind down the tongue of Lamprias, his soul, and the words he uses, just like his feet, his hands, his eyes, and his mouth.
(B) All these I bind down, I make them disappear, I bury them, I nail them down. At the court and before the judge, when they are to appear and to testify against me, that they cannot appear before a court of justice at all either in words or in deeds.

This text is made up of two very distinct parts. First, there is a list of the victims that uses the two formulas, "I bind A, his tongue, his soul, and the words he uses," and "I bind B, his tongue, his soul, and his words"; one may add "his feet, his hands, his eyes." When specifying the role of a victim, one can vary: "the words with which he helps Theagenes," "the testimony he bears in favor of Theagenes." But always, at the center of this formulary, as simple as it is flexible, is found the verb "I bind down," from which derives the name of "binding spells" (*katadesmoí*) given to these texts already in their time.

The second part is an emphatic summary ("All these I bind down, I make them disappear, I bury them, I nail them down") and the indication of the actual reason for the spell. Theagenes and the speaking voice (for brevity's sake: the sorcerer) must be confronted at the bar, and the other eight persons are friends and helpers in favor of Theagenes. Thus, the spell, which is meant to prevent them from appearing before the court, belongs to the group of *defixiones iudicariae*. It is because of this function that the text primarily attacks the oratorical and intellectual abilities; the further threat against "his feet, his hands, his eyes" intends to prevent their physical appearance in court.

But the victims are not just bound down—this we could read as a stronger (or more emphatic) way of binding, of "tying tight"—they are also buried and nailed down. These words are more than just emphasis: the victims are pushed down, into the subterranean world; are they to become the victims of the subterranean powers? The answer will become clear after a more searching analysis of the texts.

Judicial spells were very widespread in Athens between the middle of the fifth and the end of the fourth century, during the era of the greatest growth of the Athenian democracy and its judiciary institutions. However, they are attested to already from fifth century Sicily (where Gorgias is witness of the contemporary height of rhetoric), and they were not to disappear completely in the succeeding eras.[18] Cicero knows at least one (not very serious) case in his own era, and among the currently known texts, there are instances from the imperial age. An interesting example comes from the area of the Gallic *Santones*. The text was found with another of the same kind and with coins of Marcus Aurelius, dated into the year 172 A.D.

denuntio personis infra / scribtis Lentino et Tasgillo, / uti adsint ad Plutonem. / quomodo hic catellus nemini / nocuit, sic . . . nec / illi hanc litem vincere possint. / quomodi nec mater huius catelli / defendere potuit, sic nec advo/cati eorum eos defendere {non} / possint, sic ilos inimicos /. . . (followed by a whole series of enigmatic words—either garbled Latin or magical words).

I announce to the persons mentioned hereunder Lentinus and Tasgillus, that they must appear in court before Pluto. As this cat has not harmed anyone, in such a way . . . that they cannot win this trial. And in the same way that the mother of this cat was unable to defend him, let their lawyers be unable to defend them, let these adversaries. . .[19]

Much more ambiguous is a text found in Brigantium, on the Lake of Constance, whose letter-forms date back to the first century A.D.:

Domitius Niger et / Lollius et Iulius Severus / et Severus Nigri / servus advers/arii Bruttae et quisquis adve/rsus illam loqutus est: omnes perdes.
Domitius Niger, Lollius, Iulius Severus and Severus, the slave of Niger, the enemies of Brutta and all those who spoke against her, you will destroy them all.[20]

The aim of the spell is somewhat ambiguous. At first sight, the naming of *adversarii*, enemies, would suggest a judicial confrontation (of which we have other examples); the perfect tense *(adversus illam loqutus est)*, however, makes one rather think of a talking in the past, i.e., slander. The divinity invoked will have known what it was about.

These three texts present the three types of formulas used by the binding spells: (a) the mere statement in the first-person singular "I bind" (Attic example); (b) the address to a given power, often in the imperative, more rarely in the subjunctive, or, as in the text from Brigantium, in the future; and (c) more complex, the juxtaposing of two parallel facts, of which one depicts the ritual action (among the *Santones* the cruel and gruesome killing of a tomcat) and the other depicts what is wished for the victim. Since Audollent this type of formula has been called a *similia similibus* formula; Frazer preferred the rather loose term *sympathetic magic*.

Whereas in the first text, from the fourth century, one does not wish to harm permanently, but only to prevent one's adversary from appearing in court, the more recent texts are more menacing. In this case, it is necessary to *perdere*, to ruin one's adversaries, they must go to Pluto; what is sought is the death of the adversaries.

Before exploring these horrors, let us return for a moment to the formulas and their variants, notably the first one, which is fairly widespread and of which the implications are not very clear. Next to the use of the simple utterance "I bind (down)," there exist two major variations, the replacement of the verb with another, more or less synonymous one, and the addition, with the help of a preposition, of a divine name to the syntagm "I bind" and its synonymous expressions.

The large number of verbs used to express the one ritual is remarkable. The verb *katadeō* and its Latin homonym *defigo*, which are at the root of the technical terms *katadesmós* and *defixio*, are not alone, and they are not even dominant in the epigraphic texts. The literary texts and the modern terminology tend to be misleading. Even in Attica itself, where "to bind" is dominant, we also have the verb *katagráphō*, "to enroll, register," which is rather frequent outside of Attica.[21] There, it is the religious terms for "to dedicate," *anatíthēmi* and *anieróō*, that are the commonest terms, less frequent "to write down" (*engráphō*, that is unto the tablet) and "to register" (*apográphō*, as with a magistrate— although the preverb might also have the force of "to write away," "to make disappear by writing.")[22] Later, we also note "to adjure," *horkízō* and *exhorkízō*. In Latin, setting aside the derivatives of "to bind" (*ligare*, *alligare*, and *obligare*), we find the verbs *dedicare* and *demandare*, "to dedicate," *adiurare*, "to entreat," that is, a terminology formed after the Greek.

Thus, instead of the simple action of "binding" aimed at the victim, there are verbs that seek to define a relationship between the victim and a divinity: one "dedicates" a man to a particular superhuman being, "registers" him in the god's world. It is only natural that rather often, the simple structure (verb and direct object) is completed by the mention of the divinity: "I register Isias, daughter of Autocleia, with Hermes Who Detains. Detain her with you. I bind Isias down to Hermes Who Detains—the hands and feet of Isias, her whole body."[23] This example, dating from about 400 B.C. and found in Euboean Carystus, shows that the different formulas have more or less the same function: "I bind" and "I register" do not differ in their effects; the victim is still delivered to Hermes, who detains (therefore his epithet) him by tying up his limbs.

There are other texts that are even more revealing, which come from the two extremities of the ancient world, one from Cnidus, the other from Arezzo. The one from Cnidus, which dates from the end of the Hellenistic era, was found in the sanctuary of Demeter and Kore: "Nanas dedicates Emphanes and Rhodo to Demeter and Kore and to the gods around Demeter and Kore, because they received a deposit from Diocles, but did not return it and embezzled it. Let this be beneficial and salutary for me, and harmful for them who did not return the deposit, even if they are opposed to it."[24]

The other example, which comes from a mineral spring in the vicinity of Arezzo, can be dated from the middle of the second century A.D. "Q. Letinius Lupus, who is also called Caucadio, who is the son of Sallustia Veneria or Veneriosa: he is the man whom I deliver, dedicate, and sacrifice to your divine power, so that you, Aquae Ferventes, unless you prefer to be called Nymphs and by some other name, so that you kill him, slit his throat this very year."[25]

These are borderline cases and might be seen, to a certain

degree, as atypical. Although most of our curse tablets come from tombstones, these two texts were left in a sanctuary, the sanctuary of Demeter, Kore, and Pluto at Cnidus and the sanctuary of the Nymphs that was the spring itself. Although rare, these cases are not isolated: we know of other examples from sanctuaries.[26] One fact, however, is significant: all these divinities are in contact with the subterranean world; they are Demeter, Kore, Pluto, and the Nymphs. We are not as far from the graves as we might think. Instead of throwing the texts into a spring, as in Arezzo (or, later, Roman Bath), at other places the curse tablets were thrown into wells.[27] And the papyrus from the British Museum already quoted considers a whole range of what it calls a "Buried Binding Spell"—the tablet is hidden in the earth or the sea, a river, a water pipe, a tomb, or, again, a well.[28] One thus always seeks contact with the subterranean world; and if the dead in their graves constitute preferred and natural intermediaries, that state does not rule out other ways, not only through the intermediary of springs and wells but also through divinities who are concerned with the subterranean realm. This revelation confirms those ancient authors who established a close relationship between magicians and the powers of the netherworld.[29] In a reversal characteristic of the magicians, they seek the movement downward, toward the center of the earth, whereas in the daily worship of polis or family, it is the movement upward, toward the celestial divinities, the *superi*, that is sought.

The text from Arezzo shows yet another reversal. The victim is named A. Letinius Lupus, son of Sallustia Veneria or Veneriosa; he is defined by the name of his mother, not by his father's name, as was customary in Greek and Roman society (and already with their Indo-European ancestors). This is a detail found just about everywhere in the world of the *defixiones*, in which the victim and sometimes the sorcerer are defined this way. We have already encountered this usage in the text found in Carystus, where Isias is called the daughter of Autokleia. One interpretation was to see in it the vestiges of a matrilinearity, if not of a magical tradition deep-rooted in the phase of the *Mutterrecht*; but that is sheer fancy. Somewhat clearer minds have invoked the principle *pater semper incertus*: one can identify only the mother with certainty. In a domain in which, as the text from Arezzo testifies, precision was sought, the patronymic name alone would not have been judged sufficiently precise.[30] But is it really a matter of precision when we do not even know whether the mother's *cognomen* is Veneria or Veneriosa? Biology should not be confused with institutions; magic does not seek a higher precision than do the Greek and Roman civil institutions that are content with the patronymic name. Yet other scholars pointed out that the definition through the name of one's mother was a common Egyptian practice; and, after all, magic comes from Egypt.[31] This might certainly be true, but it still does not explain why Greeks and Romans took over an Egyptian custom so alien to their own ways. There exists a simple solution: the use of the mother's name, the reverse of the common practice in institutions, is yet another instance of the series of reversals characteristic of magic.

What distinguishes the two latter texts from the huge number of comparable binding spells is the resemblance with the ritual curse or imprecation (*dirae*) as it is known in the Greek and Roman religion.[32] Facts of language contributed to the resemblance: the term *devotio*, which is usual for the imprecation in Roman religion, is also the term regularly used by Tacitus to refer to accusations of magical binding. Audollent already saw it; and he went to a lot of trouble to work out the distinction between *defixio* and *devotio*.[33] According to him, the main difference would be that the imprecation is public and spoken before the whole social group, whereas the ritual binding is secret and private. In actual fact, the difference is fundamental. The famous

Dirae Teorum, the official imprecations proclaimed by the city of Teos, had to be uttered by the magistrates in the public space of the theater during the three great festivals of the polis, the Anthesteria, the Heraklea, and the Dia.[34] The funerary imprecations were inscribed in the monuments, plainly readable for those who could and wished to read them. Herodes Atticus, the extremely rich sophist of the Antonine epoch, had literally strewn his Attic land with similar imprecations engraved on beautiful steles of Hymettian marble; what we cannot know, though, is whether such funerary curse texts had been accompanied by an appropriate ritual at the time when the grave was closed.[35]

But this publicity goes together with another situation, to which we shall have to return, which is that the imprecation is a precaution taken against the possible dangers of the future, political rebellions, or the looting of graves. The future being always unpredictable, it is prudent to call on the gods as guardians of what one wants to protect, without one's being naturally able to give the name of the persons against whom the imprecation is directed. The binding spell, in return, is the result of a present crisis with its roots in the individual past. The circumstances are always perfectly clear, and the spell is directed against one person or several contemporary persons of whom it usually gives us the exact names. There are elements that blur the distinction, in that some spells (classified sometimes under the rubric of "judicial prayers") have a performer who is unable to name the victim who had harmed him in the past; also, there are instances of a community cursing someone after damage done, as did the Athenians with Alcibiades.[36] The curse that Chryses—whom Homer calls a "curser" (*arētēr*) (the translation as "priest" banalizes the term)—directs against the Greeks, at the beginning of the *Iliad*, is his reaction to a personal crisis caused by an event in the past (his humiliation at the hands of Agamemmon); Chryses, however, does not react in public, he curses the Greeks well away from them, on a lone beach.[37] Clear differentiations remain constructs, always liable to being contradicted by some facts.

We remember the tomcat from the Santones mentioned earlier. Its killer wished his adversary to be immobilized and maimed in the same way that he had immobilized and maimed the animal. This wish belongs to the category that Audollent named the *similia similibus*. The Gallic example, although late, is not different from what we find in the earlier Greek spells, as they were found from the late fifth century onwards. These texts can be put into two large groups: those that compare the fate of the victim with the fate of the dead person into whose grave the spell is slipped, and those that compare the victim with the lead tablet.

A tablet of lead, coming from a tomb in Megara and dating from the second or first century B.C., bears the following formula: "O Pasianax, when you read these letters (*grámmata*), but you will never read these letters, O Pasianax, and Neophanes will never bring a trial against Aristander, but, O Pasianax, in the same way that you lie here inert, in the same way Neophanes will fall into inertia and nothingness."[38] This is a curious text, which professes a cruel irony regarding the dead man, Pasianax. It is one of the rare case in which the name of the deceased who serves as intermediary is found attested to.

Let us be more precise. The text begins with a rather commonplace epistolary formula. After all, *grámmata* does not designate only "the letters" inscribed on the sheet of lead, but also "the letter" sent, like *litterae* in Latin. The binding spell thus takes the form of a letter addressed to the dead man. It is an element that has already been pointed out, and other textual signs have been collected that were thought to confirm the hypothesis that the curse tablets, at least originally, could have had the form of letters.[39] But examples are rare in which, as in our case, the text can be considered a letter addressed to the deceased, and a text like the Attic spell that begins by "I am sending this letter to Hermes and Persephone" is just about unique.[40] In any case, there is no example old enough for us to be able to conclude that originally the curse tablet was a letter addressed to the infernal divinities.

There is another explanation for this address, which is so often attested to, to the dead man or to the chthonian divinities. The papyri have taught us that it was necessary to recite the text while engraving it on the metal: not only was the spell recited, but also it was put in writing at the same moment. The writing thus has the goal of fixing the language spoken, of making it permanent.[41] It is but natural that often the effects of the spell were conditioned by the physical survival of the written text.[42] By lodging the text in a tomb or a well, by directing it to the subterranean powers, one tried to get these words made lasting to reach the divine, demonic, or heroic addressee. Thus, we have two actions that are not quite parallel: on the one hand, the inscribing of the text parallel to the spoken prayer shows a redundancy intended to ensure the message's arrival; on the other, lodging it close to the netherworld adds a further dimension. Putting the message in the form of a letter would be from this viewpoint merely a secondary detail. It is still true that, even in this moderate form, the dead man in his tomb becomes a kind of infernal postman who brings the text to the divine or demonic addressees. This could also explain why, in the current state of research, it seems that there exist many tablets with binding spells that were not deposited in the graves of *áhōroi* or *biaiothána-toi*, people who had died at a young age or in a violent death and who were considered the ideal helpers of sorcerers because they nurtured a grudge against the still living.[43] If the dead is only a messenger, it is not necessary to rely on such specific traits.

The opposite of death is not just life: it is the heightened life of love. Thus, it is not surprising that similar comparisons are primarily attested to in erotic binding: "In the same way that the corpse who is buried here be unable to speak or say a word, that she lie close to him [not the corpse, but her lover] in the same way and be unable to speak or say a word." In this text the contrast between death and love, silence and talking, is made very clear.[44] Some four centuries earlier, a text from Attica has it this way: "Just as this corpse is useless, so may all the words and deeds of Theodora be useless with regard to Charias and the other people."[45]

The second group consists of formulas that compare the victim and the very tablet on which the spell is written. An Attic text from the fourth century, that begins with a list of names, continues as follows: "In the same way that this is cold and 'out of the true,' let the words of Krates be cold and 'out of the true' in the same way, his as well as those of the accusers and lawyers who accompany him."[46]

Written from right to left, the text really is "out of true": in its time, the direction from left to right had long imposed itself. Its reverse, retrograde writing that is not rare among the texts of binding spells,[47] constitutes one of those reversals characteristic of the world of magic. Normally, the texts do not explain their way of writing; it is sufficient that one acts in the reverse way of what is usually done. The explanation given this time thus seems a secondary improvisation dreamed up by someone who wanted to give meaning to a traditional and independent ritual form.

Another characteristic feature is the reference to the special nature of lead: the metal is "cold."[48] Moreover, it has other properties exploited by sorcerers; lead is considered "without luster," "without value," or "useless," in the same way that the words and acts of all those whose names will be engraved on the tablet will be useless.[49]

Coldness, absence of luster, value, and utility give the impression of attending to so many personal variations on the characteristics of a metal traditionally destined to receive binding spells. This circumstance too has given rise to a scholarly debate; some scholars have emphasized that the choice of lead for these texts was originally determined by the cold and dead nature of this metal.[50] But that opinion can no longer be maintained. We have enough spells on sheets of papyrus, coming from Egypt and preserved, no doubt, because of the extremely favorable climate, to venture the hypothesis that such perishable sheets must also have existed in other areas of the ancient world from which have come down to us only texts on the infinitely more resistant sheets of lead. There are recipes on the papyri that recommend the use of papyrus, often of the highest quality ("hieratic paper"), as in one of the papyri of the British Museum that introduces the recipe for a binding spell with the words: "Take some hieratic paper or a sheet of lead."[51] From literary sources we know about binding spells written on wax tablets.[52] Wax tablets, papyrus, and lead are the three most widespread writing materials in the ancient world, lead being especially important in the archaic and classical eras. There is sufficient evidence to prove that lead was the material ordinarily used for letters in eastern archaic Greece, and much later writers still remember this use as an archaism.[53] The choice of material is thus easily explained. It is a secondary development, an *a posteriori* ritualization of a common practice of writing on lead; some of its properties were secondarily charged with an affective and symbolic value not intended in its original use.

Thus, we find the same process in the two categories of *similia similibus* formulas. The magicians exploit an earlier and traditional usage, the deposition of the tablet in the tomb, the use of lead, the use of retrograde writing, to end up with new and unexpected meanings. This permanent search for new combinations of meaning seems characteristic of the sorcerer's world. It would thus be erroneous to speak of sympathetic magic in these cases. What is at stake is not a mystical, "sympathetic" harmony between objects and people, but rather the construction of a universe in which things and acts carry a new and completely unusual meaning, entirely different from everyday life.

As to the localization of the curse tablets, we glimpse also a chronological development, although the clues are less unequivocal. The binding spells from the classical epoch all seem to come from graves; at the time of the papyri, on the other hand, there exists a whole spectrum of possibilities for the deposition of the texts.[54] In a recipe for ritual binding with the help of a magic ring, a papyrus from the British Museum recommends depositing the ring in an abandoned well or burying it in the tomb of a person untimely dead, and it gives two curiously contradictory reasons. The dead person would serve as mediator and assistant (it is the well-known theme of the infernal postman), but it would also be necessary to hide the ring, for it would retain its power only as long as it was not found.[55] This second reason is presumably a later development, deriving from the custom of seeking contact with the subterranean divinities through the dead and their tombs.

RITES

We remember the suggestion that "to bind down" would mean more than simply "immobilize," a suggestion requiring that the force of the prefix of the Greek verb be wholly spelled out. The reconstruction of the ritual (the formulae lead to the ritual) will supply this specification. It will also complicate things; "to bind" does not always refer to the same procedure, depending on the era and the kinds of ritual.

The first indications capable of providing this specification come from the Attic spell that, in a rather striking formula, sums up what the actor wants to see happen to his or her adversaries: "All of them, I bind them, I make them disappear, I bury them, I nail them down."[56] This list of actions conjures up a ritual sequence, whose object is not the very person of the adversaries, but the tablet of lead that bears their names. After "binding" the lead, one "makes it disappear" in the tomb where one had hidden it, "one buries it" and "one nails it down." We sometimes find traces of this last practice. Numerous lead tablets have holes, even preserve, though more rarely, the tool that had pierced them, an iron nail; obviously, sometimes the nail was left in the folded or rolled-up tablet.

The hypothesis of a ritual sequence that would be perceptible through our four verbs runs into two difficulties. The first is that the sequence of the actions—binding, making disappear, burying, nailing—is not logical; it would be more satisfying to let the nailing follow immediately after the binding. However, the series of verbs as it is transmitted has a much stronger rhetorical expressivity—the most aggressive act, nailing, forming the climax of the sequence—and one is, after all, in the presence of an oral rite with its own rhetoric. But even if this explanation is accepted, it is still true that the act referred to by the verb "to bind down" is not as clear as the rest. Is this really a separate rite—perhaps the tablets were tied with a thread of organic matter that left no trace in the soil? Or is it only the summing up of the three following actions, so that "making disappear, burying, and nailing down" together constitute the act of "binding"? The answer is yet open; the rituals might give a clue.

A first clue to the actual rites appears in the rare situation in which systematic and precise excavations have made it possible to preserve the whole context. Such is the case of a tomb from the Athenian Kerameikos which the vases date shortly after 400 B.C.[57] In addition to these vases and the skeleton of the deceased, the tomb contained a rather worn judicial spell, a list of nine men's names in the nominative and without patronymics (Babyrtides, Xophygos, Nikomakhos, Oinokles, Mnesimakhos, and so on) but also carried the threat that the rite was aimed at every person who "will be accuser or witness with them." This laconic formulation is not exceptional in its time. The text of eight lines is printed on a tablet of lead that also serves as a cover for a small lead container (about eleven centimeters long, six centimeters wide, and twenty-four millimeters high); the tablet held a small lead statuette of a man, with prominent genitals, whose arms are tied on the back, while the right leg bears, engraved in tiny characters, the name of Mnesimakhos, who is found on the list. In the meantime, similar figures have been recovered from two neighboring graves.[58]

Not satisfied with writing the text, this person also molded a bound figurine. The fact of tying the figurine prefigures what is going to happen to the victim. "To bind down," thus, is nothing other than immobilizing. There are, moreover, other statuettes of lead with prominent bonds of iron or bronze.[59] But that is not all. The cover of the container is pierced with two holes that are not accidental but were made by a pointed object, probably a nail, another sign of "nailing down."

The meaning of this ritual act becomes clearer yet in the few cases in which no statuettes were used, but instead live animals, like the tomcat of the Santones, were used. Indeed, we read the following on the second tablet from the same context:

> *aversos ab hac lite esse quo/modi hic catellus aversus/ est nec surgere potest,/ sic nec illi, sic transpecti sint / quomodo ille.*

Let them be turned away from this trial in the same way that this cat is turned away and cannot get up. Let it be thus for them as well. Let them be pierced through like the cat.[60]

It is not only because it was killed that the cat cannot get up, but also because it was "turned away" or rather "twisted" (aversus) and "pierced through" (transpectus). The explanation once again comes from these figurines of magical binding of which we have a rather large series, from different eras and different regions, from classical Attica to late Egypt. Among these figurines, some are truly aversi, not only tied but with the head turned rigidly toward the back, often with the feet turned in the same direction, thus barring any normal movement, so that the person is truly immobilized. The cat had also undergone the same "reversal" of the head; and Libanius gives an account of a magical chameleon: "Its head was squeezed between its backlegs, one frontleg was missing, the other was stuffed into its mouth in order to make it keep quiet." Other figurines were—and some are still—pierced with nails.[61] The most striking example comes from the Louvre; it is a figurine of a naked young woman, kneeling, her arms tied behind her back, pierced with thirteen needles.[62] The little cat was probably pierced through in the same way. (It is not by chance that it is a cat, moreover; the "deification"—to repeat the euphemism used in these texts—of a tomcat is relatively frequent in the magic papyri.)[63] As to the figurines, even when not pierced by nails or needles, they almost always have been intentionally damaged; two wax figurines, a man and a woman kissing, carefully wrapped in a papyrus bearing an erotic binding spell, are a rare exception.[64]

To obtain further details and even a kind of indigenous commentary, we must turn to the papyri. The great papyrus in the Bibliothèque Nationale contains a ritual called "a marvelous erotic binding spell."[65] The largest part of this long text is constituted of the two *logoi,* the verbal rites accompanying other rites. The text begins as follows: "Take some wax [or clay] from a potter's wheel and make two figurines, one male, the other female.[66] Make the male one armed like Ares, holding in his left hand a sword, which he aims at the right collarbone of the female figurine; let her have her arms tied behind her back and be kneeling, and let the magical essence be set on her head and around her neck." There follows a long list of magic words to be engraved on the body of the female figurine—on her head, ears, eyes, face, right collarbone, arms, hands, heart, belly, genitals, buttocks, and soles of the feet. It is necessary to write on the breast the name of the victim and that of her mother (315) (which proves that the use of the metronym is intentional, not used for lack of anything better). Then we read, "Take thirteen bronze needles, drive one into her brain," saying, "I stab your brain with the needle, NN [name to be filled in], two in your ears, two in your eyes, and so forth," each time saying, "I stab this member of this person so that she thinks only of me, NN." After the figurines, one has to prepare the tablet: "Take a sheet of lead, write the same incantation, recite it and attach the sheet to the figurines with a thread from a spinning frame, making 365 knots and saying, as you know, 'Abrasax, hold tight.'" Finally, the whole is deposited: "Set them at the time of sunset next to the grave of a person who died prematurely or by violence, and also set down some seasonal flowers."

Such is the rite of preparation and deposition. There follow the oral rites, the long incantation recited and inscribed on the sheet of lead, and the "request," the hexametrical prayer recited facing the setting sun at the moment when the tablet and the figurines are set down.

Before analyzing the texts, let us focus on the preparatory rite and especially on the figurine. What relationship is there between the representation (the figurine) and the person represented (the victim)? What is the purpose of the stabbing with nails or needles? An extensive conception of magic would suggest that the image is more or less identical to the person represented, that what happens to the image also happens to the living person, that the magical mentality is incapable of making the distinction between the representation and the object represented.[67] The facts from antiquity clarify these vague ideas. There is no doubt that the figurines represent the victims whose names, moreover, they often bear. Thus, on the thigh of the figurines held in the container from the Kerameikos is engraved the name of one of the adversaries, Mnesimakhos, and our text prescribes writing the name of the desired woman on the figurine's breast; there other instances of such a practice as well. It is therefore tempting to assume that even in the cases, the most frequent ones, in which the figure did not bear a name, it was nevertheless a substitute in a way identical to the victim.

But representation does not mean identity. The figurine does not need to be a portrait; it suffices that it bears some very superficial resemblance to the identity.[68] The spell from Carystus mentioned earlier concerns a woman, but it is nevertheless engraved on a lead figurine that is not female, which is perhaps male, but more probably of indeterminate sex; it is somewhat difficult to spot an intention of gender differentiation in this hastily executed piece.[69] A vague resemblance to the human figure is sufficient; the figurine is not the more or less identical substitute for the absent person, but the symbol for him.

The same is true for the ritual of our papyrus. The sorcerer-lover makes two figurines, not only the one of the kneeling and tied-up woman but also the one of an Ares who threatens her with his sword. With this figure of the Greek god of war, we leave the space of the simple mimesis of some reality to enter into myth, that is, symbolic representation.

A ritual detail is added. It is necessary to fix "the magical essence" (ousía) on the head or the neck of the female figurine. This essence consists of elements that have been in contact with the woman—fingernails, hair, fabric from her clothing. In rare finds from Egyptian graves, along with the binding spell on lead or papyrus, a lock of hair was preserved.[70] But not all of this is designed to perfect the identity between the statuette and the woman. We find the essence in the same rite during the recitation of the final prayer; the sorcerer speaks it "holding on to the essence of the tomb" (435). A passage of this same prayer, addressed to Helios, shows the function of the "essence": "Send to me at the hour of midnight this demon NN, whose remains I hold in my hands."[71] The "essence" does not identify the sorcerer to the deceased but instead has the role of a pointer that establishes a symbolic relationship between two points, of which one is the object referred to (the "signified": in our case, the actual girl) and the other is the sign (the "signifying": in our case, the figurine).

Since the figurine is not identical to the victim, neither is the piercing of the figurine's members with needles or nails an act of ritual binding or even magical wounding; the performer has no intention to maim or wound the victim. The aim is clearly stated in the text. Each time that he injects a needle, the sorcerer must say, "I pierce this limb of this person, so that she thinks of me alone, the NN." After all, the rite is called a "binding spell": "binding" is the central act. This verb appears only twice, both times in the lógos, and only the second occurrence is useful to us. In the last part of the prayer, the sorcerer orders the demon thus: "Carry this out, bind for all time and force this woman to be obedient to me."[72] The bond created by the demon must be lasting and never-ending.

Let us combine the two ideas. In both cases, the sorcerer seeks to monopolize the beloved woman by removing her from all other men. The members affected by the needles are those that are useful for this relationship. From this point of view, our text constitutes a veritable erotico-magic anatomy of the female body, an analysis of the way in which this total male domination of the female body functions. The eyes, the ears, the mouth, and the brain are useful for sensual and intellectual contact; the feet and the hands create the necessary physical contact (first by bringing her to the lover, than by taking hold of him); the belly and the sexual organs are destined for erotic contacts. But what is sought is not only the monopoly of erotic contact. At the end of his prayer (which the text labels a "request"), the lover-sorcerer commands the demon, "Seize her by the hair, by the entrails, by the sex, by the soul, until she comes to my home and remains without separating from me; do it, bind her for as long as my life lasts, force her to be obedient to me, let her not separate from me at any hour of my life." What is at stake is thus total submission, destined to last a lifetime.

That the goal of the piercing was to monopolize the contact between the man and the woman—to "bind her for as long as my life lasts"—may seem vague in reality. What effect did the magic have in the life of the victim? We find again some indications of it in the "request": the sorcerer-lover asks the demon to act in such a way that the woman can no longer eat or drink, nor sleep nor remain strong and healthy. These are rather commonplace consequences of the erotic desire that we find detailed in both Latin poetry and Greek romances: she has to fall in love, once and for all. The same explanation fits the wish that she not have sexual contact with another man, that her one desire makes her renounce any other liaison.

I stress this because there are cases in which a ritual binding seems to provoke illness.[73] Especially disturbances affecting sexuality are explained as the consequence of a magical attack: Ovid tries to explain his impotence by a binding spell, already Hipponax had recommended a ritual healing for it; and in the ancient East, such rituals were quite common.[74] A more serious instance comes from the Byzantine collection of miracles, the *Lives of the Saints Cyrus and John the Pennyless (Anargyri)*; a certain Theophilus had been magically tied hand and foot, and he suffered from almost unbearable pains in the extremities thus affected.[75] The saints advised him to have fishermen fish in the sea, which he did without even being puzzled by such advice, so great was his confidence in their knowledge. The fishermen brought in a small box containing a figurine in bronze that bore the features of Theophilus, with four nails piercing its hands and feet. The nails were taken out one after the other, and each time a nail was removed, Theophilus recovered the health in the corresponding member.

But this little story—as impressive as it is—does not fit in very well with the ideology of ritual binding. It remains vague about the exact nature of the ritual employed (it is his enemies who wished to do harm to Theophilus, with the help of the demon), and it does not fit into one of the five categories mentioned. It would be advisable to guard against the idea that binding spells could produce diseases by means of similar punctures made in a figurine. The perforation of the members does not have such precise and simple consequences—the mechanism is not so direct.

Another Christian story, taken this time from the *Life of Saint Hilarion*, written by Jerome, confirms this skepticism. A young man fell in love with a "virgin of God" (*virgo Dei*) in Gaza, thus an impossible love. Finally, the young man had himself initiated in magic at the temple of Aesculapius in Memphis, Egypt. Returning after a year, he buried "verbal monsters and monstrous figurines sculpted in a sheet of bronze from Cyprus" under the threshold of the virgin's house. We readily recognize the combination of the text and magic figurines, which Plato already knew were buried under thresholds.[76] The girl's reaction was unexpected: "The virgin went insane; after throwing the cap from her head, she twirled her hair, gnashed her teeth, and called the name of the young man."[77] The binding magic does not give rise to a specific disease, but to a total amorous madness.

It remains to explain the other rite, which in the papyrus is performed with the female figurine. Before sticking the members with needles, one engraves magical words on other parts of the body: head, ears, eyes, face, right collarbone, arms, hands, heart, belly, genitals, buttocks, and the soles of the feet. This list of parts covered with magical words is not identical to the list of members pierced by the thirteen needles, as is shown by simply counting; there are thirteen needles, hence thirteen parts, but sixteen members to be written on. Nevertheless, the two lists are close. There are correspondences (ears, eyes, hands, and soles of the feet); some differences are easy to understand; the head instead of the brain (the head is engraved, the brain is pierced), and the face instead of the mouth (same reason). Finally, there are some additions like the arms (for a technical reason: the arms are easy to write on even if they are tied behind the back, and it is harder to pierce them) and the collarbone, brought into relief by the gesture of Ares, who thrusts his sword into it.

Despite the differences, the lists are thus very close. The second list can be understood as the result of the man's desire to monopolize the erotic relationship with the woman. We can glimpse the same explanation for the first list, apart from the collarbone. The magic words to be inscribed on the different parts are not devoid of sense. They are the names of divinities and demons, and behind some of them appear known names. The name of Thoth is thus written on the heart, that of Ammon on the face, derivatives of the Semitic *melech*, "king," on the arms and hands (it is a widespread divine and demonic name, as on the statuette ascribed to Apuleius and called "King"), and the name IAΩ, Jahweh, on the head; there is a hierarchy. At any rate, the different parts of the body, of which the head forms the most important point, are ritually dedicated to different powers, divine and demonic, even though, at the current stage of research, several aspects of the demonology remain unknown; and the consecration concerns, with some minor variations, the same parts of the female body, which he is going to pierce later. In the world of the magician, the dedication is only a variant of the action of binding: already the text from Carystus identified the two actions. But the magician does not just pierce the members for the purpose of binding them, he also dresses a list of the parts and of their superhuman protectors on whom he has an influence. Besides, assigning the members to divinities is a well-known ritual of healing, called *Gliedervergottung* (deification of limbs) by German Egyptologists. Always, the members of the body are entrusted to the protection of specific divinities; always, as in our text, the list begins with the head and ends with the feet.[78] Seen from this historical perspective, the magical practice appears as evident reversal of this ritual of healing, creating not health but erotic fervor.[79]

This detour via Egypt could shed light on certain facts in Greece proper, beginning with the nature of the ritual act referred to by the verb "to bind." If we again follow the papyrus, after engraving the sheet of lead, the magician ties it with a thread of linen to the figurines, saying "Abrasax, hold it tight." Abrasax is the demon, the letters of whose name, when read as figures, add up to 365, the number of the days in a year; he represents duration, the year, or even better, the Great Year. The tablet itself is tied to the figurine with 365 knots; the bond should last forever, and Abrasax guarantees this. The verb used in his apostrophe, "to hold tight" (*katékhein*), also appears very often on the Attic curse tablets; the magician prays one of these infernal divinities to "hold tight" the victim, in particular Hermes, who draws from there his epithet *Kátochos*. Would it not be possible that someone tied and carefully knotted around sheets a thread that disappeared in the Greek earth over the centuries?

However that may be, in Egypt a ritual was found that combines two figurines (with the name of a victim) and one lead tablet, whereas for the rest of the ancient world, there are only very rare figurines and a huge mass of tablets. Must we conclude that the combination of tablet and figurines was necessary and that the figurines simply were lost? The possibility must be considered that the images were fashioned with other materials less durable than lead; the papyrus speaks of wax or clay, two materials that are not preserved outside of Egypt, and our literary texts, from Plato to the Augustan poets, often enough mention statuettes of wax.[80] But even in Egypt, where statuettes of clay and wax have been preserved, there are examples of texts without statuettes. The goal of the binding ritual must thus have been achieved by the single consecration of the text. This conclusion confirms what we said about the purely symbolic nature of the ritual: the effect of the binding did not depend on a "sympathetic" act performed with the help of voodoo dolls.

The concept of sympathetic magic, however, is still worrisome; there are always spirits to be exorcized, notably Frazerian spirits. It is obvious (and already said) that sorcerers did not wish to wound the victim's members in the same way that they pierced the members of a figurine. Moreover, because, as we have seen, there exists no homology between the performance of the rite and the goal sought after, the sorcerers by all accounts did not wish to kill, or bury, or pierce with nails the victims of the judiciary spell of the fourth century. What they wanted was to act so as to prevent adversaries from appearing in court or, if they did appear, to hinder them from pleading or testifying. No tablet, Athenian or otherwise, earlier than the Roman era expresses the desire to kill an adversary; and even later, the expression of this desire is extremely rare, and not only in the erotic spells, in which it had no reason for being. This sympathetic homology thus exists only in the mind of a superficial observer; it is not surprising that it appears for the first time with a Christian writer.

Another spirit to be exorcized is the psychological spirit, so dear to certain scientific ancestors. Could not psychology help to understand these violent acts, of an unconcealed hostility, that consist of sticking needles in human figurines, of driving a nail into a carefully written text of lead? Would not this be a violence directed against enemies or objects of desire that prove inaccessible, but diverted and channeled toward substitutes? The thesis is well-known, but it too raises difficulties.[81] The first is that the act of violence is an immediate and spontaneous discharge, although there is nothing spontaneous in the rituals. The binding ritual of the papyrus from the Bibliothèque Nationale is extremely complex. We must first fashion two identifiable figurines of clay or wax; how much time does that take? Next, the names of the demons, which are relatively complicated words, must be inscribed. Then, a long and complex incantation must be inscribed and recited. Finally, a hymn must be recited in hexameters. Among these acts requiring a great deal of concentration, the sorcerer pricks the figurine with exactly thirteen needles, in precise places, while reciting precise words. There is no place in this ritual for a spontaneous discharge of erotic frustrations. And even the rituals that we catch sight of behind the judiciary spell of the fifth and fourth centuries seem too complex to suggest the spontaneous outbursts of violent hatred.

But there is another fact, one much more puzzling for those who believe in a psychological approach. According to Plato, it was not the laypersons, those adversaries involved in a complicated trial, who performed the rite, but rather itinerant specialists, to whom no one would think of ascribing feelings of hatred or frustration. Other literary and juridical texts refer to these specialists, but it is the magic texts themselves that often enough suggest this hypothesis.[82] The very fact that the long, erotic binding rite in Paris comes from a book, from a carefully written collection of magic rites, shows the existence of professionals; and the complexity of the rite and its imprecations corroborates this impression. The professional knew how to make figurines, could write, and had a good memory for recalling long oral texts. This professionalism explains that the text from this book has been employed several times in real binding rituals, attested by leaden tablets and spells on papyrus;[83] the unhappy lover would thus have done nothing other than follow the ritual course indicated to him by a professional, performing a particular gesture, pronouncing a particular word—without forgetting to pay the professional afterward (the reputation of greediness has stuck to the magician over the centuries).[84] Now, such a scenario no more allows for spontaneity than it does for violence. If it is really necessary to look to psychoanalysis to understand these rituals, psychoanalysis and psychopathology can only bring to light the very distant psychological foundations of these rituals.

Another observation on the lead tablets goes in the same direction. In the cases in which we find—in Athens, Cyprus, Rome—an entire cache of texts that were not all addressed by the same person to the same adversaries, we could note that they came from the same hand (or from a small number of hands); they were obviously written by the same professional sorcerer. In addition, there was found in a hoard, next to some ten tablets all written in the same hand, with identical formulas but addressed by different persons to different adversaries, a tablet bearing the same text but clumsily written by someone who had not yet achieved sufficient ease in engraving texts of this length on small sheets of lead. Clearly, we are dealing with a sorcerer and his apprentice.[85]

But the rite in the Paris papyrus has more to show. We still have to look at the two oral rites, the spell written also on the tablet, and the hexametrical "request."

The spell is addressed to the infernal powers:[86] "I entrust this binding spell to you, infernal gods HYSEMIGADON and Maiden Persephone, Ereskhigal and Adonis BARBARATHA, Infernal Hermes Thoth [more magical names],[87] and to mighty Anubis Psirinth who holds the keys to Hades, to the infernal gods and demons, to men and women who have died untimely deaths, to youths and maidens, year after year, month after month, day after day, hour after hour." It is a variant of a well-known prayer formula, in which the sorcerer addresses all the powers of a place, those whose names are known and those referred to only by their group name, in order to make sure that no demon or god feels neglected and would therefore take revenge. Thanks to this invocation, the objects that are deposited go into the possession of the powers and must remain so forever.

Yet this is not the central goal of the invocation. Whereas the gods and the infernal demons are the guardians of the magic objects entrusted to them, certain other demons have different but no less precise functions: "I beseech all the demons of this place to stand as assistants beside this demon here."[88] The sorcerer implores the demons who inhabit this particular cemetery—all the powerful dead that there are—to help their new colleague, the deceased, who like them has died before his time and who has suffered a violent death; and it is at his grave that the statuettes and the tablet have been deposited. It is to him alone that the rest of the text is addressed. He is to wake up and to bring the woman desired; if she is unwilling and resists, let him treat her roughly until she comes: "If you perform this for me, I shall right away leave you in peace."[89]

The superhuman and infernal beings who figure in this text

thus have special tasks. A particular demon is isolated as the agent intended to fulfill the magician's desire, and the others are the guardians of the magic objects or are the assistants for their colleague, depending on their position on a topographical grid whose center is the grave selected.

The final hexametrical prayer brings in a new element.[90] The prayer is addressed to the sun: "When you have arrived in the depths of the earth at the abode of the dead, send, at the hour of midnight, this demon to me, NN, whose bodily remains I hold in my hands [this text must be uttered holding in one's hands the magical essence, some parts of the dead person], and who will come constrained by you, to carry out everything that I have in my heart, appearing gentle, harmless, and devoid of hostile thoughts toward me." This prayer is, so to speak, an action parallel to the depositing of the tablet in the grave. The goal of the deposition was to make the sorcerer's text reach the dead person, to go from our world to the infernal world, from up on high to the underworld. Theoretically, one could stop there. But the sun is also a mediator between these two worlds, notably in Egyptian thinking: present in our world, in the heights of the sky, during the day, the sun crosses the world below during the night and then encounters the world of the dead. It is significant that the sun must be addressed at the precise moment when it sets, that is, at the moment that it goes from high to low. We may, incidentally, wonder whether this frequent magical hymn to the sun points not, here again, to a reversal.[91] While so many philosophers and charismatics, models of piety from Socrates to Proclus, passing through Apollonius of Tyana, adore the sun that rises, the sorcerer, on the other hand, adores the setting sun.[92]

The prayer thus adds two things. It guarantees that the demon will arrive without exhibiting either irritation or anger regarding the sorcerer (a rather frequent preoccupation that means that the sorcerers protect themselves with amulets); and it forces the demon to respond to the sorcerer's call, which seems a superfluous action, for one might think that the deposition of the tablet in the grave suffices to bring that about. But two conceptions concerning the abode of the dead coexist here. On the one hand, the dead are considered to inhabit the grave and the cemetery (that is why one asks for the help of the demons, after the depositing of the object); and on the other hand, they are supposed to inhabit a vaguely distant world beyond, beneath the earth, where the gods also live, to whom the first invocation of the tablet is addressed, and where the sun spends each night.

The papyrus mentions the special category of beings constituted by the *áhōroi* and *biaiothánatoi*, those who have died before their life could reach its fulfillment. The concept is an old one; these beings appear already in the texts found on curse tablets from classical Athens. Since Erwin Rohde, scholars have studied these unruly souls, an inexhaustible reservoir of malevolent spirits for the sorcerers.[93] Having quit life before reaching its goal, marriage and procreation, they were reputed to be envious of the survivors and for this reason ready to put themselves at the service of magicians.

Besides the term *áhōroi*, "those who have died an untimely death," found both in the papyri and the actual spells, at least an Attic spell of the fourth century has an even more telling expression—if only it were generally accepted. The text, which deserves closer scrutiny, is written on both faces of a lead tablet; although a crucial part is mutilated, its sense is clear. The first side reads like this:[94] "I bind Theodora to the one at Persephone's side [that is, Hecate] and to the *atélestoi*. May she be herself *atelés*, and whenever she is about to chat with Kallias and with Charias, whenever she is about to discuss deeds and words and business [. . .] words, whatever he indeed says. I bind Theodora to remain *atelés* towards Charias and Charias to forget Theodora, and

Charias to forget [. . .] Theodora and sleeping with Theodora."
The meaning of *atelés* and *atélestoi* is controversial. It is clear that
in the text, the two words are set into relation to each other;
the infernal *atélestoi* have a hand in Theodora being *atelés*. Literally, both words designate someone who has not reached his or
her goal. It is not only Theodora who does not reach her aim,
the same holds true for her words and deeds; there are texts
from Sicily that bind someone into being unsuccessful.[95] It is
also obvious that Theodora is cursed to be unsuccessful in love;
the open question is only what exactly the infernal *atélestoi* are.[96]
The second face is helpful: "Just as this corpse lies *atelés*, so may
all the words and deeds of Theodora be *atélestoi*."[97] It is a *similia
similibus* formula that likens the fate of the corpse to the fate of
Theodora's words and deeds; the two Greek expressions are thus
synonymous. It could follow from this that the *atélestoi* would be
all the dead; but why would they be unsuccessful? In a context
of erotic contest, it is preferable that they be people who died
unmarried: *télos*, after all, is a common Greek word denoting
"marriage"; another text from Attica hopes that the victim, a
woman, should be "without the goal of marriage."[98] The word
atélestoi, in this text, then would be "unmarried ones," ideally
suited to help prevent poor Theodora from marrying.

THE SPELL PUT TO USE

This is what can be learned from the papyrus book in Paris. It
constitutes, as we have said, a collection of recipes; therefore it
shows blanks (NN) where individual names would be inserted.
But we also have—and this is a unique case—six texts that derive
from the recipe attested to by the papyrus.[99] A study of these
texts reveals two things. The first observation is that the copyists
used the original text very freely. They of course always put the
abstract information into concrete form, inserting concrete

names into the blanks (other papyrus recipes even prescribe to do so); but they also shortened or lengthened their original in such a way that it is impossible to say whether it is really our papyrus that serves as a model or another text of the same tradition. Again, as with the *Eighth Book of Moses*, these texts, although secret, were not transmitted with the precision and care taken with literary texts. A second and more surprising observation is that a sorcerer could not, because of this imprecision, learn to perform a rite by means of a book. The most significant indication is the making of the figurines. Although the papyrus prescribes the fashioning of an Ares and a woman, excavations have preserved only female figurines, and even the so-well-investigated city of Antinoupolis has not yielded a single figurine of Ares. In addition, the female figurines never bear the inscription stipulated by the papyrus. This second omission is more easily explained. The dedication of particular body parts to superhuman powers constitutes a ritual parallel to that of sticking with needles, which can on this account be omitted. The other omission is harder to explain. Perhaps the sorcerer left out the mythological scene because it was too complicated and did not provide any additional benefit. Thus, not only is the papyrus text more redundant, but because it contains the Egyptian rite and the Greek myth, it is also more learned and traditional than the concrete performances.

The last question, which brings us to daily life, is that of the situations, the motivations, that could lead a person of antiquity to perform a ritual binding. Christopher Faraone studied this long-neglected problem in a fine essay; to the extent to which I share the conclusions already expressed in the title of his work—"the agonistic context"—I shall be brief.[100]

Since Audollent, as we have seen, binding spells have been classified into five categories: juridical, erotic, commercial, agonistic, and against thieves and slander. To modern feelings, these categories lie on different levels: only the first four pre-suppose a common situation of rivalry (what Faraone calls an agonistic situation). There are always two opposing parties—adversaries in court, rivals who solicit the same erotic favors, circus artists or professionals, business competitors. Always—and this is the central point—ritual binding occurs at a moment when the result of this confrontation is not yet clear. The ritual is thus not an act of vengeance that accompanies the defeat, but rather is a means intended to influence the course of the com-petition.

We have seen this for judiciary spells: their goal was to make the adversaries incapable of appearing before the court. Some earlier scholars, who were disinclined to attribute to the Greeks such unfair behavior, interpreted these texts as the expression of bitterness provoked by loss at a trial. But debate over this was settled by the evidence of an Athenian text that gives the date of the trial, with the verb in the future tense.[101] Further evidence is given by the two cases in which a sudden loss of language during a trial was explained by a binding spell.[102] The same observation holds good for the erotic binding spells. The Attic text against Theodora is quite frank: "[I wish] that Theodora be unsuccessful with Charias, that Charias forgets Theodora and Theodora's child, and that Charias forgets the love with Theo-dora."[103] The situation of rivalry is obvious; to win Theodora, Charias (perhaps the father of her child?) must be removed by means of the ritual. Our modern sensibility is perhaps offended by the fact that the victim of the ritual act is not Charias, but Theodora. But the rite functions in the same way as in the erotic spell of the Paris papyrus book. There too, the recipe assumes the existence of rivals; in the spell, the sorcerer prays that the victim would be unable to have sexual relations (very precisely detailed) with a person other than the sorcerer (or his client). The actually performed ritual texts, which were based on this recipe, very faithfully repeat this manifestly very important passage. The papyrus book also considers the possibility that the victim is married. However, the husband is not cast aside, and the woman is concentrated on: "Do not let NN try to seek pleasure with another man, not even with her husband, with the exception of me" (line 374). This time the passage is not repeated in any of the three copies, because the victims pursued were not married.

There is, however, a difference between the Egyptian papyrus and the Attic text: only the latter tries to reach its goal by explicitly fostering dissension between a couple. This kind of text, which is very clear in another Attic text of the fourth century—"I turn aside Euboula of Aineas, her face, her eyes"—is attested to mainly in Greece proper.[104] Although late literary sources generally accuse the magicians of trying to separate married couples, and the papyri contain recipes in order to achieve this,[105] these texts are in reality very rare in the rest of the ancient world.[106] Here the usual proceeding is to attract, with the help of a powerful demon, the object of one's desire, whether a man or a woman, whether of the same or of the opposite sex.[107] We have seen that rivalry is not absent in these texts, whether the women are already connected with other men or whether the man is the rival of other potential suitors of the young woman.

It is Faraone who has called attention to the commercial spells. Texts have long been known in which victims were referred to by their profession and targeted by their work: "I bind the shop and the professional activity"; "I bind the helmet factory of Dionysios, his house, his activity, his work and his means of subsistence"; "I bind . . . his craft and his tools."[108] Nevertheless, this kind of ritual has not always been clearly enough distinguished from judiciary spells. It was often thought that the professions were only additional details concerning the persons aimed at. It seems evident, though, that these texts must be put in a special class, as is shown by a text on lead from the early third century B.C., coming from a necropolis in Metapontum: "I bind the first workshop of these people. I bind so that they are unable to work, but are unemployed and in misery," followed by the names of seventeen doctors.[109] There is only one explanation for this curious text: a group of (young) doctors founded a private hospital, the first in the city, no doubt against the will of an already-established colleague, who thus wishes them total unemployment.

Finally, for the agonistic spells, it is not necessary to demonstrate the situation of rivalry. Although there exist some examples from the classical and Hellenistic age, most of these texts are of a later date. The spells concerning athletes—runners, wrestlers—are almost banal.[110] More interesting are those concerning the chariot races and that come from the amphitheaters of Rome, Carthage, or other cities. All of them are of rather late date.[111] The victims of these spells are primarily drivers of chariots or their horses. A fairly typical text from Carthage begins with a long list of names of horses (these texts constitute, incidentally, the main source for the names of Greek and Roman horses), followed by an invocation of a demon, which is called by a whole series of Greek magic words (his secret names) and by a Latin invocation (of which I keep the unorthodox orthography):

excito te, / demon, qui ic convers/ans: trado tibi os/ equos ut detineas/ illos et implicentur / nec se movere possent.

I call on you, demon, who lie here [in a grave, from which the text comes]: I deliver these horses to you so that you hold them back and that they get tangled up [in their harness] and are unable to move.[112]

There are much more precise texts in which the failure of the bound driver is described in full detail (and where there is a sudden leap from horses to drivers, easily understandable to the concerned sorcerer, more confusing for the modern reader):

> I bind to them [to the horses] the race, the feet, the victory, the strength, the soul, the speed, drive them crazy, without muscles, without limbs, so that tomorrow, in the hippodrome, they will be unable to run or walk or conquer or leave the starting gates or go around the course, but let them fall with their drivers . . . Bind their hands, steal their victory, their sight, so that they are unable to see their opponents, rather, drag them their own chariots and throw them on the ground so that they fall down throughout the hippodrome, but particularly around the course, with their own horses.[113]

And as the turns had to be the places particularly favorable for falls, we see that it is not miracles that are expected of demons.

All this looks quite straightforward. Nevertheless, there are certain difficulties. Certainly, some of these rites were performed by the rival drivers themselves (which puts them in the same category as commercial spells). Towards the end of the fourth century A.D., imperial legislation is directed against those drivers who commissioned a binding spell against a rival. The law threatens capital punishment, in case they should either cover or do away with the sorcerer instead of handing the sorcerer over to the law.[114] But there are more cases in which the rituals were commissioned by their supporters:[115] in a sport which does not yet know betting, there must be different motives at work.[116] In the imperial society, the drivers constituted important social mediators between the elite of their noble patrons and the masses of their supporters, so much so that each race brought into play social structures and that the victory of one party was perceived as the affirmation of a particular social group. The agonistic situation is still present, but transferred from the individual to the group.

This circumstance becomes strikingly visible when the two conflicting groups are pagans and Christians, as shown in a story also reported in the *Life of Hilarion*. The *duumviri* of Gaza held horse races that caused numerous rivalries between the two administrators. In this exact case, the pagan colleague made sure of the help of a magician so that his drivers would win; it thus belonged to the saint to help the other *duumvir*, a good Christian, to wield a stronger magic to thwart the pagan one. The saint is first reluctant to help, quite understandably; finally, he offers holy water as an antidote—and, of course, the Christian horses win. This victory does not help just the magistrate; the crowd, disappointed by the pagan god Marnes, turns to Christianity.[117]

What all these cases of ritual binding have in common is that they are performed in the context of a crisis. It is always a situation in which a great uncertainty predominates, one that will be resolved by a future decision, while the ways to influence the result are very limited. It may be a matter of people taking part in an imminent trial, merchants or professionals faced with new competitors (like the doctors of Metapontum), or people who practiced professions based on techniques difficult to master (like bronze founders or potters whose pots broke in the fire because of incantations).[118] As a competitor in an agonistic struggle, an individual needed a strategy for overcoming a feeling of uncertainty increased by that of a certain powerlessness. The performance (or commission) of a spell made it possible to regain the initiative and the hope that one could affect the outcome. The ritual thus offered both the community and the individual a means to master emotionally an otherwise difficult crisis.[119]

The Greco-Roman culture had other strategies for putting an end to similar crises produced by the feeling of uncertainty.

Divination thus obtained information about the future, without one's thinking of manipulating the unfolding of events; it was enough to replace uncertainty by certitude. On the other hand, the performance of what we may call positive magical rites was intended to manipulate and influence the outcome of events by strengthening the individual's personal energy (whereas the ritual binding—negative magic—aimed at eliminating or diminishing the energy of the adversary or competitor). To the commercial spell, there existed a reverse process in order to protect one's shop and one's work by a charm; in the papyri this rite, which promised to enrich its practitioners, is called "Charm for Acquiring Business and for Calling in Customers."[120] To the judiciary and agonistic spells, there were corresponding practices, which were considered to procure victory, or amulets, which were capable of protecting against failure. A papyrus from the British Museum thus contains a "Victory Charm" and also a "Victory Charm for Chariot Races."[121] A papyrus from Oxyrhynchus promises "victory and safety in the stadium and the crowds."[122] Finally, the amulet of a mime was supposed to procure charm, physical beauty, and victory "to Sphyridas whom Thinousiris gave birth to."[123]

This polyvalent use of the amulet, supposed to procure both physical beauty and sexual attractiveness as well as victory, is very often found in the spells of the papyri. What our categories single out—victory in a trial, commercial success, success in love—is not always separated in the thinking of the ancients. A prayer to Helios, in the Papyrus Mimaut of the Louvre, thus furnishes a long and mixed list of desired qualities: "Come to me with a happy face, on a bed of your choice, giving me, NN, sustenance, health, safety, wealth, the blessing of children, knowledge, a good name, goodwill [on the part of other men], sound judgment, honor, memory, grace, shapeliness, beauty in the eyes of all men who see me; you, who hear me in everything whatsoever, give persuasiveness with words, great god, to the [there follow magic words, the demoniacal name of the sorcerer, who has become a superhuman being], I beg, master, accept my prayers."[124]

This rather striking list gives the portrait of the ideal man as conceived in Imperial Greco-Roman society, combining what we would call the social virtues—which serve to secure an elevated position in its society (a good name, benevolence, persuasiveness)—with what in our eyes constitute private virtues (health and the like), without forgetting "physical beauty in the eyes of others," that is to say, sexual attractiveness. It is a long list of goods necessary for social success in this society, an ideal self-portrait that has largely escaped the attention of scholars on the lookout for information about the social history of the ancient world.

This agonistic model admits of only rare exceptions. There are only few but striking cases in which instead of the term *competition*, it would be preferable to use *jealousy*.[125] An illustration is a text from Cremona, which dates from the very beginning of the Christian era and in which a certain Q. Domatius curses several persons in order to remain the sole heir, and adds, as if it were a matter of a votive gift, "I curse them at my own expense so that they perish."[126] This text might just happen to be a pathological exaggeration of rivalry. There is also the category of spells directed against thieves and slanderers, which can hardly be called agonistic. But we can understand how this category fits into our analysis and why the ancients did not separate it from other binding spells, with which it shares not only the external form of the lamella of lead but also the depositing in wells or in the sanctuaries of the chthonian gods.[127] It is always a matter of past events, misfortunes already undergone, but for which the person responsible is often unknown.[128] What this kind of spell has in common with the other categories is that here again, it is performed in a crisis provoked by a lack of information, this time concerning not some future situation but the person who can be accused of committing the crime. In this situation of uncertainty, it is once again the powers down below who help. They are considered to know the victim and to punish the crime. It could also be hoped that the sorcerer would find the guilty one; among other texts, the papyri offer recipes making it possible to find a thief.[129]

The first texts of this kind came from the sanctuary of Demeter in Cnidus, made famous by the excavations by Charles Newton. Since then, examples have been found throughout the whole ancient world, including the British Isles. The sanctuary of Cnidus, and it alone, also offers another kind of text for defending oneself against the accusation of magic. The most typical example runs as follows:

> Antigone dedicates to Demeter and Kore, to Pluto, to all the gods and goddesses who surround Demeter. If I gave poison to Asklepiades or if I intended in my soul to harm him, or if I called his wife to the sanctuary and if I gave her three half-mines for her to cast him out of the world of the living, let Antigone go up to the temple of Demeter, burning with fever and let her not succeed in obtaining the favor of Demeter, but let her suffer great pain. If someone spoke to Asklepiades against me, and if he tampered with a woman by giving her money . . ."[130]

The second part fits into the typology already analyzed, that of the spell against crimes or slander committed by persons unknown. The first part contains the defense of a woman, Antigone, against the accusation of having attempted to poison a certain Asklepiades or having incited another woman to do so. All this clearly has the air of *mageía*, of *veneficium*, and the meeting in the sanctuary to obtain the poison has a surprising parallel in Cicero.[131] The defense of the alleged witch consists of a curse against herself. She invokes the wrath of the divinity against herself in the event that she is guilty: that the goddess punishes her by sending her an illness.[132] It is a process very close to the ancient oath, which also was nothing other than a conditional curse directed against the person who took the oath; the person called for divine wrath on himself or herself if the person was guilty of perjury. We once again note the affinity existing between the binding spell and the curse.[133]

VIEWPOINT OF THE VICTIMS OF RITUAL BINDING

In what circumstances could someone think of being the victim of an instance of binding spell, and what were the defenses against such an attack? It is no easier to answer this question for antiquity than for the modern world.[134] We do not have, as a matter of fact, detailed descriptions, with the exception of three anecdotes dating from late antiquity and related earlier, the one concerning the Virgin of God from Gaza, reported in Jerome's *Life of St. Hilarion*, and the later ones on Theodorus and Theophilus, told by Sophronius.

The cases of Theodorus and Theophilus suggest a process that unfolds in two stages. Everything begins with an inexplicable illness. When the saints are consulted, they declare an attack of magic. It is then a matter of finding the magic object responsible in order to confirm the diagnosis and to undo the effects of the magic. In the case of Theodorus, the magical objects are disinterred from the threshold of his house. In the case of Theophilus, it is necessary to find the objects in the sea—an easy task for saints, one suspects.[135]

The case of the virgin is simpler and, at the same time, less logical. We are dealing with behavior that is absurd and aggressive, contrary to everything that the prior life and social role of the victim lead us to expect. A virgin, who is devoted to God and who therefore resisted the advances of a young lover, is suddenly seized by a frenzied love, ecstatic and without control. The saint is consulted; he diagnoses demonic possession resulting from an erotic binding spell and then exorcizes the demon. Although the author meticulously describes for us the making of the magical objects, he does not, however, make the success of the healing depend on the detection of these objects. It is a literary rehandling of which Jerome is fully conscious: "The saint did not wish to give the order to seek out the young man or the statuettes before the virgin is purified, to avoid giving the impression that the demon had gone away, freed of the incantations, that he believed the demon's words, for he knew that demons are deceitful and crafty in order to impose themselves."[136]

The saint obviously knows the protocol to follow in such a case, but if he had first found and destroyed the sacred objects, he would have allowed the demon to go away without having been able to make him swear never to return. In closer analysis, it appears that this departure results from the superposition and combination of two demonologies, that of possession and that of the binding spell. Although they were acquainted with possession and exorcism, the pagans did not confound them with the binding rituals, where, in their eyes, the demonic helper of the sorcerer did not possess his victim, but tortured him. It is thus the Christians who broaden the field of exorcism by making it the most common means for resolving any problem in which superhuman forces come into play. Always, they exorcize the demon with the help of a more forceful name than the one that had forced the demon into the victim: "I adjure you in the name of the living god," in a Jewish exorcism;[137] "I adjure you in the name of the Nazarene, Jesus Christ, and the holy apostles," in the Christian liturgy.[138]

The rare cases from the pagan world yield further information. Take the case of Germanicus as recounted by Tacitus. The prince, hitherto healthy and strong, is suddenly stricken with an inexplicable illness from which he dies, without any remedy capable of helping him. Someone suspects a *veneficium* and seeks traces of it: "One found in the ground and in the walls the remains of human bodies, incantations and binding spells and the name of Germanicus inscribed on tablets of lead, ashes half burned and full of rot, and other things by which one thinks of dedicating men to the infernal divinities."[139]

Sudden death leads to suspicion of magic. The search confirms these suspicions and points in the direction of a more searching diagnosis, that of a binding spell. Tacitus is explicit: he mentions the typical curse tablets of lead with the victim's name, the magical essence taken from a tomb and which must have served to obtain the help of a demon; he also explains the process of the ritual binding as an action with the goal of dedicating (*sacrare*) a man to the infernal divinities, which the non-Attic texts on lead confirm. We have already seen that the verbs with the root "to bind" are often replaced by verbs that denote consecration.

We could consider Tacitus's story an example of literature that can be exploited only with reservations. We know, however, of several inscriptions from the imperial era that report cases of unexpected death resulting from a magic intervention; in most of them, Helios is asked to punish the unknown sorcerer.[140] One text, the grave inscription for the wife of an officer who had died at the age of 28 after prolonged immobility, held an incantation responsible: "Cursed by incantations, she lay mute for a long time"—perhaps in a coma that the contemporary doctors did not understand?[141] Whatever the reason, the celestial or the infernal gods will punish the perpetrators. A metrical inscription from the imperial era, now at the museum of Verona, is even more touching: "Growing in my third year, I was captured and killed, while I could have been the delight of my mother and father; the cruel hand of a witch (*saga*) took me, while she remains on the earth and harms by her art. Parents, beware of your children so that the pain does not end up filling your heart."[142]

The situation is ambiguous: are we facing a sudden and unexpected death attributed by the parents to the intervention of a witch, or is it a matter of one of those child sacrifices mentioned by so many stories? We shall never know. The first hypothesis, however, seems more probable.

There are still other cases. There is the funny anecdote reported by Cicero about Curio, who attributed his forgetfulness to an incantation made by his adversary. Because the story is not completely serious, we must not expect concrete proofs of it. It is nevertheless significant that we are dealing again with someone who proves incapable of playing the role that was expected of him, like the virgin of Gaza.

Libanius, another orator stricken by a malevolent magic, speaks of it in his autobiography.[143] In the middle of a highly successful career, he was attacked by headaches so violent that he wanted to die: "I avoided all the books containing the works of the ancients, I avoided the writing and composition of my orations, and my eloquence was undone, even though my pupils loudly demanded for it."[144] To this malady was added another, an arthritis that hampered his movements. The cure is performed in two phases. A dream first revealed that Libanius was the victim of witchcraft, then his friends began looking for traces and remedies.[145] Libanius did not believe in the diagnosis—but he had to yield to the facts: "However, a chameleon turned up in my classroom, coming from I don't know where. It was a very old chameleon and had been dead for several months, but we saw that its head was tucked between its hind legs, that one of its front legs was missing while the other closed its mouth to silence it." Although no lead tablet was found, this discovery pointed to ritual binding. The chameleon had its head turned around like the cat of the Santones, a symbolic expression of all the misfortunes that had to befall the victim, and the missing leg and the leg that closed the mouth more specifically represented what someone wanted to see happen to Libanius, the loss of movement and speech. After this discovery, the healing was not long in coming. In another discourse, Libanius suggests that it was some colleagues who had practiced this feat of magic; the fact that these same colleagues in turn suspected Libanius of having worked magic might explain the skepticism he affects in his autobiography.[146]

The final case belongs to quite a different category. It is an oracle that was published not long ago and that poses very interesting problems; the text was found in the Ephesus excavations, but it concerns another town in western Asia Minor, difficult to identify. The town had suffered from the great plague brought by the armies of Lucius Verus from Mesopotamia in 165 A.D. An oracle was then consulted, probably that of Apollo at Clarus (we know other oracles regarding this plague and who came from this sanctuary), and Apollo gave a strange answer. The townspeople should obtain a statue of Ephesian Artemis, all in gold and carrying two torches (not the image, thus, of the *multimamma* that does not carry torches); install it in a sanctuary of Artemis Soteira, the "Savior"; and organize a festival. During the festival, the torches of the goddess then would melt the wax figurines made by an unknown sorcerer.[147]

The plague thus was attributed to the binding spell of a sorcerer. Sorcerers could be thought to act against a whole town; when contrary winds had slowed the supply fleet for Constantinople and thus created a public uproar, the emperor Constantine executed the philosopher Sopater because he had, "through an excess of cleverness," magically bound the winds.[148] Sopater presumably had done nothing at all; he just happened to be a pagan philosopher hated by some powerful figures at court. The sorcerer who had worked the plague remained unknown: it was the crisis—the plague, like the hunger in Constantinople—alone that produced this response; nor were magical objects found. The cure was obtained solely by divine intervention that melted down the figurines, and if humans did not know where to find the figurines, Artemis knew. The destruction of the magical objects alone, here even only symbolic and imaginary, sufficed to free the town of the consequences of this magic attack.

There are particularly two situations in which the ancients suspected magic and, more precisely, ritual binding: disease or sudden death that was medically inexplicable; and unexpected and inexplicable professional failure. We might hesitate to classify the madness of the girl of Gaza rather as a disease or a professional failure. What matters is that not every case of professional failure or disease finds such an explanation; but only those that escape the reasoning of the medical or professional technician. The plague under Lucius Verus belonged to this category; in other oracles, the plague is explained by the wrath of the gods or of the infernal heroes, which enters into the same explanatory scheme. The ailments of Libanius, arthritis and headaches, are also of those diseases against which amulets could provide protection, such as epilepsy or the fever.[149] As in the era of Hippocrates, magic always served to explain what escaped medical diagnosis; even the skeptical Pliny knows of ailments for which a magical cure might be advisable.[150]

Professional failure is even more revealing of what the accusation of magical binding implies in the ancient societies. The lawyer who forgets his speech for the defense, the teacher of rhetoric who no longer wants to speak, the chaste *virgo Dei* who runs about the streets, her hair flying in the wind and shouting the name of a young man: all are behaving in an unexpected way contrary to what the society expects of them. Such behavior, which would be completely remiss if it were under their control, might jeopardize their privileged social position. Therefore, explanations attributing odd behavior to a binding spell implied that other people, sorcerers and demons, were responsible, and an exorcism could reestablish the former social position. It must be stressed that society accepted this strategy. It is not an individual subterfuge meant to protect oneself from the consequences of a reprehensible act (even in the case of Jerome's virgin, in which the saint seems to have had some doubts: Hilarion had a long talk with her and pointed out that one never should give a hold to demons. . . .); but rather, it is a legitimate way offered by society, not the least to its prominent members, to resolve a limited crisis that, ultimately, could have endangered its cohesion, even if, in the case of Curio, Cicero was certainly not the only one to smile. It is also an efficient strategy to explain maladies that defied scientific medicine, without jeopardizing the status of scientific medicine as such. That does not mean that the strategy was not vulnerable to personal misuse. Curio, after all, came rather close to it.

We do not know whether Curio really went to the trouble of searching for the magical object; it seems doubtful that he did. At any rate, the scarce information we have about how to undo ritual binding makes one thing clear: the most important step was to find the magical object. This fact clearly appears in the stories about Theodorus, Theophilus, and the *virgo* from Gaza, as well as in the experience of Libanius and in the papyri; in each case the spell loses all its power as soon as the lead tablet and the other ritual objects are found. That is why they must be hidden as much as possible, even thrown into the sea; at least one lead tablet was found in the sands of the Mediterranean. On the other hand, it could be important to undo the binding again; therefore, one papyrus advises marking the spot where a curse tablet was buried. There is even the advice to hang the magical ring or tablet on a cord into the sea or river in order to recover it again for undoing.[151] Perhaps it was enough to find the magic objects, but more probably it was also necessary to destroy them: that is what Theodorus did. In the Ephesian oracle, the destruction of the figurines is paramount.

On the other hand, there were cases (like that in the Ephesus oracle) when it was unnecessary to find an object; at least the account about "godly" Plotinus concentrates on the battle of the minds. Plotinus wards off the magical attacks of an enemy (typically enough, an Egyptian philosopher), relying solely on his powerful soul. The philosopher Maximus, Julian's teacher, saved his pupil Sosipatra (one of the few female philosophers of later antiquity) in a similar way, having heard that she was plagued by erotic magic.[152] In the spiritualized world of theurgy, the countermeasures against harmful magic take philosophical and spiritual forms; there was no necessity to rely upon the material world. The story that Saint Hilarion talked to the demon and made him leave the virgin of Gaza long before the magical objects had been found, expresses a similar concern, this time in the service of powerful Christian spiritualization.[153]

If in the imperial era, it was apparently enough to find the curse tablets or the other magical objects and to destroy them, things are less clear in earlier times. Countermeasures seem to have been more complicated: the ritual binding asked for a ritual unbinding. This could be difficult; a spell from Republican Rome even asserts, "Nobody shall undo me if not he, who did this."[154] Despite this assertion, there existed specialists for these counterrituals. The comical poet Magnes, a contemporary of Aristophanes, combines interpreters of dreams and "untiers," and a late lexicon on the Attic classics explains that "to cleanse ritually" means "to untie a man under a spell."[155] Such rites were cathartic and brought healing, as did the dreams; witness the popular healing sanctuaries of Asclepius or Amphiaraus.

The most spectacular evidence from the classical epoch, however, remains more than doubtful. The tomb of the Kerameikos, which contained not only a binding spell but also a figurine in its container of lead, surprised its excavator.[156] When the flagstones were opened that had remained intact since the classical era, an unusual fact was discovered. The content of the grave was so much in disarray that the excavator thought that the body of the deceased had been cut into pieces, and that the container, the cover bearing the inscription, and the figurine had been intentionally separated from each other. This he took to be a countermeasure against a binding ritual introduced immediately after the burial and detected shortly after this. Such a proceeding, however, appears highly improbable in the light of the evidence investigated so far; and the final publication of the grave refrains from such an interpretation, and rightly so— although it would have been a most spectacular case.

AN EASTERN PREHISTORY

Magic, the Greeks and Romans tell us, comes from the East, from the Persians and especially from the Egyptians. We have seen that this assertion must not be considered an objective and true historical account, but a definition of the place occupied by magic in the thinking and society of the Greeks and the Romans. It is not enough, however, to brush aside the question of the relations between Greek magic and Eastern magic.[157] After all, the *mágos* appears for the first time in Greek with a subject of the Persian kings, Heraclitus; and in the domain of ritual binding notably, a certain number of Eastern practices make it possible to establish extremely suggestive parallels with Greco-Roman magic.[158]

These parallels, however, point neither to Persia nor to Egypt, but to Mesopotamia, which has had a long tradition of magic. Although the texts attesting to it come mostly from the royal library of Assurbanipal in Nineveh, we glimpse a scholarly transmission that continued over the centuries and that survived at least up to the era of the Seleucid kings, if not until later epochs.[159] The history of this tradition is still widely unknown; however, the indications that we have point to a consistent picture. In the walls of the chamber of the palace in Antiochia where Germanicus was the alleged victim of binding magic, magic paraphernalia were found; and the chameleon was found, after a long search, in Libanius' lecture room, presumably thus on the floor or in the walls. Now the Assyrian texts, in their accusations of witchcraft, describe the depositing of magical objects in the walls.[160] A Greco-Egyptian recipe on papyrus gives directions to perform a rite "on the banks of the river, where no man's foot has trod"; we find the same instruction, almost literally, in an Assyrian rite that is also otherwise rather close to it in detail.[161] Even more significantly, the name of Ereskhigal, the queen of the Sumerian hell, disappeared from documents for almost two thousand years only to reappear in the magic papyrus books and on the curse tablets.[162] The same tradition stands behind the Ephesian oracle that advised the melting down of the wax figurines that had caused the plague. To burn or melt figurines is a current practice in Mesopotamian cathartic and exorcistic rituals, thus giving its name to the main ritual books on the topic.[163]

What strikes the observer in these two magic cultures are the affinities between the texts (and the rites) of the Assyrians and those of the Greeks, notably in the world of ritual binding. Certainly, many of these resemblances are not specific. It is rather common in many cultures to make figurines of the victim,[164] to determine its identity with the help of what the Greeks call "magical essence," for example, hair or pieces of fabric from a garment belonging to the victim,[165] and finally, to tie the victim's figurine up in fetters.[166] The custom of depositing these figurines in graves is much less frequent; as for their deposition in the grave of close relatives, it is mentioned only in the Assyrian Maqlû and in Plato.[167] It is also very rare that the victim's name must be inscribed on the left thigh, which is stipulated in the Assyrian texts and is found on a figurine from Attica and two figurines from Etruria.[168] To deposit a figurine under the doorstep is a way of making certain that the victim will, sooner or later, get into contact with it; this procedure appears in the Maqlû, in Plato, and, much later, in the Christian fictions.[169]

The list of functions allotted to these rituals is nearly as close.[170] If we set aside the more important role devolving upon the magic rites in the protection against malicious demons in Assyria and the absence of agonistic spells in societies that did not have sports, the list is still the same: assistance in erotic affairs, either to make a conquest of the person loved or to get him or her back; assistance in commercial activities; and, finally, in the Babylonian and Assyrian society, in which hierarchy is much more important than in Greece, assistance for calming the anger of a superior, which returns, much later, in the magical papyri of imperial Egypt.[171]

These resemblances are too obvious to be only the result of convergences. Now, the Babylonian and Assyrian magic is the business of well-trained specialists, possessors of considerable knowledge, who therefore enjoy a rather high social position; these specialists converse with kings, even Seleucid kings.[172] They also can travel. Walter Burkert has stressed the important role that these itinerant specialists had in the orientalizing epoch of early Archaic Greece. Yet the most similar practices that concern us here date from the fifth and fourth centuries, and for the same era Plato attests, for Greece, the existence of itinerant specialists in magic and ritual.[173] We recall that we have traced the history of these specialists since the era of Heraclitus, an era in which the Mesopotamian world, through the Persian empire, reached the borders of Greece. Nothing would be simpler than to imagine contacts through these itinerant magi, traveling on the excellent roads of the Persian empire to Ionia and Attica.

There is a fundamental difference, however. In the Mesopotamian world, we can make out two types of magic texts, the exorcisms built on the accusation of magic, and active magic, two types of magic that are strictly separate. Exorcism, represented by some great books like the Maqlû and the Shurpu, serves to heal or to protect oneself.[174] The rite will lead to the healing of illness, but will also repair the social failures and lack of success caused by the intervention of a demon, triggered by a sorcerer or witch. Also, the rite constitutes a precaution for guarding against attacks foreseen by divination. In the thinking of the neo-Assyrian texts, the sorcerer's intervention destroys the protection of the gods who usually defend humans against the demons' evil influences. The purpose of exorcism was thus to restore this protection and this divine benevolence. Active magic, moreover, attested to by many so far uncollected texts, concerns practices for providing assistance in various personal problems, such as love, commerce, and social status.[175] All this is what can be called positive magic; whereas negative, harmful magic is punished with death, all these practices, according to the Assyrian laws, are perfectly legitimate.[176] Injurious magic, on the other hand, is not attested to in the archaeological material from Mesopotamia; there are neither voodoo dolls nor lead tablets from the Near Eastern Bronze age, in marked contrast to the Greco-Roman world. We know of these rituals only through the accusations contained in the exorcisms; and these accusations depict an entirely fantastic and surrealist image of the sorcerers and their rites. There is an obvious conclusion, that these rites existed only in the imagination of the exorcists—a situation that closely corresponds to what Evans-Pritchard found among the Azande. Harmful magic, the binding magic performed with the help of figurines, did not exist in the Assyrian society.

The Assyro-Babylonian world thus knew of the binding spell only in the theory of the accusation, whereas the Greeks practiced it. This surprising difference is explained by the very mechanisms of transmission. In the Babylonian society, these rites were indeed conceived of, but, out of a fear of sanctions, they were not carried out. The absence of their practice did not prevent people from believing in their effectiveness, however. When these rites were transplanted to a different society, which was unacquainted with such sanctions (and Plato explicitly attests to this for Athens), there was a great temptation to make these rites a reality, and nothing stood in the way. Quite the contrary: the competitive and unhierarchical society of the Greeks incited the use of this means of self-affirmation.

One question, however, remains open: that of chronology. While in Attica, the attestations begin in the course of the fifth century, there are texts from Sicily and Magna Graecia that already date to the later sixth century.[177] There are two possible explanations. Either the practice started in Attica, but then the Athenians wrote their early spells exclusively on perishable matter, such as wood, papyrus, and wax, and only later started using lead; it is a perfectly reasonable option. Or the rite came from Sicily and Magna Graecia into mainland Greece; this origin would tie in with many details of afterlife and eschatology developed in Western Pythagoreanism and brought later to Athens.[178] For the moment, there is no convincing answer. But it has become increasingly clear from archaeology that, in Greece, the practice of ritual binding had begun well before the fourth century (a date favored by an earlier generation of scholars) and that it did not originate from a breakdown of Greek enlightenment.[179]

6

LITERARY REPRESENTATION
OF MAGIC

THE LITERARY and epigraphical documentation for ancient magic and its rituals sets in towards the end of the sixth century B.C. The lead tablets begin to be numerous in the later part of the fifth and the first half of the following century; this first peak is caused mainly by the Athenians and their passion for writing. Curse tablets become much rarer in the Hellenistic era to peak a second time in the imperial epoch; here, they are omnipresent, from Arabia to Britannia. The Egyptian finds belong to the same epoch, both the large papyrus books and the single spells on small sheets of papyrus, whose number is still rapidly growing. On the other hand, in the Hellenistic epoch and the beginning of the empire, there exist some literary texts that describe magical practices in colorful detail. It is tempting to use them in order to fill the gap in the epigraphical documentation, and too many scholars have uncritically yielded to this temptation.[1]

But this procedure is dangerous. Works of literature have their own laws, and it is always risky to disregard laws—although in this case, the literary critics long concurred in taking seriously what their text presented as religious facts.[2] It is not that these texts—from Theocritus to Lucan and to Heliodorus—were devoid of interest; but their interest bears less on the understanding of magic than that of literature. Two questions seem paramount: the first is the use these authors make of the motif of magic for their own poetic and sometimes psychagogic objectives, and the second lies with the intertextual dialogue of these texts in the closed world of the Alexandrine and Imperial literature, where every later text reacts on its precursors and models. Ancient literature, as we know, does not know any anxiety of influence. Even in the rare cases in which a poet works out new motifs, the poet does so not so much in reaction to religious and cultural realities as to contribute to this discourse between poets and texts in a new and unexpected way.[3]

THEOCRITUS AND THE EROTIC SPELL

To illustrate these problems, let us focus on erotic magic, which is, after all, very much present in the literature, from Theocritus to Virgil and up to the Roman elegiacs.

For the Roman authors, Theocritus's second *Idyll* (*Pharmakeutriai* or *The Sorceresses*) constitutes the key text, the indispensable though often implicit reference. The first part of this text (lines 1 to 62) brings onto the scene a magic ritual, as the title announces. In the middle of the night, under the shining moon, two women are practicing magic, Simaitha and her slave Thestylis. The goal of the rite is to win back the love of a young man, Delphis, who was for a time the lover of Simaitha, but has henceforth turned to other loves.

The rite as Theocritus describes it follows a precise course, carefully presented after the introduction, in nine strophes of four lines each, separated by the refrain "iynx, draw this man to my dwelling, my lover." The poem opens with the preparations for the rite. Required are laurel and *phíltra*, an extremely vague term referring to the ingredients for erotic magic, and a vase adorned with purple wool (1–2). Then unfolds the actual rite, which follows very distinct stages.

The first stage takes us up to the moment when the goddess Hecate appears. Simaitha has three objects to burn: the sacrificial barley (*álphita*), which she spreads over the flames, saying "I scatter Delphis's bones"; some laurel leaves, whose burning is accompanied by the wish "that his flesh burn in the same way"; and some husks of corn (*pítura*). After this, Simaitha begins a prayer to Artemis-Hecate. The prayer is interrupted: dogs are heard, a sign that the goddess has arrived at the crossroads, and to protect herself, Simaitha must sound a gong.

A nonritual strophe marks the transition to the second phase of the rite. The goal of the actions of the first phase was to make the love (the fire) come back to Delphis's body; now it is a matter of breaking down his resistance and enticing him. Simaitha makes some wax melt ("let him melt in the same way," melting being a common metaphor for that love without resistance); she makes a rhombus turn ("let him turn in the same way to my door"); and she offers three libations, each time praying for him to forget any other love.[4] A new nonritual strophe marks a second pause.

Now comes the third phase. Up to this point, Delphis has been only very indirectly concerned by these metaphorical processes, but now, the rites come closer to him. Simaitha begins by tearing off a piece of his coat and throws it into the fire. Then, she orders Thestylis to rub some *thróna* underneath the threshold of Delphis's house and to say "let his bones be rubbed in the same way." The scholiasts simply state that *thróna* are *phármaka*, without further specifications. Simaitha herself sets about crushing a lizard to make a drink of it for her lover. Here ends the ritual; there follows a very long passage in which

Simaitha recalls her past love. At the poem's end, however, she announces other, much more terrible rites in case Delphis would not let himself be won back.

To this ritual, Theocritus seems to give a very precise name. Three times Simaitha speaks of "binding," in introducing the rite (line 3), announcing the rite itself (line 10), and summarizing it (line 159). We are thus in the presence of a binding spell, a *defixio*.[5]

That is the first problem. The rite, as Theocritus describes it, does not correspond to the love spells that we know. Although, at the beginning, Simaitha uses a thread of wool, this thread binds nothing, but rather adorns a vase. Later on, Simaitha speaks of wax, which can be a way of designating a wax manikin, even if nothing proves it; but the wax is melted, and the figurine does not remain tied as a symbol of permanent submission. And although she makes use of the formula *similia similibus* several times over, this formula does not follow the known forms.

Besides what the papyri call the "erotic binding spells," *philtrokatádesmoi*, there is a second category of erotic rites called "spells of attraction," *agōgaí*, or, more rarely, "erotic rites," *philtra*.[6] Their objective is the same as that of the binding spells, that is, to attract a beloved woman by ritual means. In a single case, this rite is even described as capable of "binding down" (the technical term for a *defixio*). Nevertheless, the rites that we possess follow rather a different procedure from the one described by Theocritus, although it is closer to the other binding spells.

Many of these "attraction rites" make use of fire to offer fumigations. The objects burned are extremely varied, and go from simple myrrh[7] to a recipe as complex as this one: "Take a field mouse and drown it in the water from a spring, take two lunar beetles and drown them in the water from a river, a crayfish, some fat from a spotted goat that is virgin, some dung from a dog-faced baboon, two ibis eggs, two drachmas of resin of styrax, two drachmas of myrrh, two drachmas of saffron, four drachmas of herb of Italian Cyprus, four drachmas of an uncut incense, a single onion. Pour all this into a mortar with the mouse and all the rest, and grind the whole."[8]

This process is typical. When dealing with a long and complex list of ingredients, the magician never burns the various elements one after another, as in Theocritus, but combines these ingredients into one specific fumigation, sometimes in the form of a pill. Nor are the materials that Theocritus has Simaitha burn (barley, laurel, husks of corn, cloth) often attested in the papyri; barley, husks, and cloth are absent, laurel is found once only, in a binding spell with the help of Apollo (whose sacred plant is laurel).[9] Sprinkling the flames of an altar with barley flour, on the other hand, is a fairly widespread ritual—but not in magic: it opens the Greek Olympian sacrifice. Simaitha thus gives the opening of her ritual a sacrificial look, so to speak, and the servant who helps her to carry out the rite fits into this. It is thus the rites of sacrifice that Theocritus evokes and not those of actual magic. Odder yet is the cremation of a piece of cloth taken from the beloved's coat. In the magic of the papyri (and elsewhere), such a piece represents the so-called magic essence, which usually indicates the path to the victim or to a dead person, but which was not the object of a symbolic destruction and substitution.[10] When Theocritus has her tear and burn, he thus inserts this rite in that series of "sympathetic" acts brought particularly into relief in his text as in the popular conceptions of magic.

Another problem is posed by the instruments that Simaitha uses. The poem mentions two of them, the iynx and the rhombus, the iynx being mentioned in the refrain, the rhombus only once, in one of these "sympathetic" passages: "As this rhombus of bronze turns by the power of Aphrodite, let him turn in the same way around my door" (line 30). From the most ancient commentaries on Theocritus to the most recent ones, there has been a scholarly discussion on the question of whether iynx and rhombus must be distinguished as different instruments. The scholiasts identify them with each other; most modern commentators distinguish between them, which seems more convincing. Simaitha, indeed, turns her iynx, a small magical wheel manipulated by two strings, at regular intervals, and once, she also makes the rhombus turn, an instrument that gives off a sound and that British social anthropologists would compare with a "bull roarer." But there is a much greater difficulty: neither of these instruments appears in the papyri. The rhombus is rather poorly in evidence anyway, whereas the iynx has been attested to in the literary texts since Pindar and on fifth century Athenian vase paintings and magnificent fourth century gold earrings, where it is primarily manipulated by Eros.[11] Later the attestations are limited to literature, and we can assume that it was no longer in use during the era of the papyri. In this situation, it is impossible to reach an unequivocal conclusion; we cannot tell whether Theocritus is referring to a practice that is contemporary or—and I am rather of this opinion—whether he is using a purely literary tradition that raised the iynx above the realities of the ritual.

Among all the rites that Theocritus has Simaitha perform, one single fumigation does not fit into the series of "sympathetic" rites: the sacrifice of the husks of corn. It is the moment when Theocritus brings a little ritual drama on the scene. While burning the husks, Simaitha does not go through her "sympathetic" litany but invokes Artemis-Hecate. Nevertheless, after a brief invocation of a line and a half, she interrupts herself, frightened: the goddess has arrived at the crossroads, and self-protection is called for.

It is important to emphasize that Simaitha begins a prayer but does not even go on with it to the end of the invocation: "You,

Artemis, who also move the brass doors of Hades and everything that is as strong . . ." Such an invocation had to mention other mythic and ritualistic qualities of the goddess before reaching the *narratio* of the prayer, the second part of the traditional prayer (in which an earlier occasion is recalled when the divinity granted her help), to end with the *preces* expressing the actual wish.[12] Simaitha does not even finish the first part of this canonical tripartite structure, interrupted as she is by the divinity's arrival.

The comparison with the papyri shows that Theocritus's description is a skilled and highly informed game. The sacrifice of husks is found only once in the rites of attraction, and this in a particular subspecies, the ritual insult, *diabolé*. In this rite, instead of offering a prayer, the magician addresses the divinity with a calumny supposed to emanate from the person she wants to attract. Consequently, the goddess, angry at the victim and ready to do him harm, pushes him straight ahead to the magician. The husks (of wheat) appear in a long list of horrible ingredients of a fumigation: "fat of a dappled goat, blood and dung, the menstrual fluid of a dead virgin, and the heart of a person who died young, the magical essence of a dead dog, a woman's embryo, fine-ground husks of wheat, sour rubbish, salt, fat of a dead doe, horseradish, myrrh, black laurel, barley, and the claws of a crab. . . ."[13] All this is the perversion of an ordinary ritual ("NN offers you, goddess, a horrible fumigation") in order to arouse the divine wrath against someone: burning husks is the reversal of burning barley. A psychological interpretation might be that this sort of ritual proves the guilty conscience of that man who aspires to possess a woman, but recognizes that it is to harm this woman that the goddess is propelling her to him. But more to the point than such explanations is the fact that the magician is using a traditional Egyptian ritual.[14]

The very content of the calumny is highly varied. In the same rite of attraction, the sorcerer asserts that his victim "said that you, goddess, slew a man and drank the blood of this man and ate his flesh; and she says that your headband is his entrails. . ."; in another rite, in a prayer to Isis-Selene: "I shall reveal to you calumnies of that wicked and impious NN; for she has revealed your holy mysteries to the knowledge of men. It is she, NN, who told, and not I, that you left the celestial vault and walked the earth, with a single sandal, a sword, and shouting a foul name. It is she who said: 'I see the goddess drinking blood.'"[15] At least a trace of this type of rite appears also outside the Egyptian papyri: we remember the dream of Libanius, that his enemy sacrificed two children who were then buried in the temple of Zeus, a dream that roused in Libanius the suspicion that magic attacks were the source of all his problems. This makes sense only if these acts serve to arouse Zeus' anger and thus are ritual slander as well.[16]

Thus, in Theocritus the sacrifice of the husks of corn, that worthless refuse, which must be thrown away and not offered to the goddess, is an element of ritual slander that, however, is not explained; Simaitha does not say an explanatory prayer, unlike the sorcerers in the papyri. Now, the ritual slander forms the most effective means for attracting a divinity, but also the most immoral and hence most dangerous means. It is necessary not to play with this rite that necessitates a ritual protection: "Do not use without due consideration [this is the warning on the papyrus], but only in case of need. There is a protection against the fall from on high, for the goddess has a custom of raising into the air those who do not protect themselves and of letting them fall from on high."[17] We now understand Simaitha's concerns. Her third sacrifice is the most hazardous, for it attracts a goddess, but an angry goddess. Therefore, one has to watch out and protect oneself from the outset.

The instruments employed in this rite of protection are not

the same in Theocritus and in the papyri. In the papyri, the protection normally devolves on an amulet that can be made earlier and used in different magic acts or that, in the case of a more dangerous rite of slander, as ours is, is specially made and hidden under a person's right arm. In Theocritus, it is the gong that must chase out Hecate. The gong always signals the presence of subterranean power: it is one of those instruments that are played, like the trumpet, in marginal situations. In the mysteries of Eleusis, the gong was sounded when Kore arrived. In Rome, the gong was used during a lunar eclipse, which is also a liminal moment of crisis.[18] The gong opposed to Hecate is thus not an isolated practice. But to the extent that it primarily appears in the Eleusinian ritual, often exploited by literature, we cannot rule out that it is a literary idea, without parallel in actual contemporaneous magic.

The slander rite ends by a rite of separation. In the ritual considered before, it is necessary to leave the space where the rite has taken place, in this case the roof, walking backward, and the door must be opened, because the efficacy of the rite is such that the woman loved could arrive in a great rush and could die out of desire if she found the door closed. There is nothing of the kind in Theocritus, who continues with something quite different: Simaitha makes the wax melt and offers a triple libation with its formula. We have already spoken of the wax; this action, which is also "sympathetic," is found in other magic rites, which are not necessarily erotic, and is never combined with a slander spell. The libation is much more commonplace, as was the sacrifice of barley. The magical character is due only to the threefold repetition of the incantation. A similar observation holds for the rites at the end: a person can perform binding spells (erotic and otherwise) at a threshold, and there is even an attraction rite that must be carried out in front of the magician's door.[19] As to the crushed lizard, an indication of its power for magical attraction lies in the fact that the *Cyranides*, the collection of magical stones, recommends the "lizard stone," the *líthos saurítēs*, for a rite of erotic attraction. On the other hand, a papyrus from the third century A.D., now in Leipzig, gives the recipe for an attraction rite performed with the help of a gecko that must be dried and burned.[20] With the crushed lizard, Simaitha prepares an "evil drink." The closest parallel is furnished by one of the papyri of Leyden that gives the recipe for a love potion whose main ingredient is some hornets gathered on a spider web.[21] As a pretty symbol of the desired effect, the tiny spider even succeeded in capturing those large insects.

The appearance of Hecate in Theocritus deeply disturbs Simaitha. The goddess reveals herself at some distance, and immediately Simaitha begins to protects herself—which would be a completely erroneous reaction in a rite intended to be realistic: the magician makes the divinity appear only to be aided by her even if, as a general rule, it is not one of the major gods who appears, but demons. Characteristic is this prayer to Selene, conceived as the supreme divinity, in which the magician prays to her to send him a helpful messenger (*ángelos*) who can go fetch the woman desired. If at that moment the moon became red, she had really sent this demoniacal helper: "But recite the prayer several times, and he will bring her and bind her, and she will love you for the rest of your life."[22]

The conclusions are thus clear. Theocritus does not realistically describe an actual ritual scenario and does not play the ethnologist, but rather constructs a mosaic, a kind of superritual capable of activating in its readers all sorts of associations connected with magic, and he constructs it following ritual facts that are well-informed but, taken as a whole, would not work. In short, this poem does not constitute a source of information for contemporary magic. This is true as well for the details whose ritual references escape us, like the use of the iynx. No one can guarantee that it is an authentic ritual fact rather than a literary reminiscence. A further complication, incidentally, is added by the fact that the scholiasts affirm that Theocritus imitates a poem of Sophron, an obscure author of the fifth century. The specialists discuss, without bringing in convincing arguments, whether fragments of Sophron can be compared with the Theocritan *Second Idyll*.

This conclusion does not mean that the text is devoid of all value and interest for the study of ancient magic. It shows what magic represents for the cultured contemporaries of Theocritus, who viewed these rites with amusement and in a detached way. We see that, from their intellectual and enlightened perspective, magic involved mainly strange sacrificial fumigations practiced with aberrant substances, but much less aberrant than those that we find in the papyri, and according to a suggestive "sympathetic" process: the categories of sacrifice and "sympathetic" practices dominate in Theocritus's imagery much more than they did in actual magic.

It remains to tackle a question that has not yet been mentioned, but that is of the utmost importance, the one concerning the identity of these practitioners of magic. In Theocritus as well as Virgil, or in the elegiac poets, and generally in the great majority of the literary texts, it is women who practice magic, whether erotic or of another kind. This situation amounts to an astonishing reversal of what we find in the epigraphic texts and the recipes on the papyri. In the papyri, most commonly a man tries to attract, bind, and possess a female victim. It is almost always, with one or two exceptions, *ho deîna*, so-and-so (accompanied by masculine forms), that designates the sorcerer, and it is *hē deîna* (or rather *tēn deîna*) and feminine forms that designate the victim. On rare occasions the recipes mention a homosexual relationship, but it is always a relationship between men. The same observation can be made for the erotic defixions: it is almost exclusively men who seek to bind a woman or, in the rare case of seduction, who seek to drive away a rival for a woman. There is one small, consoling detail (however consoling it is): it is not already married women who are targeted in actual practice. Whereas the recipe for a love spell in the great Paris papyrus offers a blank in which to insert the name of the desired woman's husband, the actual curse texts do not make use of it. They are out for (as the papyri say) "a woman for one's whole life."

This rather curious detail can help us answer two questions that now must be asked. How can one explain the fact that it is almost exclusively men who tried, clandestinely and by magic, to obtain women, not for the purpose of an affair, but for one of marriage? Why, on the other hand, do these same men, when they are well-educated, always imagine the reverse situation and represent women practicing erotic magic in order to possess men?

The first question admits of two answers, of which the second modifies the first. We can first place the erotic spells back in the context of general social competition, along with the struggles to achieve success and social benefits aimed at by the professional and commercial binding spells. In this framework, it is pointless to dwell too long on the role that the woman could have in the struggle for power in ancient societies, Roman or Greek. Through marriage, the daughter could bring her family benefits resulting from relations with another house. As a source of potential benefits, she was strictly guarded; the access to young women, especially of "good families," was never easy. The erotic binding spell and the rite of attraction offered a path, clandestine but thought to be effective, toward this source of benefits. That is why what is sought in our texts is almost always permanent union, that is, marriage. That is also why the masculine sexual attractiveness, to appear beautiful in the eyes of the world, is a good that can help the ancient male to acquire some social status.

The problems encountered by Apuleius in Oea are thus indicative on more than one count. His plea in his defense clearly brings out that at the origin of his difficulties, there were questions of wealth and social standing. He who would marry the rich widow would have access to her fortune and could thus enjoy whatever social standing this fortune would bestow. It is thus a sign of perspicacity on the part of Apuleius to stress, at the beginning of his speech, that he, Apuleius, was not gaining as much from this marriage as might be believed, for his own family was already rich and powerful, and his personal fortune was not as slight as his itinerant philosopher's clothing would lead one to suppose. It was not the opposition between a romantic marriage and a marriage for money that was at issue in the governor's court in Sabratha. We also understand the trouble that Apuleius goes to in order to lower the social position of his adversaries. The more they have to gain through marriage to the rich widow, the more credible become his own efforts to reduce the accusation to a mere manifestation of their envy. We then understand why, rather curiously, he is accused "of being handsome," *formosum philosophum*. If we admit that male beauty served as a weapon in the social contest and could be obtained, preserved, and even increased by magic, we catch sight of the implications contained in this accusation.

Erotic magic, however, remained a secret weapon, unworthy of the ideal warrior of the world of men, who for this reason always steered clear of it. An anecdote, once again taken from Lucian's *Philopseudes* ("The Lover of Lies"), demonstrates the way that men could talk about it. Glaukias, a young man of eighteen who had recently become the heir of a fortune through the death of his father, falls madly in love with Chrysis, his neighbor's wife. His philosophy teacher cures him in a rather surprising way: he brings in a Hyperborean magus who performs an attraction rite. After having invoked Hecate and called down the moon (and, amusingly enough, after having invoked the spirit of the deceased father to consent to the relationship), he fashions a small Eros and sends it to fetch Chrysis. The god brings her, and she arrives full of desire. In the morning she returns to the women's quarters of her husband.[23]

It is a racy story worthy of Boccaccio. Young Glaukias gets a bedfellow for a night, not a wife. Lucian leaves no doubt about the fact that Chrysis herself had neither the character nor the inclination to maintain a stable erotic relationship. In this rather frivolous milieu, a milieu of men and "casino," in which one-night stands are boasted of, one could invoke erotic magic.

The disparity thus is obvious between principle and reality. In theory, men never used the practice of magic (or only for a short adventure); in practice, this resort seemed indispensable. This conclusion, however satisfying it may seem, must nevertheless be qualified. Indeed, the sociological model for the transferring of power and fortune through women does not explain everything. According to this model, the true transfer would never be done through the will of the woman, but through the will of the heads of the families concerned, whereas in the papyri and inscriptions it is always the women from whom one wishes to obtain not only love but a mad, unbridled passion. Never is a charm addressed to those fathers, recalcitrant owners of amorous daughters. Even more disturbing for this analysis is the existence of erotic magic practiced by women on men, where these same social constraints are not in effect. There is, moreover, homosexual erotic magic, feminine as well as masculine, in which the social problem is posed in quite a different way. In Athens, at least in the classical era, a homosexual relation could confer prestige on the beloved.[24] Our texts, however, come neither from Athens nor from the classical era, but from

Roman Egypt, where homosexual relationships did not confer any social prestige.[25] Thus, it must be admitted that it is not just a matter of struggles for position and social goods, although this is very often an important aspect of the problem, but that we can also be in the presence of an individual's emotional crisis, provoked by the mad love that he bears for a person who seems out of reach. Erotic magic thus offers a way to resolve this personal and even intimate crisis, and that is why the same processes can serve for loves lacking a social purpose (which, later, the Christian polemist was to call *amor inconcessus*).[26]

We begin to catch a glimpse of the answer to the second question—why, in literature, is it always the women who perform erotic magic?—or at least an aspect of the answer. These stories remove erotic magic still further away from the world of men; they are thus a means for getting rid of what should not exist. At the same time, though, they reveal the real existence of this magic; however, although practiced by men, it is in reality a concern of women. That is why a man using magic steps over the borderlines of male behavior; a true man does not need erotic magic—the only male sorcerers are those funny foreign specialists. But this is only one aspect of the question; the other aspect involves a well-known theme. We have spoken of those Roman ladies of the republican era who practiced *veneficium*. The women, marginalized and excluded from the society of men, on this account constituted a danger. They are capable of all sorts of disguised attacks, threatening either the life of their husbands or the body of some desired man. In this perspective, these stories of love spells also talk of the danger that women's love constitutes for the autonomy of the men.

It could be imagined that these stories of feminine erotic magic have a third function, which would be to provide an explanation for the mad love that a man has for a woman. Such behavior contravened the social rules, and it had to be explained.

The accusation of magic then becomes a way meant to excuse social faults, such as the mad love felt by a young woman pledged to chastity or the spectacular memory lapses of a Roman orator. But in the case of mad love felt by men, the argument of magic does not seem to have been used at the time, a fact that is all the more surprising as it is very much used in modern Greece.[27] Would this be due to some lacuna in our sources? Or could gender asymmetry in antiquity even mean that mad love in man was excused and was censured only in women?

MAGIC DIVINATION: LUCAN AND RITUAL PRACTICE

Another text helped build the image of the witch in the post-ancient literature even more than the one of Theocritus or his Virgilian transformation: the description that Lucan gives of the necromantic ritual performed by the Thessalian witch Erictho when consulted by Sextus Pompey, son of Pompey the Great. Because the text is complex, I shall try only to understand the rite without taking up more far-reaching literary problems.[28]

Lucan introduces his theme with a long passage on divination, which leads him to the magic divination of the Thessalians (VI, 425–506). But he is content to contrast this magic, which is considered commonplace, with the unprecedented arts practiced by Erictho, a sort of superwitch (a "witches' witch," in W. R. Johnson's felicitous expression), whose image the poet fills with all the features characteristic of extreme marginality (506–569). She lives away from houses and towns, in empty tombs, in direct contact with the world of the dead. She collects interesting cadavers, those of hanged persons, and of young men and young women who died early—if necessary, she kills them herself. Although serving as an intermediary between the world of the living and that of the dead, she seems decidedly inclined toward the dead. She also brings death; under her steps, fresh growths wither in the fields, and everywhere she goes, she poisons the air. Correspondingly, she puts herself outside the civic rites, and she is even their enemy. She never says prayers, never offers sacrifices. On the contrary, she defiles the sacrifices offered to the Olympian gods by mixing the pure fires of the altars with the fire of the funeral pyres, and she disturbs the order of funerals as well as the rituals intended for the dead by stealing the incense from funerary altars. Here again she does not steer a middle course between the gods from down below and those from on high, but sides with the infernal powers. The gods on high thus fear her, in the way that they fear the underworld. They are so fearful that they grant her everything she wishes as soon as she utters her first incantation, because "they are afraid to hear a second spell."[29]

After a narrative interlude in which the Younger Pompey meets Erictho, greets her, and flatters her while she consents to a divinatory rite, Lucan concentrates on the long description of the rite (624–830). Erictho leaves for the field of battle in search of a useful cadaver (the desired property: it must be capable of speaking, thus to have lungs and all the other necessary organs). Once she has found it, she lodges it in a dark hollow in the middle of a dense forest, which does not let the sunlight come through, on the threshold between our world and that of the dead, but there again, rather on the side of the infernal beings (649ff.). Dressed in multicolored clothing (*discolor*), crowned with snakes, she makes the cadaver's blood flow afresh, washes it, and smears it with lunar poison (*virus lunare*).[30] A long catalog relates the ingredients, from the foam of rabid dogs to the poisons invented by her (671–684). Then she begins her *carmen*, her magic incantation. She first utters sounds unrelated to human language, cries of sinister and nocturnal animals (dogs, owls, snakes, wild animals) and the roaring of natural forces (sea, winds, thunder); then in "a Thessalian song" she addresses the infernal divinities, from the Eumenides to Charon, and recalls for them her earlier benefits, her prayers "in an impious and contaminated voice" (706), her human sacrifices, especially of children, and commands them to help her: "obey my prayer" (711)—that they give the cadaver the knowledge necessary to make prophecies to Sextus Pompey.

This prayer was intended to revivify the dead man and make him speak. But a strange thing, the soul hesitates to return to the body. Erictho needs another *carmen*, this time with a threatening aspect: she will reveal the most intimate secrets of Tartarus, if the gods do not force the recalcitrant dead man to help her. The threat produces its effect—the cadaver begins to come back to life and is ready to answer the witch's questions. But before interrogating him, she promises him, if he answers her questions, a sepulture that will in the future protect him against any magical threat. To guarantee the truth of the prophecy, it is necessary to win the zombie's benevolence. After a vague *carmen*, he begins to make predictions or rather to tell what is known of the future in the world of the dead, a story that becomes a reversed version of Virgil's "Catalog of the Romans" in *Aeneid* VI. Once the story has ended, Erictho fulfills her promise and burns the cadaver.

The ritual is clear and straightforward. After the preparatory acts—the search for the cadaver, its transport to the forest, Erictho's change of dress—the rite proper begins. The cadaver is prepared with the help of the "lunar poison"; it must be ready once again to receive its soul. Next comes the long prayer, with its clear divisions. The first part is alien to human language; the witch speaks the languages of nature, that of the nocturnal or dangerous animals and that of the destructive forces of nature. The second part adopts, in an almost pedantic way, the structure of a commonplace Greco-Roman prayer.[31] It begins with the *invocatio*, the call to the divinities by their names, their places of worship, and their functions, an enumeration structured by anaphorical invocations and relative clauses, which ends with the invitation to appear and to hear the prayer ("listen to my prayers," 706). Next comes the *narratio*, the essential part that must establish the credibility, so to speak, of the person praying, most often by the recall of earlier sacrifices or of help already given that confirm the right to the future services of the divinity. Erictho enumerates her earlier sacrifices by a formula common in all prayers that uses the anaphorical *si . . .*; already the Homeric Chryses justifies his request with the words, *"If* I ever built you a splendid temple, *if* I burnt to you fat thighs of bulls and goats, (so help me now)." The prayer ends with the actual request, the *preces*, as in any private or public prayer.

Lucan thus stresses the almost tritely religious character of what happens, but reading him more closely, we note that it is a cleverly perverted religious practice. The divinities whom Erictho is addressing are those of the infernal world. The list of them begins with the negative and destructive powers— "Eumenides, Stygian Crimes, Punishments of the guilty, Chaos eager to confound innumerable universes" (695f.)—threatening the whole universe, and not just our world. She continues with the great divinities—Dis "Master of the Underworld," Styx, Persephone, infernal Hecate (described as the mediator between Erictho and the Manes), and then she ends with the mythological figures of Cerberus and Charon.[32] Her prayers and sacrifices constitute a deliberate inversion of the usual worship; she prays with an "impious and sullied mouth" (706), sacrifices human victims, and makes libations of human blood. At the end is not a wish, but an order: "Obey my prayers, *parete precanti.*"

When this prayer does not have the desired effect, she resorts to a second prayer, this time designated as a *carmen*, uttered in a fierce and threatening tone: "She barks at the dead and shatters the silence of their reign" (829). Thus, she succeeds in performing the rite. We recall that the theme of the second prayer had already appeared in the introduction. Lucan there said that the gods would never expect this *carmen secundum*: we now understand the reason for the gods' fear.

What Lucan describes for us is one of the most interesting—and most influential—necromancies in literature. In this first part, we already noticed some precise ritual details. Lucan describes a rite that puts our world in relation to the one down below, through two mediators; the first is the witch, who (as a human being) comes from the world of the living, and the second is the soul of a dead man, fallen on the field of battle, who is forced to come back from down below, bringing his knowledge with him: being a young warrior who died in battle, he is both *áhōros* and *biaiothánatos*. We understand, moreover, that Lucan presents Erictho's mediating function in two slightly contradictory ways. In the descriptive part, she is decidedly inclined toward the world of the dead, whereas in the description of the ritual, she goes from the world of the living to meet with a revivified cadaver who made the reverse journey. This inconsistency must be attributed to the tension between the literary will to present Erictho as a superhuman, almost infernal figure and the precision with which the poet reports the ritual.

Greek and Latin literature contains a whole series of necromancies, starting from the Homeric *Nekyia* (which, moreover, reappears among the divinatory texts of the papyri)[33] and Aeschylus's rite of *The Persians* down to the fictions in the late novels and the parodies in Lucian. None is as detailed.[34] But what concerns us here is not this intertextuality (still widely unexplored by researchers, moreover), but the relationship between Lucan's description and the comparable recipes of the papyri, research that leads to a hitherto barely mentioned domain, that of magic divination.

We have seen that binding spells had the role of helping the individual immersed in a crisis brought on by a situation of competition or social conflict (a trial, commercial rivalry, athletic contest, or sexual conquest), whose outcome is still undecided. Through the rite, an individual sought to influence the course of events, and the *defixio* was a means for gaining control of the future. Another means for achieving these ends, divination was much more widespread, and it plays a considerable role both in the papyri and in the popular or literary conceptions of magic. Arnobius, the Christian of the fourth century A.D., draws up a long list of what in his eyes a sorcerer perpetrates against his fellow humans:[35]

> Indeed, who does not know that these people make every effort to foresee what is imminent, what necessarily happens, whether they wish it or not, by virtue of the order of things; that they send a mortal illness to whom they please, or that they break the bonds of affection between the members of the same family, or that they open without keys what is locked, or that they sew up mouths shut to keep them silent, or that they weaken, stimulate, slow down the horses at the races, that they arouse in the women and children of others, boys or girls, ardors and frenzied lusts of an illicit love, or that, if they seem to attempt a useful undertaking, it is not their own strength that makes them capable of it, but the power of those they invoke?

He begins with the most commonplace activity: sorcerers attend to the divination of the imminent future. The objective is thus completely practical and amounts to knowing the weather tomorrow or the price of olives in two months. The sorcerers also seek to influence this future, an undertaking that the Christian makes fun of. But they are also quite capable of doing harm, of inducing sudden deaths or fatal disease, and can undo family affections. The first accusation derives from the *veneficus* of the Roman tradition, the second is found in the papyri as a charm under the name of "charm to create disunion," *diákopos;* several cursing tablets coming mainly from mainland Greece attest to its actual performance.[36] Other texts underscore the divinatory function of magic even more; the same Arnobius calls the sorcerer "the brother of the soothsayer," and in the influential encyclopedia of Isidorus of Seville, the magicians are specialists of divination. In addition, already in early imperial Rome, the Magi served as soothsayers, together with the Chaldeans, the astrologers: the Romans never sharply differentiated the two kinds of funny Orientals.[37]

The list continues, mentioning some more specific feats. The magician can enter everywhere and without a key. This power, which in this text has a negative connotation, is nevertheless considered as a sign of the extraordinary power possessed by Apollonius, who left his prison unaided; it is feared in the Christian martyrs Perpetua and Felicitas; and it is also found in the papyri as a charm called "Door-opener" or "Release from bonds," as a feat meant to impress the crowds at fairs.[38] The magician can "sew up mouths to keep them silent" and can "weaken, stimulate, and slow down horses at the racetracks": we are in the domain of judiciary and agonistic *defixiones.* Also mentioned is the erotic defixion, in a fine definition that combines binding spell and spell of attraction; the sorcerers "cause ardors and raging desires of an illicit love" in women and the children of others, boys or girls—*amor inconcessus* being a polemical formulation that repeats the literary stories of extraconjugal love as well as homosexual love.

Divination thus constitutes only a part of that magic world appearing in highly diverse forms in the recipes of the papyri. First there are multifunctional rites that allow for a varied range of actions; when a demoniacal or even divine parhedros has been procured, it can do almost anything. But there are other ways that make it possible to have access to divination. For example, one may use three lines from Homer as a potent spell; written on an iron tablet, they bring back a fugitive slave, make a corpse prophesy, secure success in a trial and in love. The papyrus book in the Bibliothèque Nationale presents a long list of useful functions.[39] Among the specialized rites of divination, there are the simplest charms, like one that makes it possible to foresee everything; before speaking to someone, a person must put a finger under the tongue and murmur a little incantation to Helios.[40] However, most of the recipes are much more complex. It is always a matter of making contact with a superhuman being (divinity, demon, dead person) to profit from the being's knowledge. In this domain, we can distinguish, roughly, several ways of proceeding, depending on the modes of contact:

(a) The rites seeking direct contact with a divinity, without mediation: the papyri call them "direct visions."[41]

(b) The rites seeking contact with a divinity through divinatory possession, which uses a medium in a trance, especially a boy.[42]

(c) The rites seeking contact through divinatory dreams and that often use a lamp, once even a small statuette of a god.[43] One of the papyri of the British Museum (PGM VII) has collected a great number of these dreams, including a recipe deriving from Pythagoras and Democritus; its author was clearly a specialist.

(d) The rites using an object, particularly a container filled with water, with a little oil (the lecanomancy), more rarely a lamp (as did the witch in Apuleius's *Metamorphoses*) to establish the contact. But this category is complex, for the vase or the lamp, in the papyri, can also be used for divination by dreams, like the one done through the intermediary of a medium or a direct vision.[44]

(e) The rites seeking contact with the dead to obtain information about the future. Technically, this could be a rite of "direct vision"; in practice, the rites fall into the category of necromancy.

DIVINATION AND THE DEAD

In the papyri, there are a few divinatory rites that resort to the assistance of a dead person. The most important one is a text in a threefold version preserved in the magic papyrus in the Bibliothèque Nationale.⁴⁵ The first is named *Erotic Attraction Spell of King Pitys.* It is followed by a second *Erotic Attraction Spell of Pitys,* which is much longer and more detailed and takes the form of a letter of Pitys to one King Osthanes, and by a very short formula, *Consultation of a Skull According to Pitys the Thessalian,* a radical but obvious abridgement of the *Letter.* Of this letter, the addressee is clearer than the writer. Osthanes was not a king, but simply a counselor to King Xerxes, whom he accompanied to Greece, importing magic with him, according to Pliny.⁴⁶ Pitys, on the other hand, is less easily identified. Perhaps he is Bithus of Dyrrhachium, a magician mentioned by Pliny and no doubt transformed into an Egyptian priest under the name of Bitys in Iamblichus.⁴⁷ Even more remarkable is the fact that Pithys is a Thessalian; it was the Thessalians who immediately collaborated with the invading Persians of Xerxes: if this is not pure chance, the Thessalians being the paramount sorcerers in antiquity, the fiction in the papyrus tries to attain historical plausibility, which might point to a date of its origin in Hellenistic times when such facts still were remembered.

The manipulation of the skull clearly is essential in these texts, and suggests necromancy. Nevertheless, it is not a matter of resuscitating a dead person, as the rite in the first text shows. The magician prays to the Sun to send him a demon, this *nekuodaímōn* whose skull he possesses. The magician will question him not directly, but in a dream. So before going to bed, he has to write the questions on leaves of ivy, the plant of Osiris-Dionysus, and put them inside the skull. The rite of the *Letter* is structured in the same way, if only in that the preparation is more complicated and the dead person has all the functions that a demoniacal assistant can perform. Among the latter, the erotic attraction is so important that it gave the title to the whole recipe. Although a skull, i.e., a dead person's head, must be manipulated, this is not a necromancy. The skull functions as magical essence: it is merely the indicator that will allow for the Sun to find the skull's former possessor. There is even a formula for the case in which the magician indeed would have a skull, but not that of a *nekudaímōn;* it is not so easy to find such skulls.

This clarifies the relation between the first and the second version. Their designation as "Erotic attraction spell," *agōgḗ,* is misleading, because they do not serve for erotic magic. This suggests that the original ritual had a much wider function, comparable to the second version, among other things that of an erotic attraction: therefore its title. Thus, the second version comes closer to the original, of which it also preserves the epistolary form; it goes without saying that, in this sort of wild transmission, we cannot tell how close the second version came to the original. The abridged version, which transformed it into a divinatory ritual, retained the more appealing but now misleading title—and it retained another now misleading piece of information; its title claims that it can be performed "over any skull cap." Its actual text, however, asks for the specific skull of a "man who died a violent death"; the ritual, which prepares an unsatisfactory skull, is added in the second version, presumably again from the original.

The fact that the papyri do not contain necromantic rites does not mean that they do not contain rites for resuscitating the dead, but they are not used for divination. A very short passage from *Moses* VIII contains a spell intended to make a dead man walk, but without any indication of the ritual details or the functions of the spell.[48] More relevant is the promise contained in the book of the Bibliothèque Nationale. If three verses of book X of the *Iliad* are written on a lamella of iron, one has a powerful charm: "Hang it around the neck of a man who has been executed and tell him the verses in his ear: he will tell you anything you want."[49] It is thus again a man who died by violence, like Lucan's warrior, but the resuscitation is rather peaceful and purely symbolic. The rest of the text describes the consecration of this tablet, a rite that will have the effect that the executed man will live for another three days to serve as a *párhedros* for the sorcerer, which is inscribed in a well-known series in which a dead man, a *nekudaímōn*, becomes the sorcerer's demonical assistant.

But that, after all, is what we expect. The rituals of the papyri must function in an empirical world, as difficult to believe as it may sometimes seem to us. In the empirical world, the dead do not easily set about walking and talking. A sorcerer thus leaves cadavers in their graves and manipulates only some magical essence, a skull or something else; the sorcerer always relies upon the same symbolic processes to make a *párhedros* appear. It is not surprising that often this demoniacal assistant makes his or her prophecies in a dream. Throughout the ancient world, it is in a dream that one encounters the gods, the demons, and the dead.

LUCAN AND THE MAGIC RITES

The rite described in Lucan, with its resurrection of a cadaver for divination, has no full parallel in the papyri. Nevertheless, there are interesting parallels in the level of details. Erictho begins her long prayer by "murmuring sounds that are discordant and very different from human language," *murmura dissona et humanae multum discordia linguae* (6,686), that is, sounds issuing from nocturnal and wild animals or natural forces. This sound-making can seem a fantasy, but it plays a certain role in the vocal rites. In the initial invocation of *Moses* VIII, the sorcerer must whistle and make the tongue click, even imitate the chirping of birds. These sounds have an obvious function: the bird cries translate the name of the god in the language of the birds.[50] The sounds thus constitute merely an extension of those magic words that to us—and already to ancient observers—seem so strange.[51] For the sorcerer, they are "barbarian names," *onómata barbariká*, but only in the sense that they are divine names in a foreign, powerful language. In uttering them, the sorcerer demonstrates immense knowledge as well as the capacity for approaching the gods. The sorcerer knows all their names, even those belonging to the most distant languages or to the language of the birds; it is a splendid instance of this claim to superior wisdom that already had irritated the author of *On the Sacred Disease*. The same explanation holds for the other sounds, as is confirmed by a strange myth of creation told in the continuation of *Moses* VIII. Frightened, the Creator whistled, and the earth became round. Frightened again, he made his tongue click and a second god was born. Finally, he shouted IAO (Jahweh), and a third god appeared. The sorcerer repeats these sounds, and in repeating them, he shows anew the intimate knowledge he has of the Supreme God. These sounds are thus functional, but in a very different context from the one mentioned by Lucan. It indeed seems that Lucan knows only that the sorcerers use such sounds, animal cries and other noises. He uses them to underscore the destructive and superhuman powers of Erictho, which her marginal position associates with the nocturnal animals and destructive forces of nature, humanity's permanent enemies.

After the failure of the first invocation, Erictho resorts to threats, which seems again to reflect the witch's diabolical character. But here again, the process is known through the papyri. They contain a group of spells that they call "constraining words," (lógoi) epánankoi. These spells have a precise function, which is to constrain the divinity or the demon in the rare cases in which the first prayer does not eventuate in an immediate success because the god or the demon is taking so long. These second spells are not always threatening. Some of them are rather friendly: "When he delays, say these words after the prayer to the gods, uttering them once or three times: 'The great god, he who lives, commands you, he who exists from eternity to eternity . . . enter, appear before me, Lord, joyous, kindly, peaceful, glorious, without anger, as I entreat you in the name of the Lord IAO . . . enter, appear before me, Lord, joyous, kindly, peaceful, glorious, without anger.'"[52] Here it is the reference to the Supreme God, with whom the sorcerer seems to be intimate and familiar, which will constrain the demon. Nevertheless, threats are not unknown: "In another copy, I found the following version: When he does not obey this way, wrap the figurine in the same cloth and on the fifth day throw it in the oven of a bath, and after the invocation say: God of gods, king of kings, now also force a benevolent and divinatory demon to appear to me, so that I do not resort to punishments more violent than the leaf."[53] In this text, the divination is performed with the help of a demon whose nature cannot be determined (the beginning of the text has been lost), but which indeed throws light on Lucan's text.

Lucan's text thus shows two fundamental differences in relation to the one of Theocritus. One difference concerns the course of the ritual. In Theocritus, the ritual ended with a rite that never could have worked in reality. It has no continuous and closed structure, because Theocritus tinkers with heterogeneous elements. Lucan, on the other hand, constructs a rite that has a perfect internal logic and that is completely consistent within the general framework of magical ritual: it might even have worked, when tried out. Certainly, it is a matter of a literary construction, and Lucan must be placed in an intertextual network whose references begin with the Homeric *Nekyia*. It is up to specialists in literature to decode this game that few Latin authors play with such brio. What the historian of religion must point out, however, is the resemblance of some particular details with the very real rites of the papyri, details that seem drawn from a precise knowledge of contemporaneous magic; it is not inconceivable that Lucan might have access to the respective books.[54] Although it is not legitimate to read this poem as if it were a source for the history of magic rites, it remains no less true that, with the one of Theocritus, it testifies to the imaginary world of magic.

Which leads us to the second difference, that of the descriptive code of the rites. In Theocritus, magic remains a petit-bourgeois act. The almost family activity of these two young women is considered with uppity benevolence; symptomatically, the poet sometimes uses a language from a cookbook to describe the rites. It is necessary to "dredge" the altar with flour, to "melt" the wax, to "scramble" the lizard, to "knead" the herbs—activities belonging to the realm of cooking. Although sacrificial action always takes place in proximity to the culinary space, this language reflects the social condition of the two female magicians. Lucan, who brings onstage the terrors of magic, resorts to the language of religion in his narration of the rite. The long initial passage already informs us that it is indeed a matter of religion. Lucan gives a list of oracles whom Pompey does not consult and whom it would have been "pious," *fas*, to consult, if it were not that Pompey seeks the *nefas*, the infernal gods. Thus he happens upon Erictho, the radical enemy of the gods on high *(superi)* who is given over to perverting all civic and private rites and who is totally dedicated to the world of the dead and the infernal powers. Lucan uses this to depict magic as a radical perversion of the civic religion, and he pushes this description well beyond what the papyri attest as the realities. Whereas in Lucan, Erictho's divine protectors are Pluto, Persephone, and the other powers of the netherworld, in the papyri it is always a supreme god, Helios, or even the Jewish IAΩ, who protects and helps the sorcerer in his deeds. The papyri do not confirm the radical opposition of religion and magic found in Lucan—as it will be found, later, in the Christian authors. But it is not in a spirit of religious (or enlightened) criticism of magic that Lucan is writing; the literary aim of all this radicalization characterizes Pompey the Younger, who, *Magno proles indigna*, perverts the republic and defiles (again, the code of religion) the triumphs, *polluit triumphos* (420–422). This perverse career finds its narrative climax in the encounter with Erictho.

7

WORDS AND ACTS

AT THE END of this journey through ancient magic, two questions that have long intrigued historians of magic have been regularly brought up without being fully clarified. What is the nature of magic ritual, and, more generally, what makes magic seem something quite specific? It is time to address these questions—not so much in order to propound a definitive theory than to bring up some suggestions for future debate.

SYMPATHEIA

One of the most prominent features of magic ritual, which has been stressed already by ancient observers like Theocritus, is what is still called—out of convention, laziness, or for want of anything better—"sympathetic" magic. That term, made familiar by Frazer's highly influential scholarly work, is much older than this work.[1] As a good Hellenist, Frazer took it from the Greek Stoics, who explained the functioning of astrology by *sumpátheia*, that is, an intimate orchestration that connects the whole cosmos and the planets to our everyday life. But it is particularly the alchemists and magicians of the imperial epoch who thus explain the "relationships established . . . between the fires of the sky and the occult forces that fill with attractions and repulsions the most distant kingdoms of nature."[2] Or, to cite Plotinus, that magician's enemy who had an intimate knowledge of theurgy: "Magical actions, how does one explain them? Certainly by sympathy, because there exists both harmony between similar things and repulsion between dissimilar ones, and because there exist numerous forces which are focussed unto one living being. Many things are being attracted and enchanted, although no one sets them in motion: true magic, thus, is the love there is in the cosmos and its opposite, the hate."[3] It is thus a term already considered technical in the occult arts of later antiquity that Frazer took up and adapted for his own purposes. He used it to describe the cosmology of "primitive man" whose "magical thinking" started with the same assumption that there is a sympathetic cohesion among things; this thesis forms the basic supposition for Lucien Lévy-Bruehl and his "La mentalité primitive" (1925). Since the notion of "primitive thinking" has melted away like snow in sunlight, sympathy also will have to disappear. An explanation is still needed, however, for the ritualistic facts to which it referred. As Theocritus could have taught us, the so-called "sympathetic" rites constituted, for the contemporary observer, a prominent feature of ancient magic.

Among the explanations of the moderns, one of the most recent ones that have seemed appealing is the one given by the ethnologist Stanley Jeyaraja Tambiah. Tambiah, who has always been concerned with problems of ritual, introduced into the contemporary debate about the nature and function of ritual what he called the dimension of "performativity."[4] The term has been coined in general linguistics: here, it denotes a special aspect of verbal use in which the verb does not describe an action (as in "the witness swears an oath") but where action and linguistic utterance coincide (as when I am a witness taking an oath with the words "I swear to God"); it was Ludwig Wittgenstein, in his critical remarks on Frazer, who would introduce the concept into linguistics.[5] Any rite has theatrical aspects, and what matters to the participants is the way in which they take part in the rite: this interest in the theatrical aspects brings Tambiah (who in other domains sometimes seems rather an heir of Frazer) closer to Victor Turner.[6] Tambiah has written a fascinating article on the magic of words in which he draws the attention of ethnologists to the set of ritualistic acts and words that constitute the magical rite.[7] He also has reexamined the Frazerian terminology and established a distinction between "empirical analogy" and "persuasive analogy." The former characterizes the science used to predict the future, whereas magic has the aim of influencing future events.[8] Although this reasoning is indisputably appealing, it must be rethought in relation to antiquity.

The texts of the *defixiones* recorded both on the lead tablets and in the papyri are prayers, ritualistic utterances to which writing gives an unalterable permanence. At the same time that the spell was engraved on lead, it was spoken. The simple sentence "I bind so and so (to Persephone, and so on)," or "Persephone, bind so and so in order that he be unable to appear in court," or the *similia similibus* formula "that so and so be also twisted as this writing, as cold, as useless as this lead," are all three oral rites that both accompany and describe the ritual action.

There is a set of rites that should be compared, although they, according to general opinion, have nothing to do with magic.[9] When the people of Cyrene founded their city, they took an oath never to return to Thera, from which they had emigrated. Later, under unstable political conditions, they repeated this oath; an inscription from the fourth century B.C. has preserved it for us. This inscription thus described the central rite: "After making figures of wax, they burned them, uttering together an oath and performing together a sacrifice, men, women, boys, and girls: 'Let him who breaks this oath and commits contrary acts, let him melt and be liquefied like these figures, him and his descendants and his fortune.'"[10] Livy tells how the Romans concluded an alliance (*foedus*). They sacrificed a pig, and in killing it with a silex blade, the priest made the following vow: "Let him who breaks the alliance be killed like this pig."[11] These are only two examples of the same conception of the oath. One could easily cite other cases from Greece, Rome, or other cultures—especially from the Near East—that attest to the same ritualistic behavior.

In all cases, a solemn oath is taken. The oath is always conceived as an imprecation against the one who utters it and against his entire group. This imprecation is always accompanied by a rite whose meaning is clarified by the accompanying words: what happens to the object of the ritual act will happen to him who breaks the oath. It would be tempting to speak of a rite directed against an object that was the substitute for a person. This was done for Cyrene: the manikins (*kolossoí*) are unmistakable substitutes for the Cyreneans.[12] But the presence of the pig for the Romans or of the ewe in another oath, in Homer's *Iliad* III, cannot be explained in this way, not to mention the onion in a cathartic Hittite ritual in which one peels an onion while saying the following words: "Let the offender be dismembered in this way."[13] In fact, it is not the object manipulated by the rite that ought to hold our attention, but the action itself: one kills, one dismembers, one melts, and one liquefies. Aside from the sacrificial animals, the object is very often chosen in function of the action performed on it. The onion with its detachable layers can be easily peeled, and wax melts at a low temperature; in another rite of the Cyreneans, in the course of which the manikins are deposited in the countryside, they are made of unburnt clay so that they will not last very long, as the ritual expects.[14]

These acts, moreover, do not all have the same significance. There are those where the jump from the signifier (the rite) to the signified (the future transgression) is easily made: whoever breaks the treaty, will be annihilated by the wrath of the gods, as the pig is killed by the priest; the Roman *foedus*-ritual could almost be described as allegorical. There are other rites for which the translation is not as simple, and that are metaphorical expressions, like "melt" and "liquefy" in the rite of the Cyreneans. It is a matter, moreover, of metaphors that are not common, even in indigenous use. It is the context that gives them all their semantic value.

In all these cases, someone could, as was done in other oaths, confine himself or herself to speaking these words: "Let any person who breaks this oath be struck by such and such a calamity—himself, his descendants, all his house and his fortune." But we see what the ritual act that accompanies these words can bring. The message of the rite takes on quite a different intensity; the recipients of this message receive it through other codes than just the linguistic one. They must first decipher the metaphor, and, above all, they see, hear, and feel the figurines melt and the pig die. They receive an overdetermined message, accompanied by redundancies that have an emotional character. The result is perfectly clear: the message will be better committed to memory.

It is necessary to be more precise about what is meant by persuasive analogy. Persuasion requires a recipient. Someone always persuades someone else, and in our rites it is the group that persuades itself. The rite is an act of communication, which must be understood like other acts of communication. As always in the art of persuasion, a person plays on different registers to get the message across. It is enough to read Quintilian to measure the complexity reached by the different ways of signifying.

The model of ritual communication follows the model of any communication: there are senders, receivers, and a message. Usually, the senders of the ritual message are also its agents, whereas the recipient is the social group that attends the ritual, and the message is always important for the group. In this scheme of communication, ancient magic assumes a slightly aberrant form: the group is missing. There is no doubt about this for the papyri. Only the sorcerer performs the rite, alone, and there is never a group; the very rare cases in which the sorcerer allows a colleague to participate do not contradict this fact, so rare are they. The situation may be somewhat less clear in the Attic binding spells from the classical era, but we still have the impression, even though the documentation on this point is incomplete, that the *defigens* acts alone. The magic rite thus seems to short-circuit the communication: the sender and the recipient are identical. The corollary would be that the message concerns only the sorcerer and is of importance only for the sorcerer. These reflections are still pertinent even if it is admitted that the differences are exaggerated for the sake of the argument. It might just be that in the communal rite too, there is not always a very clear distinction between the sender and the recipient, for the rite does not separate as clearly those who are acting from those who are observing. Ovid's *spectandum veniunt, veniunt spectentur ut ipsae* would be rather the rule of any communal ritual. But the essential fact remains: the message of the communal ritual concerns everyone, agents and onlookers, whereas the message of the magic ritual concerns only the isolated agent who is the sorcerer.

Hence arise all the psychological explanations that follow a similar pattern. The magician is someone who speaks only to and of himself and herself, an eternal narcissus. When the magician pierces the lamella of lead and says, "I bind down, I nail down all these persons," this is not a demonstration meant for others, but a satisfaction, a personal "abreaction." The difficulties connected with this conception have already been mentioned: a magic ritual is anything but spontaneous. Even worse, the psychological approach construes magical acts as products of mental degeneration; from there comes the view that magic is debased religion, where the sacrifice of the noble bull has degenerated into the immolation of a common cat.[15] This theory, to say the least, misunderstands differences in structure for historical developments. Magic does not historically follow after religion, neither is it earlier: religion contains magic, as one specific religious form.

We must not disregard another difference between the rites of oaths and these magic *similia similibus*. The case just cited—"I nail down all these people"—is rather close to the situation of the oath, witness the Roman *foedus* ceremony, except that here the comparison is not made explicit and the metaphor "to nail" rests unexplained; but its sense is clear. More important, the same semantic structures in the magic rites and in those oaths that are self-imprecations virtually never coincide. Whereas the communal imprecations emphasize action, the magic rites of the *similia similibus* kind concentrate on an object and its quality: "Let so-and-so be like the dead, as is this leaf . . ." The lone exception is the rites brought onstage by Theocritus, who puts the accent on the action: "Let Delphis burn, melt, turn in the same way as such-and-such an object." It is this difference that confirms the importance of differentiating the communicative situation. In literature, magic is addressed, like the oath, to a human group, to the public of the listeners and readers who follow the literary rite. That is why its dramatic structure corresponds to that of the oath and not to that of the magic rite.

This communicative situation has its own effects. In all the cases considered here, the message uttered and brought on the scene does not record a fact, as do the nuptial or funerary rites that announce and perform a change of status, but is a means for influencing the course of future events. Hence the important problem: how can the words and acts be made to remain living and efficacious after the rite? For the oath, the thing is easy. All the participants in the oath of Cyrene saw the manikins melt, and they heard or uttered together the formula of comparison that accompanied the ritual and by which they condemned themselves in the case of a transgression. All this will remain in everyone's memory, and as the rite is repeated, each generation commits itself anew and preserves the memory. It is only in the fourth century that people began to distrust the collective memory and put the rite in writing; it is telling that this event happened in the century of Plato, who, in his *Phaedrus*, made this decline of memory manifest. The situation of the magician is much more precarious. When confronted with the crisis that he too wishes to resolve, by influencing the course of events, he has only his own memory to keep alive the words and also the perpetuity of the objects that he manipulates. That is why he does not melt the figurine of wax but ties it up, saying, "I bind so-and-so"; by doing so, he makes a kind of icon, a lasting condensation of his words, and he hides it in a place protected from the (accidental or voluntary) destructive effects of people. As the magician inclines toward the powers from below, it is in a tomb, in a sanctuary of the internal divinities, or, later, in the sea, a river, a well that he is going to hide them. Or the magician inscribes the words on a lamella of metal, a tablet of wax, or a sheet of papyrus, on which he "freezes" his words into a text that preserves the memory of the ritual act. Again, it is not by chance that these written rituals appear at about the same time as the so-called Orphic gold leaves that perpetuate ritual instructions for the afterlife.[16] But the writing does not simply perpetuate the ritual by saying, "I bind so-and-so." The similia-similibus formula makes explicit what the sorcerer wishes, and does so by using again things that guarantee duration: "Let so-and-so be like this lamella of lead." Then the magician pierces the tablet with a nail of which the holes remain, and often even the nail (which disappeared only because iron disintegrates in the soil much faster than lead): "I bind such-and-such a person." This is not a metaphor for "I kill this person," but for "I immobilize this person," for the nail is not a weapon, but a means for making things fast. The sorcerer even uses the dead person as a durable sign whose tomb served as a hiding place. There are rare indications of this intention of the sorcerer in the Attic formula that does not make use of the term "I bind," but of "I register," a quasi-juridical formula: the victim's name is deposited with the gods from below. Some centuries later, a comparable concept is found in the Cypriotic binding spells in which the binding spell is a "deposit" (parathḗkē), an object left with the demons who, in their tombs, are prayed to in order to transmit it to the infernal divinities.[17]

Seen from this perspective, the *similia similibus* rites as well as the existence of these texts of *defixiones* are a consequence of the isolation in which the magician acts, an isolation that seems to constitute the fundamental difference between the rites of magic and those of the civic religion.

These formulas draw our attention for another reason. In the context of communication established by the ritual, there exists, in addition to the horizontal axis connecting the human interlocutors, the vertical axis of the relationship established between humans and the gods, those on high or down below. Even if we admit that the communication conveying messages functions only at the horizontal level and that the gods are only symbolic objects making it possible for the communication to exist, it is still no less true that in the fiction of the ritual—theatrical, if you will—action there is another, vertical communicative axis. Humans address the gods through the intermediary of prayers and sacrifices, through the smoke that rises, and through the blood that flows, and we expect a certain number of reactions from the potential recipients of the rite. First, we expect immediate signs that the sacrifice has been accepted or rejected, perceived through the inspection of the entrails and the observation of the flame; then we expect signs that the gods will grant the wishes for the future, will grant the help and benevolence prayed for. This vertical communication is played out differently from the horizontal one and is conscious and carefully staged by the human actors: it is this communication that is spoken about by the indigenous people. The chance observer from outside, uninformed about theology and mythology, perceives only the interaction of the horizontal ritual messages whose signifiers are determined by an ancestral cultural tradition.

When we consider the situation of the magician, who is both the sender and the lone recipient of the ritual message, we understand how in such a situation the vertical axis, which leads to the gods and to the demons, can assume some importance, for it is indeed necessary, after all, to have interlocutors. That is precisely what the writers of the imperial era, Apuleius and Iamblichus, confirm for us. Magic is the search for a close communication with and participation in the divine sphere—the *communio loquendi cum dis* of Apuleius or the *methousía tôn theôn* of Iamblichus: both insist on the dialogue that is established between the magician and the gods.[18]

A theoretical consequence of this construction is that the separation between the agent practicing magic and the external observer is not as clear as the theory would have it. By a pirouette à la Magritte, the two spaces enter into communication.

THE MAGICIAN'S PRAYER

While revealing his difficulties, the orator Libanius makes a curious remark. He resisted his friends who implored him to counteract ritually the magic of his enemies and was content to offer prayers. There thus were countermeasures, presumably magic rites, about which, however, the orator had scruples, probably religious ones. We glimpse the existence of a contrast between the different forms of ritualistic behavior; and from this perspective, it appears that the prayer constitutes the most religious and the least reprehensible means, the furthest from superstition, which Libanius, in an enlightened spirit, wished to avoid. He is not at all alone: some centuries earlier, Plutarch had attacked magic as part of superstition and excessive dread of the gods.[19]

Perfectly comparable reactions are found in the modern history of research on the magic papyri. The papyri contain a certain number of hexametric hymns that are interesting documents for imperial religious poetry that otherwise is badly attested to and not well-known, thus accounting for the scholarly interest in them since Albrecht Dieterich.[20] Nonetheless, for Dieterich's generation, these hymns seemed to have such a "religious" color that most contemporary scholars, from Dieterich to Martin Nilsson—and especially Richard Reitzenstein—were convinced that these hymns were written in and for a context that was not magical, but religious, and that the magicians appropriated them, satisfied to insert in them those primitive elements that are the magic words.[21] For these scholars, it was inconceivable that magicians, deeply involved in a world of superstition and barbarism, were capable of conceiving documents that give such impressive evidence of a spiritualized religiosity. This attitude derives from the Frazerian dogma, according to which the magician is distinguished from the religious person by the lack of humble and disinterested submission to the divine will, and by the magician's will to force and constrain the divinity. This position still has its partisans.[22]

We find the same preoccupation in the famous thesis of Dieterich, that the magicians transformed and introduced into their world a whole liturgy of mysteries, the so-called "Liturgy of Mithras." It was obvious that this text expresses in its prayers a religious search for which the Greco-Egyptian sorcerers were denied credit. Dieterich thus preserved the Frazerian dichotomy without giving up the attempt to find traces of the true religion in the magicians. But we should not be surprised to read in Father Festugière, another defender of religion against magic, that the "Mithras Liturgy" was not a text of mysteries, but a simple text of Osirian magic ornamented by a bit of hermetism.[23] This point of view is inscribed in the argumentation of Festugière, who combats all those who, like Reitzenstein or Nilsson, claimed to find in the papyri vestiges of "true" religion; in his eyes, the papyri contain nothing other than magic, and to recognize in them the slightest trace of religiosity smacks of delusion. We can understand his position. For Father Festugière, who has lived in a system that still is acquainted with and sometimes even practices exorcism, the struggle against magic is a much more tangible reality than for his Protestant German colleagues.

It must be repeated that there is no doubt that the sorcerers uttered prayers. Nor did the ancients doubt it. In Lucan, the witch Erictho formulates a prayer that could belong to a textbook on religion; more important is that Plato already speaks of the "prayers" (eukhaí) as well as of the "incantations" (epōidaí) uttered by the begging priests and seers. What is more, prayers as formally correct as that of Erictho are found on the curse tablets as well as in the papyri. Although here the term currently used for this oral rite is *lógos,* "speech," the attestations to "prayers" and "to pray" are not lacking.[24] The human actors are well aware of these religious stances, and they often enough make use of formula attested in prayers as well—as in a spell from the first half of the first century B.C., which was found in Sevilla and which ends with a current formula from religious dedications: "When you do it, then I will fulfill my promise to you according to your merits," *si faciatis, votum quod facio solvam vestris meritis.*[25]

One example will suffice to introduce us to the specific problems posed by the magic prayer; it is a spell from the third century A.D. found in a Cypriot tomb.[26] The spell begins with the invocation to the dead formulated in more or less perfect hexameters: "Demons who live on earth and demons who are the fathers of fathers and mothers, similar to men, who reside and have their seat here, who previously received in your heart, a soul full of pain . . ." The prayer is thus more and more precisely addressed to the dead who have become demons: the spell proceeds from all the dead to those of the cemetery in question and finally to those who feel the weight of their death more than the others, those who died before their time.

Next comes not the *pars epica,* but the third part of the canonical prayer, the *preces,* a perfectly legitimate and functional inversion of the traditional formula. To stress the urgency of the prayer, the supplicant first omits the long narrative part: "Receive the animosity and anger that Ariston has against me, Soteirianos, also called Limbaros, take away his energy and his strength, make him cold, mute, and breathless, cold toward me, Soteirianos, also called Limbaros." The coldness being sought is not that of death, but the coldness accompanying the disappearance of the "hot" anger against the performer of the spell, a judiciary *defixion.*

What follows constitutes the so-called *pars epica* intended to show the credit of the person who prays: "I entreat you in the name of the great gods . . ." Next follow magic words, then new *preces*, which concern another victim and repeat the preceding structure. In our example, the *pars epica* is thus constituted of magic words alone instead of containing that reference to the earlier sacrifices that we encountered in Erictho, or that reminder of the help previously furnished by the personal goddess as she appears in the famous prayer of Sappho.[27] An identical process is sometimes found in the papyri, and we have already referred to it. The magic words are the secret, barbarous names of the divinity, and the sorcerer demonstrates by the knowledge that he has of them that he is worthy of receiving divine assistance. The most instructive case is found in a prayer of the *Charm of Astrampsychus*, whose objective is to obtain success and happiness. The prayer begins with a beautiful invocation: "Come to me, Lord Hermes, like babies in the belly of their mother, come to me, you who collect the food of the gods and men, come to me, Lord Hermes, to the so-and-so." Next comes the expression of the wish: "Grant me charm, food, victory, happiness, sexual attractiveness, beauty of face, strength regarding all women and all men." Instead of the *pars epica*, there is another list, each section of which is introduced by "I also know your forms, your wood, your identity, your origin, your homeland"; and, at the end, after the repetition of the invocation and of the wish, comes the affirmation: "I also know your barbarous names."[28]

This brings us to a theme already mentioned. The use of "foreign names" in magic goes back to the classical era, and it is Euripides who first mentions this phenomenon. Iphigenia, preparing the sacrifice of Orestes, "shouted barbarous words, as a true witch": it is a supreme irony to put this in the mouth of an indigenous messenger of the Taurians.[29] Much later, there were to be some theoretical reflections. The skeptical Pliny proposes a psychological explanation: "It is not easy to tell whether foreign and unpronounceable words take away belief in magic, or rather the unexpected Latin ones which sound ridiculous, because one always expects something which is immense and which is able to influence the gods or rather to give them orders."[30] In Iamblichus, the neo-Platonist philosopher, the theory is more serious and more detailed; he speaks of these names in the seventh book of his treatise on *The Mysteries of Egypt*, a philosophical defense of magic. In reality, they are not barbarian names, even less of names with no meaning, as his interlocutor has it, but the Assyrian and especially Egyptian names of gods. The gods love to be called by these names because they are "co-natural" to them: they are the most ancient names that were preserved without change; what is perpetual and unchangeable is appropriate to the nature of the gods, which is itself eternal and immutable. It is also necessary to read the passage that follows. "If it was a convention that decided the establishment of the names/words [the Greek *onómata* has both meanings], one could readily use some for others. But if these names/words depend on the nature of beings, those that come closer to it are more agreeable to the gods. Which shows how right it is to prefer the language of the sacred peoples to the languages of other men, for in translation the names/words do not perfectly preserve the same meaning."[31]

This passage recalls a text by Origen, mentioned already much earlier. Like Origen, the neo-Platonist philosopher is opposed to the common practice of *interpretatio graeca* (or *latina*) of divine names, for he believes in the existence of nonarbitrary relations between signifier and signified, name and divinity. That does not mean that any historical language is the language of the gods; Iamblichus states, "So leave aside the ideas that depart from the truth. As if the god invoked was Egyptian or spoke that language! Rather, say: because the Egyptians were the first to receive the prerogative of communication with the gods, the latter love to be invoked according to the rules of this people. This has nothing to do with the contrivances of sorcerers."[32] Because the gods have an absolute existence, one cannot speak of the "gods of the Egyptians" or of the "gods of the Greeks," and because they are beyond human nature, they do not speak a human language. The magicians would agree to this; the final sentence underscores that once again Iamblichus is writing within the framework of an apology of magic.

The use of a special, supposedly ancient, language for the invocations is not so rare in magic. Tambiah has collected examples concerning India in which a rather complex system is used, employing several levels of ancient languages for the invocations to the gods.[33] More simply, the use of Coptic in Greek, of Greek in Latin spells, like that of Latin in Reformation England, could provoke an accusation of magic.[34] The Greco-Egyptian papyri write only of "barbarian, foreign names," while the learned Iamblichus is in a position to specify that the names are Egyptian, and the Christian Jerome suggested a Jewish origin (both theories are partly correct).[35] Structurally, the use of these foreign languages once again consists in a reversal of regular linguistic behavior, of the ordinary prayer formulated in a language understood by everyone; the not very rare practice of writing a Latin spell in Greek letters comes rather close.[36]

There is still something else. In the ordinary "religious" prayer, it is the ritual act that legitimates the asking for divine favor: to emphasize one's own merits in order to commit the divinity to help, a person mentions the sacrifices or dedications that the person has already offered. In the magic of the papyri, it is knowledge that makes possible communication with the gods. The person who knows the intimate details of divine nature thereby demonstrates that he or she is close to the god and commits the god to react favorably. Magic thus has a well-defined theological and epistemological aspect. It could be thought that this is a late, neo-Platonic or gnostic development, but the author of the book *On the Sacred Disease* has already noted that the ritual healer was laying claim to a higher knowledge. In this respect, the gap between magic and civic religion exists already in the fifth century B.C. On the other hand, this theology makes magic close to the mystery cults; the initiated also used a higher knowledge to gain access to the divinity. A case in point, again, are the so-called Orphic gold leaves, which in fact belong to the Bacchic mysteries; the special fate, the eschatological happiness promised to initiates, depends on the right answer that they could give to the infernal guardians of the Lake of Memory or to Persephone and her court. Another feature shared by magic and mysteries is the quest for memory. The magicians seek to acquire a good memory so as not to forget what the god or the demon reveals to them in a dream, while for the initiate it is essential not to forget the instructions received during the initiation in order to be able to conduct oneself properly in the world beyond.

This circumstance explains why terminology specific to the mysteries is so often found in the papyri. It is not just a superficial embellishment nor even a relic of the older use of these same texts in mystery rites, nor is it only the result of a structural similarity between the initiation of the magician and the initiation of the follower of a mystery group. The spirituality of the magicians is akin to the spirituality of the followers of the mysteries, in that both take part in this quest for the divine that is characteristic of imperial antiquity.

We thus encounter, and not just in the hexametric hymns, the expression of what to a Frazerian is the sole prerogative of religion, the simple submission under God's wish and will. It is not rare that the god is called "Lord" (*kúrios*), which expresses some hierarchical subordination. The corollary, the fact that someone describes oneself as a slave, is not absent either: "Lord gods, give me an oracle on such-and-such a business this very night, during the coming hours. I pray to you with all my heart, I implore you, I your servant whom you have placed on the throne," an expression that once again refers us to the mysteries, this time those of Corybants and of their rite of enthronement.[37] The sorcerer again calls attention to himself as an initiate in order to benefit from the intimate relationship between the gods and the initiates.

This intimacy between the god and the magician finds other, more direct expressions as well, such as in a passage from the *Charm of Astrampsychus:* "Come to me, Lord Hermes, as babies do to the womb of women"; or in the "rite of encounter," the *sústasis,* with Helios where the rite culminates in the common meal of man and god, both sitting "face to face"; we have also read the prayer in the papyrus Mimaut: "Come close to me with a kindly face, on a bed that you yourself have chosen . . . I pray to you, Lord, accept my prayers"—another *sústasis* where god and human meet for a common meal.[38]

We therefore cannot separate the hymns from the rest of the corpus of magical papyri, thus creating a simplistic dichotomy between magic and religion. Sentiments of this kind are found in prayers in prose as well as in the metrical hymns. The distinctions—if distinctions there are—obey other laws.

MAGIC AND COERCION

A great number of binding spells from the imperial period address the god with the formula "I entreat you." This time, it is not a matter of convincing the gods through a higher knowledge; the magician coerces them simply through an invocation. This seems to confirm a modern opinion that sees coercion of superhuman beings as the defining property of magic. In the words of a contemporary scholar, "The magician does not implore the gods, he forces them; he has no intention to obey the gods or to submit himself on his knees and with a guileless heart." Is this correct, and where does this concept, which today appears to be firmly linked to the name of James G. Frazer, have its origin?[39] The question has, up to now, been touched on here and there in this book, but never properly discussed.

Already in the papyri, we find spells, which their authors called "spells that constrain," *epánankoi:* the idea of constraining superhuman powers is not unknown to magicians. We have also noted, in Lucan and in the papyri, that this coercion is simply an additional process that is used only if a more benign charm has not achieved its goal. Magicians had thought about ritual coercion and judged it a dangerous action; they always preferred to act without it.

There exist, moreover, different ways of constraining the divinity. First, there is the constraint by trickery; we recall the initiatory ritual in which Seth-Helios comes to the aid of the sorcerer who claims to be the victim of an attack led by Isis and Horus,[40] or the "slander rites," *diabolaí,* in which a person brings down the divinity's wrath on another person whom the person defames by accusing him or her of an impiety, ritualistic or otherwise. Then, there is the constraint by extortion, so to speak. In a divinatory rite described in the papyrus book in the Bibliothèque Nationale, a trap is set for a (unspecified) god or demon. In the middle of a circle of food—the leftovers from the sorcerer's meal—which is supposed to attract the demon to a common meal, a beetle is suspended above a lamp arranged in such a way that the flame does not yet touch the animal: "Stay calm after you have thrown out the morsels, enter your house and close yourself in; the one you have summoned will arrive and by threatening you with his weapons, try to force you to release the beetle. But you, you will not move it or release it before he has given you an oracle."[41] The beetle is the sacred animal of Helios, the superior god whom all the demons are thought to obey, from which comes the demon's interest in the animal. Incidentally, the coercion of a divinity in order to obtain an oracle, as this rite puts it to work, is a well-known mythical theme in Greece and Rome; to obtain an oracle or any other vital information, in a situation of crisis Menelaus or Aristaeus seizes the divine prophet Proteus, and king Numa captures the gods Picus and Faunus by force or trickery.[42] The narrative structure and the structure of the ritual are rather close, whatever their exact relationship is. Another rite makes it possible to seize hold of Persephone by resorting to blackmail. The sorcerer calls the goddess, but when she approaches, torches in hand, a charm will extinguish her torches. "The goddess will thus be sad and will complain," and the sorcerer promises to relight the torches if she helps him by sending him a dream or by killing an enemy.[43] (We notice the ease with which the magicians move in the two religious worlds: in the Egyptian one, Helios and his scarab; and in that of the Greeks, Kore and her torches. It is obviously inaccurate to attribute such stories to a uniquely Egyptian origin.)[44]

And finally, there is the purely verbal coercion of the coercion spells, the *epánankoi*. Ordinarily, these threats as well are accompanied by special rites, rites that can symbolically forestall the tortures with which the demon is threatened. The magician draws a portrait, wraps it up in a piece of cloth, and then throws it into the oven or a bath or suspends it above a lamp.[45] Other rites are reversals of the sacrificial rites: one offers the brain of a black ram; one fumigates with the dung of a black cow; as a final resort, one suspends the normal rules of worship.[46] Besides the direct threat, there is also the myth. A coercion spell of the papyrus of the Bibliothèque Nationale is addressed to a long list of the infernal gods and implores them to send "gladiators and heroes" (that is, those who have fallen in combat). It continues thus: "Isis came, bearing on her shoulders her husband, her brother. Zeus came down from Olympus and stood awaiting the phantoms of the dead who were lead to such-and-such a woman and did such-and-such a thing. All the immortal gods and goddesses came to see the phantoms of these dead. So do not hesitate and do not delay, gods, but send the phantoms of these dead."[47] Here we have a little mythical story, a *historiola*, partially modeled after the famous story in the *Odyssey* that tells how the gods came running to gaze at Ares and Aphrodite who were caught in a trap.[48] Because, according to our myth, the gods from on high already have come to witness the spectacle of the dead attacking a woman, their example will prompt the infernal gods to do the same. Thus, the spell does not apply crude coercion, rather persuasion by an *exemplum*; it is a well-known rhetorical strategy to which these *historiolae* own their popularity. Whereas this *historiola* blends Greek elements with Egyptian ones, juxtaposing Isis and Zeus in a quasi-Homeric situation, another coercion spell in the Paris book presents another blend. The magician threatens Aphrodite: "But, if as a goddess you act slowly, you will not see Adonis rise from Hades; immediately, I shall run and bind him with steel chains; as guard, I shall bind him on another wheel of Ixion; no longer will he come to light, and he will be chastised and subdued. Wherefore, O Lady, act, I beg." Although the Greco-Phoenician cult of Adonis was popular in Hellenized Egypt, the netherworld here is purely Greek.[49]

There is no doubt that coercion belongs to magic.[50] But it constitutes only one element in a set of religious behaviors that range from the cruelest constraint to the most obsequious submission. The variety of religious behavior that the magician makes use of is accompanied by a very precise organization that structures the superhuman world that the magician addresses. The following coercion spell gives an illustration of it: "Listen to me, I am going to say the great name, AOΘ, that every god reveres, that every demon fears, to which every messenger (*ángelos*) obeys."[51] We see a very strict hierarchy: at the top there is the "great name," the name of the supreme god to whom the other gods are subject, then come the demons and finally the messengers. It thus suffices for the sorcerer to become the intimate of the supreme god to get himself obeyed by the whole hierarchy; this intimacy manifests itself through the knowledge of the name. Another coercion spell of the Paris book is no less revealing: "If he delay, after the prayer to the gods, say these words once or three times: 'The great god, he who lives, who commands you, who exists from eternity to eternity.'"[52] The magician can claim even the powers of the supreme gods. Demons are dumb.

The hierarchy of the superhuman world is thus perfectly functional. But it does not belong only to the theology of the magicians: it is a hierarchization that finds its most subtle expression in neo-Platonic thinking, from Plotinus to Proclus, in much more elaborate and complex constructions. From neo-Platonic thinking, this hierarchization spread in the religion of the era, where it constituted a theological response to the growing hierarchization of the imperial society. For the magicians who draw their theology from this religious stock, already present, moreover, in the texts earlier than the fourth century, like *Moses* VIII, what matters is only the existence of two levels. On the one hand, there is the Supreme God with different names (among them, the Israelite IAΩ, or Jahweh, is not without importance) toward whom all want to ascend and with whom they seek to become intimate; he is exempt from coercion. On the other hand, there are those demons and messengers whom the magician calls into his service with the help of the supreme god; towards them, constraint can be used in the last resort. There is also an intermediate area, that of the minor gods, which is rather poorly defined: some gods—Kore or Aphrodite—can be coerced; Hermes, the holder of a supreme knowledge, is treated much better.

An analysis of African systems by Clifford Geertz addresses the question of hierarchies. He pointed out that there existed, in a certain number of African societies, a magic theology distinguishing two levels of superhuman beings.[53] But there is one crucial difference towards the Greco-Roman material. The African dichotomy is a function of the aim pursued by the magic rite: the lower level includes the demons and the lesser beings invoked in everyday magic and minor affairs, whereas the second degree includes the highest beings, the gods, who are invoked only in important matters. The Greek dichotomy, on the other hand, is one of ontological status; in order to command the lower beings, the Greco-Egyptian sorcerer always needs access to the higher gods. Instead of being a real parallel, the African cases help to sharpen our understanding of the specificity of Greco-Egyptian theology.

Thus, coercion, although present, is not really constitutive of Greco-Roman magic, but is only one of the elements of a much more complex ideology. Why, then, is it invested with such importance in European thinking about magic?

The first time this notion becomes visible is in the treatise *On the Sacred Disease,* whose author censured the healers for claiming powers that belong only to the gods, for even claiming to have a power higher than that of the gods, the power to coerce them and use them like slaves. All this reduces the gods to nothing, for the divine is defined by its absolute superiority relative to humankind.[54] Thus, the theological thinking of the sophists' epoch interprets the magicians' affirmations in this sense and uses them as an argument against magic. Plato follows suit.

Although he does not speak of "coercion," he does say that the magicians "persuade" the gods. Now, persuasion is nothing other than a subtle form of coercion that resorts to words. We have seen that well-chosen *exempla* can coerce the gods.

Later writers repeat these criticisms, the pagans in a more qualified way than the Christians.[55] It is thus not surprising that Iamblichus devotes a paragraph to coercion of the gods to respond to his interlocutor who has noticed (which the enlightened doctor had already said) that it was incompatible with the divine nature to allow itself to be forced. This, therefore, is an argument that was widely used in the polemic against magic. The philosopher's response is revealing: "In sum, the so-called 'obligations of the gods' are obligations of the gods that manifest themselves in a way fitting to the gods. It is thus not from the outside nor by violence, but because the good is necessarily useful, that they use their ever-even and unvarying dispositions."[56] Iamblichus does not deny that there are "obligations of the gods" (he knows magic well enough). But he reverses their interpretation; it is not the sorcerers who force the gods, instead it is their own divine nature, which is pure good. We think of Seth, who feels compassion for the presumed victim of Horus.

There thus existed a whole ancient polemical tradition that accented this definition of magic by the coercion of the gods, a tradition first adopted by Platonism—and which on that account belongs to an important stream of ancient thought—then upheld by the polemic of the Christians. So it is not surprising that both the intellectual Frazer and the religious Father Festugière had recourse to this definition. Another, less shocking definition disappeared from sight: the one given by Apuleius. According to him, the magician derives his powers from the *communio loquendi*, the conversation and dialogue with the gods: "*magus* is properly he who, doing business with the immortal gods, has the power to effect everything he wishes through the mysterious force of certain incantations."[57] This definition would have been much less vulnerable to Christian polemics.

MAGIC AND REVERSAL

In the course of this analysis, we have come across a number of those reversals that characterize magic and especially magical ritual—intentional inversions of everyday practices or ordinary ritual.[58] Already in the binding spells from the fifth and fourth centuries B.C., we noticed several of them, like the retrograde writing or the use of the mother's name; for lack of more precise facts about contemporary magical rites, we must confine ourselves to this sketchy information. The later texts attest to the magician's isolation in the performance of the rite, the specific form taken by these rites and the role played by the infernal divinities—which can be seen as so many reversals. The following paragraphs try to present them more comprehensively.

The isolation in which the magician finds himself when performing the rite contrasts the magical with the communal rite, which is performed in a group—the household, the tribe, the entire town—but also with the mystery rites. The differences, however, must not be exaggerated. Though the magician's isolation is indeed real in the *defixio,* that harmful magic condemned by Plato, one will be less affirmative for the magic of healing of which the doctor speaks in the treatise *On the Sacred Disease.* In most cultures, ethnographic or European, ritual healing concerns the entire group—the patient, the patient's family, the village; the same holds true for ancient exorcisms. Healing thus represents a domain that must be considered separately. Especially in this domain, the divisions between religion and magic are far from clear-cut and seem to have varied considerably with time. Behind the polemical description of the author of the treatise *On the Sacred Disease,* we glimpse not only the dietary prescriptions of the cathartic priests but also extensive healing rituals. Later, the description of such rituals appears in literature, for example, in Cato (who, however, does not range them with magic) or in that curious little rite performed by Tibullus for his sick Delia, which again has no negative connotations:[59] the negative evaluation is confined to the Hippocratic doctor. Nor is it in these cases ever a matter of rites performed by an isolated healer, but always rites performed in groups made up of the healer, the patient, some assistants (at least in Cato and in Tibullus), parents, and family. In other cultures, ritual healing may take the form of ritual drama, requiring the presence of a proper audience.[60]

In the papyri, on the other hand, although there is a whole series of magic recipes against illnesses (migraine, gout, fever, scorpion stings, dog bites), they are never rites performed in groups, but simple oral or written prayers. "To fight migraine, take some oil in your hands and say this formula: 'Zeus planted a grape seed, it parts the soil; he doesn't plant it, it does not sprout.'"[61] It is again one of those *historiolae* that gave an exemplum. Here is another one: "Against the same: write on a piece of scarlet parchment ABRASAX (and what you desire). Dunk it and put it on your temple."[62] A wet piece of parchment against headache makes sense, with or without a spell. In the eyes of the people who wrote the magical books, all these recipes belong to the same domain of magic as that of the other magic instructions in their books: nothing justifies our separating them.[63] And what they have in common with the other rites is the fact that they do not refer to group actions, but instead constitute small aids for the isolated individual.

In the world of the papyri where we grasp the rite with a rare precision, we see a whole set of reversals, which, however, must be distinguished from each other. Fumigations and libations are perfectly regular rites—only that, in the common worship, one burns incense, one pours wine, milk, or honey; the libations of milk, water, and honey already are extraordinary rites, confined to a few specific rituals. Magic ritual thus uses the common ritual forms, changes only the substances to be burned or libated; at least the slander spells make deliberate use of rather disgusting substances.[64] The differences are more unmistakable in the bloody sacrifices, first of all in the choice of animals. Those of the civic rites—pig, sheep, and cow—are absent, and in their place we find birds, especially the rooster, or the donkey, rare victims that as such express a clear-cut reversal in relation to civic religion. The magician uses signs that are easily identifiable. Sacrificial meals are not lacking, but the magician eats the sacrificial meat without human company. A different form of meal is used in the *systasis*, the "ritual encounter"; it is conceived as a banquet where the sorcerer and the god dine together and can be seen as transformation of the ordinary Greek symposium, only that it never includes the meat from a previously offered sacrifice. Nor is the way of killing the victim the same. When the victim is meant to be eaten in the magic rite, it is strangled; blood, the carrier of vital energy, may not be shed. In an initiatory rite, on the other hand, one drinks the blood of a sacrificial victim; on the banks of the Nile (in a marginal place), the sorcerer builds an altar, lights a fire with some wood from an olive tree, cuts off the head of a rooster, throws its head into the Nile, and then drinks the animal's blood.[65] Finally, there is the holocaust offering in which entire animals are burnt, as in the ritual consecration of a magic ring. Outside the town or in a graveyard (again in a marginal place, that is), a large hole must be dug, an altar is built above this hole, a fire is lit with the wood from fruit trees, and then the magician burns a goose, three roosters, three pigeons, and incense, a sacrifice explicitly described in the papyrus as holocaust.[66] Here again, magic uses traditional forms, sometimes organized in new combinations.

THE SEARCH for contact with the infernal divinities and the dead, that is, the ritual movement downwards, always constitutes a radical reversal, both in the framework of Greek or Roman civic religion as in that of magic. Once more, it is necessary to be specific. The fixation of magic on the powers from down below is totally true only for the classical era, and solely for the domain of binding spells. For the other rites, we lack information, apart from the too-general remark in Plato that magicians "convince the gods": more precision would damage his polemical position.[67] It is more important to note, in a diachronic perspective, that in the epoch before the papyrus books, we have no indication of the two-level system in which the magician addresses the divinities on high to use their aid in order to coerce the dead, the heroes, and the demons. Basically, these two levels correspond to the common dichotomy that opposes the Olympian gods (whom the magician does not touch) and the chthonic ones, whom the magician addresses; but it would not be legitimate to project this system back into hellenistic, classical, or archaic times.[68] The emergence of the two-level system constitutes the most important change that can be noted in the development of ancient magic. First, it reflects the transition from a more or less homogeneous pantheon to the extremely hierarchical pantheon of the imperial era. Moreover, it also refers to the fact that the magic of the imperial era went from a technique intended (not without the influence of the Near Eastern books of exorcism) to harm one's adversaries to a technique that approaches the gnostic and neo-Platonic quest for the knowledge that derives from the experience of the divinity. Although already the polemical author of *On the Sacred Disease* noted some signs of an epistemological claim of the cathartic priests, this aspect seems to have gained considerable ground only after the Hellenistic epoch. It was only in imperial times that magic became a knowledge providing access to the Supreme God, and it was only at that moment that the sorcerer acquired, through this knowledge, an assistant that accompanied the sorcerer throughout his or her career. From this derived that attempt of the neo-Platonic theurgy to use magic techniques to acquire knowledge about the Supreme God; from this also derived the ambiguity in the status of the philosopher and the charismatic "divine man," Apollonius of Tyana or Jesus, who, depending on the viewpoint adopted, could be presented as a great sage or a great sorcerer. It is obvious that this change reflects a fundamental change in society; the earlier, agonistic society with its low hierarchy and its large need for support in competition changes into a much more highly hierarchized society in which competition is the concern of a narrow elite, while the rest of society turns to the care of spiritual well-being.

NOTES

1. INTRODUCTION

1. This does not imply that these papyri are equally valid evidence for all ancient magic, both inside and outside the Greco-Egyptian culture—see the reservations of Smith, 1978, p. 119.

2. Karl Preisendanz (ed.), *Papyri Graecae Magicae: Die griechischen Zauberpapyri*, 2 vols. (Leipzig/Berlin: Teubner, 1929–1931); second ed. by Albert Henrichs (Stuttgart: Teubner, 1973–1974); the third volume, with the indices already printed separately, was destroyed during the bombing of Leipzig. English translation with useful commentaries and Coptic texts by Hans Dieter Betz (ed.), *The Greek Magical Papyri in Translation Including the Demotic Spells* (Chicago/London: University of Chicago Press, 1986, second ed. 1992); a second volume with the indices is forthcoming.

3. The collection of the *PGM* already contains a large number of them. Among the texts more recently found, the collection of Wortmann, 1968, pp. 56–111, is the most interesting; Robert W. Daniel and Franco Maltomini (eds.), *Supplementum Magicum*, vols. 1 and 2 (Abhandlungen der Nordrhein-Westfaelischen Akademie, Sonderreihe Papyrologica Coloniensia, vol. 16:1) (Opladen, 1990 and 1992) began a reedition with shorter but important commentaries.

4. Although old, the basic editions are those of Wünsch 1897 and of Audollent 1904; a more recent catalog is that of Jordan 1985a, pp. 151–197; a selection in translation with commentaries, Gager 1992.

5. See n. 2 for the basic collection *PGM* and its English translation with short commentaries *PGMTr* (p. XLI, the comparison with the texts of Qumran or of Nag Hammadi). Among the oldest is a book from Berlin from the first century A.D. not yet known to Preisendanz-Henrichs; see W. Brashear, "Ein Berliner Zauberpapyrus," *ZPE*, 33, 1979, pp. 261–278, translated in *PGMTr*, CXXII, pp. 316–317.

6. Origen, *Against Celsus*, IV, 33, attests these books for the second century A.D.; *Acts of the Apostles* 19,19 for the first. The papyri are dated from the handwriting; see Festugière, 1981, p. 281 n. 2, in which a chronological table (with the numbers of Preisendanz) is given; see the two lists of papyri in *PGMTr*.

7. The papyri contain formulaic remarks ("In another copy, I found such and such") that attest to the comparison of different versions; see *PGM* II, 55; IV, 29, 500, 1277; V, 51; VII, 204; XII, 201; XIII, 731. Already an Assyrian letter shows the importance of the philological work in the magic texts; see Jean Bottéro, "Le manuel de l'exorciste et son calendrier," in *Mythes et rites de Babylone* (Geneva/Paris: Droz, 1985), pp. 65–112, original publication *École Pratique des Hautes Études. IVe section, Sciences historiques et philologiques, Annuaire 1974/75*, pp. 95–142, especially p. 123.

8. See for this library, purchased in the nineteenth century by Anastasi, Karl Preisendanz, *Papyrusfunde und Papyrusforschung* (Leipzig/Berlin: Teubner, 1933), pp. 91–94; Fowden, 1986, pp. 168–172. In connection with the interest of the gnostics in magic, see Clement of Alexandria, *Miscellanies* I, 15, 69,6.

9. *Acts of the Apostle*, 19,19: the books had a value of 50,000 pieces of silver. In light of the close kinship between magic and divination (following note), recall the burning of the divinatory books under Augustus, Suetonius, *Lives of the Caesars: Augustus*, XXXI, 1 (where Kieckhefer, 1989, 20, talks about "magical scrolls"). Paulus, *Sententiae* V, 23, 18 (*FIRA* 2, p. 401): "libri magicae artis apud se neminem habere licet; et penes quoscumque reperti sint, bonis ademptis, ambustis his publice, in insulam deportantur, humiliores

capite puniuntur. non tantum huius artis professio, sed etiam scientia prohibita est." Ibid., V, 21, 4 (*FIRA* 2,406); "non tantum divinatione quis, sed ipsa scientia eiusque libris melius fecerit abstinere."—*Digestae*, ed. Th. Mommsen/ P. Krueger in *Corpus iuris civilis*, I, 1954,[10] reprinted Dublin/Zürich: Weidmann, 1966, XLVIII, 8, 1, 13, "(Modestinus) ex SC eius legis poena damnari habetur, qui mala sacrifia fecerit habuerit" (which includes the books).

10. Zacharias, *Life of S. Severus* 61, see Trombley, 1993, vol. 2, p. 36. For the burning of books, see Luciano Canfora, *Libro e libertà* (Bari: Laterza, 1994).

11. The VIIIth book of Moses is dedicated to his daughter, *PGM* VIII, pp. 341–343; Lucian, *The Lover of Lies*, 35ff. tells us the well-known history of the sorcerer-apprentice, and such an apprentice appears behind a text of the Athenian Kerameikos, Jordan, 1985b, p. 211. Other texts are dedicated by their authors to kings, e.g., to Psammetichus, *PGM* IV, p. 165. For the medieval tradition (father to son or daughter), see Kieckhefer, 1989, p. 59.

12. For *Moses VIII*, see n. 20; for the divination of Pitys, see Chapter 6, n. 44.

13. An exemplary case: the *philtrokatadesmos* (erotic defixion) of the great papyrus of the Bibliothèque Nationale, *PGM* IV, pp. 296–466, of which we have five texts of actual performances, see Chapter 5, n. 75.

14. Ritner 1993, e.g., 99f., where he writes about "the inherently *traditional Egyptian* basis of most PGM ritual" (the italics are his); see also his paper on the demotic spells, "Egyptian magical practice under the Roman empire. The demotic spells and their religious context," in *Aufstieg und Niedergang der Römischen Welt* 2:18:5 (Berlin/New York: De Gruyter, 1995), pp. 3333–3379. Following Ritner, Heinz J. Thissen, "Ägyptologische Beiträge zu den griechischen magischen Papyri," in U. Verhoeven and E. Graefe (eds.), *Religion und Philosophie im alten Ägypten: Festgabe für Philippe Derchain* (Orientalia Lovanensia Analecta 39) (Louvain: Peeters, 1991), pp. 293–302, presents a long list of Egyptian etymologies for the names of the magicians in PGM (p. 295f.) and for some *voces magicae* (pp. 297–302); Elisabeth Stähelin proved Egyptian origin for a detail, "Bindung und Entbindung," *Zeitschrift für Ägyp-*

tische Sprache 96 (1970), pp. 125–139; see Merkelbach 1993. Smith, 1987, p. 119, already warned of the danger there was in assuming that the papyri concerned only Greco-Roman magic. For Bowersock's view, see Glen W. Bowersock, *Hellenism in Late Antiquity* (Cambridge: Cambridge University Press, 1990).

15. Therefore, it was a sound, reasonable decision to include them in *PGMTr.*

16. For Rome: Richard Wünsch, *Sethianische Verfluchungstafeln aus Rom* (Leipzig: Teubner 1898); there is no good reason to attribute them to the gnostic sect of Sethians, as Wünsch and Audollent, 1904, nrs. 140–187, did; see Karl Preisendanz, *Akephalos: Der kopflose Gott* (Beihefte zum Alten Orient 8) (Leipzig: Teubner 1926), pp. 23–37; Gager, 1992, p. 67 n. 84. Cyprus: T. B. Mitford, *The Inscriptions of Kourion* (Philadelphia: American Philosophical Society, 1971), pp. 85–107. Athens: Jordan, 1985b, p. 245f. A text of unknown origin in Paul Moraux, *Une défixion judiciaire du Musée d'Istanbul* (Académie Royale de Belgique. Classe des lettres, mémoires 54), Bruxelles, 1960; Gager, 1992, no. 54; more in Moraux, op. cit., pp. 15–19.

17. Nock 1972: p. 190.

18. For Jewish magic, Ludwig Blau, *Das altjüdische Zauberwesen* (Budapest: Jahresbericht der Landes-Rabbinerschule, 1898, repr. Graz: Akad. Druck- und Verlagsanstalt, 1974); Peter Schäfer, "Jewish magic literature in late antiquity and early middle ages," *Journal of Jewish Studies* 41 (1990), pp. 75–91. Several important categories of Jewish magical texts are now accessible: Charles D. Isbell, *Corpus of the Aramaic Incantation Bowls* (Chico, Calif.: Scholars Press, 1975); Joseph Naveh and Shaul Shaked, *Amulets and Magic Bowls: Aramaic Incantations of Late Antiquity* (Leyden: Brill, 1985); and esp. Peter Schäfer and Saul Shaked (eds.), *Magische Texte aus der Kairoer Geniza* 1 (Tübingen: Mohr, 1994).

19. The current tendency to wish to separate these papyri from the rest of the ancient world (see n. 14) is surely a reaction to the attitude of the scholars who made them into prime documents of Greek religion, like Martin P. Nilsson, *Die Religion in den griechischen Zauberpapyri* (Lund: Gleerup, 1949); more cautious, Arthur Darby Nock, "Greek magical papyri," *Journal of Egyptian Archaeol-*

ogy 15, 1929, pp. 219–235 (Nock 1972: pp. 176–194); see also Karl Preisendanz, "Zur synkretistischen Magie im römischen Aegypten," in Hans Gerstinger (ed.), *Akten des VIII: Internationalen Kongress für Papyrologie* (Mitteilungen der Papyrus-Sammlung der österreichischen Nationalbibliothek; 5), (Vienna: Hollinek, 1956), pp. 111–125.

20. Its textual history was analyzed by Morton Smith in "The Eighth Book of Moses and How It Grew (P. Leid. J 395)," in *Atti del XVII congresso internazionale di papirologia,* (Naples, 19–26 May 1983), Naples: Centro Internationale per lo studio di papiri ercolanesi, 1984, pp. 683–693.

21. Compare Philolaus, *Die Fragmente der Vorsokratiker* 44 A 11; Walter Burkert, *Lore and Science in Ancient Pythagoreanism* (Cambridge, Mass.: Harvard University Press, 1972), p. 467f.

22. Cicero, *Somnium Scipionis* (*De republica* 6) 12: "Septenos octiens solis anfractus reditusque . . . duoque hi numeri, quorum uterque plenus alter altera de causa habetur"; see also Macrobius, *Commentarii in Somnium Scipionis* 1,5; 2,2. Franz Joseph Dölger, *Antike und Christentum* 4 (1934), pp. 153–182; W. Burkert, op. cit. p. 474f. Johann Jakob Bachofen treated the Octoas in several of his *Antiquarische Briefe* (vol. 2, 1886, nos. 31–41).

23. See John G. Gager, *Moses in Graeco-Roman Paganism* (Nashville: Abingdon, 1972); id., "Moses the magician: Hero of an ancient counter-culture?," *Helios* (1994), pp. 179–187. An amulet from Acrae in Sicily tells how Moses became a magician after climbing the sacred mountain, Kotansky, 1994, no. 32 (with earlier bibl.). For the initiation to the sacred mountain, see Chapter 4, n. 25ff.

24. *Acts of the Apostles,* 7,22.

25. Pliny the Elder, *Natural History* XXX, 11 ("It is another magic sect [*magices factio*] that is connected with Moses, Iannes, Iotapes, and the Jews").

26. Bidez and Cumont, 1938, vol.1, p. 170 (but the fragments of Hermippus do not mention Moses); an unambiguous attestation in Lysimachus, FGrHist 621 F 1; see W. Fauth, in the commentary by H. Heubner and W. Fauth on book 5 of Tacitus's *Histories* (Heidelberg: Winter, 1982), p. 34ff.

27. *Exodus* 7,8; 8,15: the first plagues of Egypt are part of that struggle between the pharaoh's magicians and those of Iahve.

28. For the explanation of these two names, see Bidez and Cumont, 1938, vol. 2, p. 14, n. 23.
29. For Jacob and magic, see *PGM* XXIIb and the amulet in G. Manganaro, *Rendiconti della classe di scienze morali, storiche e filologiche dell'Accademia dei Lincei* (series 8), 18, 1963, p. 71ff.
30. *PGM* V, 109.
31. Another work of Moses the magician is the *Didaché* in *PGM* VII, 620; already mentioned is the amulet of Moses coming from Acrae in Sicily, see n. 23.
32. See the chronological table in Festugière 1982, p. 281 n. 2 (he dates our text to the year 346 A.D., without giving cogent reasons).
33. Betz, *PGMTr* (n. 2). Betz's papers are mostly collected in *Hellenismus und Urchristentum: Gesammelte Aufsätze*, Bd. 1 (Tübingen: Mohr, 1990). After his 1982 dissertation at Brown University, *Contributions to the Study of Greek Defixiones* (Ann Arbor: 1985; University Microfilm Nr. 8226275), Jordan published several important papers, among them the highly useful index "A Survey of Greek Defixiones Not Included in the Special Corpora," *Greek, Roman and Byzantine Studies*, 26, 1985, pp. 151–197. Faraone elaborated on aspects of his 1988 Stanford dissertation *Talismans, Voodoo Dolls and Other Apotropaic Statues in Ancient Greece* in his "Binding and burying the forces of evil: The defensive use of 'voodoo dolls' in ancient Greece," *Classical Antiquity* 10 (1991), pp. 165–205, and in *Talismans and Trojan Horses: Guardian Statues in Ancient Greek Myth and Ritual* (New York: Oxford University Press, 1992) (compare Simon Goldhill, Irene Winter, Geraldine Pinch, and Joyce Marcus, *Cambridge Archaeological Journal* 4, 1994, pp. 270–289); together with Dirk Obbink, Faraone edited a pioneering collection of papers, *Magika Hiera: Ancient Greek Magic and Religion* (New York: Oxford University Press, 1991). Much more superficial, the collection by Georg Luck, *Arcana Mundi: Magic and the Occult in the Greek and Roman World* (Baltimore: Johns Hopkins University Press, 1985); see further, John G. Gager (ed.), *Curse Tablets and Binding Spells from the Ancient World* (New York: Oxford University Press, 1992); Marvin Meyer and Richard Smith (eds.), *Ancient Christian Magic: Coptic Texts of Ritual Power* (San Francisco: Harper, 1994). Much less innovative are David E. Aune, "Magic in early Christianity," in *Aufstieg*

und Niedergang der römischen Welt 2:23:2 (Berlin/New York: De Gruyter, 1980), pp. 1507–1557; and C. Robert Phillips III, "Seek and go hide: Literary source problems and Graeco-roman magic," *Helios* (1994), pp. 107–114.

34. Jean Annequin, *Recherches sur l'action magique et ses représentations* (Besançon: Université, 1973); Anne-Marie Tupet, *La magie dans la poésie latine*, 1: *Des origines à la fin du règne d'Auguste* (Paris: Belles Lettres, 1976) (important for magic as a literary topic); vol. 2 could not appear because of the untimely death of the author, who had published a part of it as "Rites magiques dans l'antiquité romaine," in *Aufstieg und Niedergang der römischen Welt* 2:16:3 (Berlin/New York: De Gruyter, 1986), pp. 2591–2675.—André Bernard, *Sorciers grecs* (Paris: Fayard, 1991). See also Marcel LeGlay, "Magie et sorcellerie à Rome au dernier siècle de la République," in *Mélanges Jacques Heurgon* (Paris: Presses Universitaires de France, 1977), pp. 525–550; and Benedetto Bravo, "Une tablette magique d'Olbia Pontique: Les morts, les héros et les démons," in *Poikilia: Etudes offertes à Jean-Pierre Vernant* (Paris: Editions EHESS, 1987), pp. 185–218.

35. Raffaella Garosi, "Indagini sulla formazione del concetto di magia nella cultura romana," in Paolo Xella (ed.), *Magia: Studi di storia delle religioni in memoria di R. Garosi* (Rome: Bulzoni, 1976), pp. 13–93. Garosi died in a right-wing terrorist attack on the train from Rome to Milan.

36. Reinhold Merkelbach and Maria Totti, *Abrasax: Ausgewählte Papyri religiösen und magischen Inhalts*, vols. 1 and 2 (Opladen: Westdeutscher Verlag, 1990–1993); Reinhold Merkelbach, *Abrasax: Ausgewählte Papyri religiösen und magischen Inhalts*, vol. 3: *Zwei griechisch-aegyptische Weihezeremonien: Die Leidener Weltschöpfung, Die Pschai-Aion-Liturgie* (Opladen: Westdeutscher Verlag, 1992); from the same school comes the inspiration of Daniel and Maltomini, 1990 and 1992 (see n. 3).

37. Richard Gordon, "Aelian's peony: The location of magic in Graeco-Roman tradition," *Comparative Criticism* 9, 1987, pp. 59–95; Hendrik S. Versnel, "Some reflections on the relationship magic-religion," *Numen* 38, 1991, pp. 177–197; Christine Harrauer, *Meliouchos: Studien zur Entwicklung religiöser Vorstellungen in griechischen synkretistischen Zaubertexten* (Wiener Studien. Beihefte 11) (Vienna:

Verlag der Österreichischen Akademie, 1987); compare Karl Preisendanz, *Akephalos: Der kopflose Gott* (Beihefte zum Alten Orient 8) (Leipzig: Teubner, 1926).

38. For the Middle Ages: Richard Kieckhefer, *Magic in the Middle Ages* (Cambridge: Cambridge University Press, 1989); and Valerie I. J. Flint, *The Rise of Magic in Early Medieval Europe* (Oxford: Clarendon Press, 1991). For Byzantium: Henry Maguire (ed.), *Byzantine Magic* (Washington, D. C.: Dumbarton Oaks, 1995). For the Renaissance: Paola Zambelli, *Magia, astrologia e religione nel rinascimento* (Wroclaw: n.n., 1979); and *L'ambigua natura della magia: Filosofi, streghe, riti nel Rinascimento* (Milan: Il Saggiatore, 1991; 2nd ed., 1996). For the present: Jeanne Favret-Saada, *Deadly Words: Witchcraft in the Bocage,* trans. Catherine Cullen (Cambridge: Cambridge University Press, 1980) (orig. *Les mots, la mort, les sorts: La sorcellerie dans le Bocage* (Paris: Gallimard, 1977; fundamental for method).

39. Augustus Audollent, *Defixionum Tabellae* (Paris: 1904) (reprinted, Frankfurt: Minerva, 1967); Richard Wünsch, "Appendix continens defixionum tabellas in Attica regione repertas," in *IG* II/III: *Corpus Inscriptionum Atticarum* (Berlin: Reimer, 1897); id., *Sethianische Verfluchungstafeln aus Rom* (Leipzig: Teubner, 1898; id., "Neue Fluchtafeln," *Rheinisches Museum* 55, 1900, pp. 62–85, 232–271; Albrecht Dieterich, *Papyrus magica musei Lugdunensis Batavi* (1888), reprinted in *Kleine Schriften* (Leipzig, Berlin: Teubner, 1911), pp. 1–47.

40. Ulrich von Wilamowitz-Moellendorff, *Reden und Vortraege* (Berlin: Weidmann, 1925–1926), p. 254 (the passage is quoted in Hans Dieter Betz (ed.). *The Greek Magical Papyri in Translation Including the Demotic Spells,* p. LI n. 31).

41. "Ausgewählte Stücke aus den griechischen Papyri": the story is told by Karl Preisendanz in the preface to the *PGM,* p. V.

42. Ulrich von Wilamowitz-Möllendorff, *Der Glaube der Hellenen,* vol. 1 (Berlin: Weidmann, 1931, p. 10); see A. Henrichs, "'Der Glaube der Hellenen': Religionsgeschichte als Glaubensbekenntnis und Kulturkritik," in W. M. Calder III et al. (eds.), *Wilamowitz nach 50 Jahren* (Darmstadt: Wissenschaftliche Buchgesellschaft, 1985), pp. 263–305.

43. For this whole group, see Hans Joachim Mette, "Nekrologie einer Epoche: Hermann Usener und seine Schule," *Lustrum* 22,

1979/1980, pp. 5–106, as well as A. Momigliano (ed.), *Aspetti di Hermann Usener filologo della religione* (Pisa: Giardini, 1982).

44. See the short history of the research in Christoph Daxelmüller, *Zauberpraktiken: Eine Ideengeschichte der Magie* (Zürich: Artemis, 1992), pp. 33–36.

45. *Papyrus magica Musei Lugdunensis Batavi, denuo edidit commentario critico instruxit prolegomena scripsit A.D.* (diss. Bonn, 1888).

46. Albrecht Dieterich, *Eine Mithrasliturgie*, 3rd edition ed. by Otto Weinreich (Stuttgart: Teubner, 1966). For a more recent evaluation of Dieterich's ideas, see Marvin W. Meyer, *The "Mithras Liturgy"* (Missoula: Scholars Press for the Society of Biblical Literature, 1976) and especially Merkelbach 1992: pp. 25–40 passim.

47. Especially (concerning magic) Richard Reitzenstein, *Poimandres: Studien zur griechisch-aegyptischen und frühchristlichen Literatur* (Leipzig: Teubner, 1904); see also Richard Reitzenstein and Hans Heinrich Schrader, *Studien zum antiken Synkretismus aus Iran und Griechenland* (Studien der Bibliothek Warburg; 7) (Leipzig/Berlin: Teubner, 1926).

48. There is a constantly growing literature on Frazer; see the recent works by Robert Ackerman, *J. G. Frazer: His Life and Work* (Cambridge: Cambridge University Press, 1987); *The Myth and Ritual School: J. G. Frazer and the Cambridge Ritualists* (New York: Garland, 1991); and William M. Calder III (Hrsg.), *The Cambridge Ritualists Reconsidered*, Proceedings of the First Oldfather Conference, Held on the Campus of the University of Illinois at Urbana-Champaign, April 27–30, 1989 (Illinois Classical Studies. Supplement 2. Illinois Studies in the History of Classical Scholarship vol. 1), Atlanta, 1991. For Tylor, see Robert A. Segal, "In Defense of Mythology: The History of Modern Theories of Myth," *Annals of Scholarship* 1, 1980, pp. 3–49. Tambiah 1990, p. 42 represents Frazer as no more than a footnote to Tylor.

49. Frazer felt specially obliged to the work of Wilhelm Mannhardt, a pupil of Grimm, "without which, indeed, my book could scarcely have been written," *The Golden Bough*, 1st ed. (London: Macmillan, 1890), p. IX (p. XII of the 3rd ed., London: Macmillan, 1913). For Frazer and the Grimm brothers, see Ackerman,

J. G. Frazer (n. 48) p. 212; Robert Fraser, *The Making of the Golden Bough: The Origins and Growth of an Argument* (London: Macmillan, 1990), pp. 191–195.

50. Ludwig Deubner, *Magie und Religion*, 1922, reprinted in *Kleine Schriften zur klassischen Altertumskunde* (Beiträge zur klassischen Philologie, 140), (Königstein/Ts.: Hain, 1982), pp. 275–298.

51. Published in two volumes, *Papyri Osloenses.* Fasc. 1, Oslo, 1925; and, with the collaboration of Leiv Amundsen, *Papyri Osloenses*, Fasc. 2, Oslo, 1931.

52. On Eitrem, see the obituary of Father A. J. Festugière, *Comptes-rendus de l'Académie des Inscriptions et Belles Lettres*, 1966, pp. 413–417, and the bibliography by Leiv Amundsen, *Symbolae Osloenses*, 43, 1968, pp. 110–123; a chapter of his manuscript has now been published with a short biographical introduction in Faraone and Obbink 1991: pp. 175–187.

53. A revealing example in Marteen J. Vermaseren, "La sotériologie dans les papyri graecae magicae," in Ugo Bianchi and Marteen J. Vermaseren (eds.), *La soteriologia dei culti orientali nell'Impero Romano*, Atti del Colloquio Internazionale (Leyden: Brill, 1982), pp. 17–30, esp. 17–20 (18: "le magicien ne supplie pas les dieux, il veut les contraindre; il ne veut pas obéir aux dieux ou se mettre à genoux en toute simplicité du coeur").

54. Despite the corrections by Nilsson, 1960, pp. 369–371 ("Letter to Professor Arthur D. Nock in some fundamental concepts in the science of religion," *Harvard Theological Review* 42, 1949, pp. 71–107, here 94–96).

55. Among a multitude of syntheses, here are three: Jan Skorupski, *Symbol and Theory: A Philosopical Study of Theories of Religion in Social Anthropology* (Cambridge: Cambridge University Press, 1976); Hans G. Kippenberg, "Einleitung: Zur Kontroverse über das Verstehen fremden Denkens," in Hans G. Kippenberg and Brigitte Luchesi (eds.), *Magie: Die sozialwissenschaftliche Kontroverse über das Verstehen fremden Denkens* (Frankfurt: Suhrkamp, 1987), pp. 9–51; Stephen Sharot, "Magic, Religion, Science and Secularization," in Neusner, Frerichs, and Flesher 1989: pp. 261–283.

56. For an evaluation of the work of Malinowski, see Raymond Firth (ed.), *Man and Culture: An Evaluation of the Work of Bronislaw Malinowski*

(London: Routledge & Kegan Paul, 1968), especially the article of S. F. Nadel, "Malinowski on Magic and Religion," pp. 189–208; E. Leach, "Frazer and Malinowski," *Encounter*, 25, 1965, pp. 24–36; K. E. Rosengren, "Malinowski's Magic: The Riddle of the Empty Cell," *Current Anthropology* 17, 1976, pp. 667–685; a shorter updating by A. Métraux, "Bronislaw Malinowski," in D. L. Sills (ed.) *International Encyclopedia of the Social Sciences*, vol. 9, 1968, pp. 541–549.

57. Stanley J. Tambiah, "The Magical Power of Words," *Man* 3, 1968, pp. 175–208, reprinted in *Culture, Thought, and Social Action* (Cambridge: Harvard University Press, 1985), pp. 17–59; Tambiah follows the ideas of Peter Winch, "Understanding a Primitive Society," in B. Wilson, *Rationality* (Oxford: Blackwell, 1970), pp. 78–111, reprinted in Winch, *Ethics and Action*, 1972, pp. 8–49. For a discussion, see Chapter 7.

58. The classical study of Arnold van Gennep, *Les rites de passage* (Paris: Émile Nourry, 1909), does not follow the Frazerian dichotomy; for a convincing analysis of it in a specific culture, see Godfrey Lienhardt, *Divinity and Experience*, Oxford: Clarendon Press, 1961.

59. Magic as a "semantic trap": Dorothy Hammond, "Magic: A Problem in Semantics," *American Anthropologist*, 72, 1970, pp. 1349–1356.

60. See the clear and radical discussion by Hendrik S. Versnel, "Some Reflections on the Relationship Magic-religion," *Numen* 38, 1991, pp. 177–197. Michael Winkelman, "Magic: A Theoretical Reassessment," *Current Anthropology* 23, 1982, pp. 37–44, considers magic a universal human phenomenon to be explained by parapsychological theories.

61. Marcel Mauss, "Esquisse d'une théorie générale de la magie," *L'Année Sociologique* 7, 1902/03, reprinted in *Sociologie et anthropologie* (Paris: Presses Universitaires de France, 1973), pp. 1–141.

62. Edward E. Evans-Pritchard, *Witchcraft, Oracles and Magic Among the Azande* (Oxford: Clarendon Press, 1937) (edition abridged by Eva Gillies [Oxford: Clarendon Press, 1976]). For Evans-Pritchard, see F. O. Beidelmann in *International Encyclopedia of Social Science* (n. 56), *Biogr. Supplement* (1979), pp. 176–180.

63. Jeanne Favret-Saada, *Deadly Words: Witchcraft in the Bocage*, trans.

Catherine Cullen (Cambridge: Cambridge University Press, 1980); for late antiquity, Brown, 1972, pp. 131–136 has shown the usefulness of Evans-Pritchard's model, as does Clerc, 1995.

64. See the highly useful reflections of Natalie Zemon Davis, "Some Tasks and Themes in the Study of Popular Religion," in Charles Trinkaus and Heiko A. Oberman (eds.), *The Pursuit of Holiness in Late Medieval and Renaissance Religion* (Leiden: E. J. Brill, 1974), pp. 307–336, esp. 309–313.

2. NAMING THE SORCERER

1. Among the discussions of the history of the term, that of Arthur Darby Nock, "Paul and the Magus," in Nock 1972, pp. 308–330 (originally in F. J. Foakes-Jackson and Kirsopp Lake (eds.), *The Beginnings of Christianity* (London: Macmillan, 1920), pp. 164–188, remains indispensable.

2. For the Persian facts and their Greek transformation, see the still-fundamental book of Bidez and Cumont (1938); and, for the classical era, the synthesis of Elias J. Bickerman, "Darius I, Pseudo-Smerdis, and the Magi," *Athenaeum* 59, 1978, pp. 239–261, reprinted in E. J. Bickerman, *Religions and Politics in the Hellenistic and Roman Periods*, ed. by Emilio Gabba and Morton Smith (Como: Edizioni New Press, 1985), pp. 619–641; on the Greeks and the Persians, see also the fine chapter in Arnaldo Momigliano, *Alien Wisdom: The Limits of Hellenization* (Cambridge: Cambridge University Press, 1975), pp. 123–150.

3. Herodotus, *Histories,* I, 101 (γένος); VII, 43, 113f, 191 (sacrifices); I, 140 (funeral rites); I, 107ff, 120, 128; VII, 19, 37 (interpretation of dreams and other marvels). See also Fabio Mora, *Religione e religioni nelle storie di Erodoto* (Milan: Jaca Book, 1985), p. 152; Pericles George, *Barbarian Asia and the Greek Experience* (Baltimore: Johns Hopkins, 1994) p. 194f. Xenophon, *Cyropaedia,* VIII, 3, 11 (οἱ περὶ τοὺς θεοὺς τεχνῖται).

4. Plato, *Alcibiades,* 122 A. The debate on the authenticity of the first *Alcibiades* need not concern us here, for the author in any case belonged to the Academy of the fourth century. See H. J. Kramer,

in H. Flashar (ed.), *Die Philosophie der Antike. 3: Ältere Akademie, Aristoteles-Peripatos* (Basel: Schwabe, 1983), p. 124.

5. Apuleius, *Apologia* 25; Philostratus, *Life of Apollonius of Tyana*, I, 6. For the moderns, see Konstantin Franziskus von Khautz, *De cultibus magicis eorumque perpetuo ad ecclesiam et rempublicam habitu liber primus*, Vienna 1767, 4: "Magia omnis . . . nihil aliud quam sapientia credebatur . . . fuitque cultus deorum" (cited in Christoph Daxelmüller, *Zauberpraktiken* [Zürich: Artemis, 1992], p. 24).

6. The Old Persian text of the inscription in Rüdiger Schmitt, *The Bihistun Inscriptions of Darius the Great: Old Persian Texts* (Corpus Inscriptionum Iranicorum I:1, Texts 1) (London: Humphries, 1991); a new (German) translation in W. Hinz, "Die Behistan-Inschrift des Darius," *Archäologische Mitteilungen aus Iran* 7, 1974, pp. 121–134; for recent discussions, see Françoise Grillot-Susini, Clarisse Herrenschmidt, and Florence Malbran-Labat, "La version élamite de la trilingue de Behistun: Une nouvelle lecture," *Journal Asiatique* 281 (1993), pp. 19–59; and Rüdiger Schmitt, *Epigraphisch-exegetische Noten zu Dareios' Bisutun-Inschriften* (Sitzungsbericht Wien, 561) (Vienna: Oesterreichische Akademie, 1990).

7. Heraclitus, DK 12 B 14 (Clement of Alexandria, *Protrepticus*, 22).

8. Miroslav Marcovitch, *Eraclito, Frammenti* (Florence: La Nuova Italia, 1978), 322 frg. 87 (original edition, Cambridge: Cambridge University Press, 1966) judges that μάγοις was the wording of Clement; but see Charles H. Kahn, *The Art and Thought of Heraclitus: An Edition of the Fragments* (Cambridge/New York: Cambridge University Press, 1979), frg. 115 and p. 262 (the attribution to Heraclitus would be "more probable"); Marcel Conche, *Héraclite, Fragments* (Paris: Presses Universitaires de France, 1986), pp. 167–170, frg. 43; T. M. Robinson, *Heraclitus: Fragments* (Toronto: University of Toronto Press, 1987), p. 85f.

9. Plato, *Republic*, 364 B; papyrus of Derveni (*Zeitschrift für Papyrologie und Epigraphik* 47, 1982, after p. 300), col. 16,3ff. I understand the Heraclitean *nuktipolois* as an adjective that qualifies the following nouns ("nightwandering").

10. Walter Burkert, *The Orientalizing Revolution: Near Eastern Influence on Greek Culture in the Early Archaic Age* (Cambridge, Mass.: Harvard University Press, 1992), pp. 41–85; see also "Itinerant Diviners

and Magicians: A Neglected Element in Cultural Contacts," in Robin Hägg (ed.), *The Greek Renaissance of the Eighth Century B.C.: Tradition and Innovation* (Stockholm: Swedish Institute in Athens, 1983), pp. 115–119.

11. Sophocles, *Oedipus Rex*, 387f. (the translation is Hugh Lloyd-Jones's, in his Loeb edition). For the different categories of seers, see Jan N. Bremmer, "Prophets, seers, and politics in Greece, Israel, and early modern Europe," *Numen* 40, 1993, pp.150–183.

12. Plato, *Republic*, 364 B.

13. Otto Kern, *Orphei Fragmenta* (Berlin: Weidmann, 1920), frg. 232; compare Plato, *Phaedrus* 244 E. For the role of Bacchic mysteries in the so-called Orphic eschatology of the Bacchic gold-leaves, see Fritz Graf, "Dionysian and Orphic Eschatology: New Texts and Old Questions," in Thomas Carpenter and Christopher Faraone (eds.), *Masks of Dionysos* (Ithaca, N.Y.: Cornell University Press, 1993), pp. 239–258.

14. See Jordan 1988a, pp. 273–277. For the details, see Chapter 6.

15. For a very provisional publication of the Derveni text, see *Zeitschrift für Papyrologie und Epigraphik* 4, 1982, after p. 300; for the theogony, Martin L. West, *The Orphic Poems* (Oxford: Clarendon Press, 1983), pp. 75–11; for the philosophical background, Walter Burkert, "Orpheus und die Vorsokratiker: Bemerkungen zum Derveni-Papyrus und zur pythagoreischen Zahlenlehre," *Antike und Abendland* 14, 1969, pp. 93–114.

16. See later, Chapter 4, n. 35.

17. Euripides, *Orestes* 1493ff.

18. For example, Preisendanz, *PGM* I, pp. 247–262.

19. Euripides, *Iphigenia Taurica* 1336f. For the *onomata barbara* later, Chapter 7.

20. Plato, *Symposium* 202 E.

21. Plato, *Menon*, 80 B. See Michelle Gellrich, "Socratic magic: Enchantment, irony, and persuasion in Plato's dialogues," *Classical World* 87, 1994, pp. 275–307.

22. Plato, *Laws* 10, 909 B. The parallel *Republic* 364 B proves, I think, that Plato does not speak about necromancy, as has been suggested.

23. See Fritz Graf, *Eleusis und die orphische Dichtung Athens in vorhellenistischer Zeit* (RGVV 33) (Berlin/New York: De Gruyter, 1974),

pp. 35–38; A. Henrichs, "The Sophists and Hellenistic Religion: Prodicus as the Spiritual Father of the Isis Aretalogies," *Harvard Studies in Classical Philology* 88, 1984, pp. 139–158; the adjective used by Plato, θηριώδης, belongs to this specific terminology.

24. Gorgias, DK 82 B 11,10. See Jacqueline de Romilly, *Magic and Rhetoric in Ancient Greece* (Cambridge, Mass.: Harvard University Press, 1975).

25. Keith V. Thomas, *Religion and the Decline of Magic* (London: Weidenfeld and Nicolson, 1971); compare also Thomas, "An Anthropology of Religion and Magic II," *The Journal of Interdisciplinary History* 6, 1975, pp. 91–109; Tambiah: 1990, pp. 18–24.

26. Aeschylus, *Persae*, 687. For *goēs* and shamanism, see Walter Burkert, "Goēs: Zum griechischen Schamanismus," *Rheinisches Museum* 105, 1962, pp. 36–55; protest in Jan N. Bremmer, *The Early Greek Concept of the Soul* (Princeton, N. J.: Princeton University Press, 1983), pp. 24–53.

27. *Odyssey*, IV, 221 (Helen); X, 290, 317 (Circe's drug); 287, 302 (moly); 392 (undoing the transformation).

28. *Iliad*, IV, 190; XI, 846; XIII, 392; *Odyssey*, IV, 230; XI, 741; XXII, 94 (healing). *Odyssey*, I, 261 (poisoned arrows); II, 329 (the suitors).

29. *Odyssey*, XIX, 455ff.; see Robert Renehan, "The staunching of Odysseus' blood: The healing-powers of magic," *American Journal of Philology* 113, 1992, pp. 1–4; and in general, William D. Furley, "Besprechung und Behandlung: Zur Form und Funktion von ἐπωιδαί in der griechischen Zaubermedizin," in Glenn W. Most, Hubert Petersmann, and Adolf Martin Ritter (eds.), *Philanthropia kai Eusebeia: Festschrift für Albrecht Dihle zum 70. Geburtstag* (Göttingen: Vandenhoeck, 1994), pp. 80–104. Plato, *Republic*, 426 B; see also Pindar, *Pythia* IV, 217; Sophocles, *Ajax*, 582.

30. Aristotle frg. 36 Rose. The tradition gives Aristotle or "Rhodon" as the author (that is, the peripatitic Antisthenes of Rhodes from the second century B.C.), Suidas s.v. *Antisthenēs Athēnaios.*

31. Edward B. Tylor, *Primitive Culture: Researches into the Development of Mythology, Philosophy, Religion, Art and Custom* (London: John Murray, 1873), vol. 1, *The Origins of Culture,* (New York: Harper, 1970), pp. 113–117. For Scandinavia, see also Carl-Herman Tillhagen, "Finnen und Lappen als Zauberkundige in der skandinavischen

Volksüberlieferung" in *Kontakte und Grenzen: Probleme der Volks-, Kul-tur- und Sozialforschung* (Festschrift für Gerhard Heilfurth) (Göttin-gen: Schwartz, 1969), pp. 129–143; for the ancient Near East, Volkert Haas, "Die Dämonisierung des Fremden und des Feindes im Alten Orient," *Rocznik Orientalistyczny*, 41:2, 1980, pp. 37–44.

32. Charles Stewart, *Demons and the Devil: Moral Imagination in Modern Greek Culture* (Princeton, N. J.: Princeton University Press, 1991), pp. 38–42.

33. Heraclitus, DK 12 B 15.5.

34. *On the Sacred Disease* 2 (in the Loeb edition of Hippocrates, ed. W. S. Jones, vol. 2, p. 140; whose translation is modified).

35. *On the Sacred Disease* 4 (p. 148).

36. *On the Sacred Disease* 3 (p. 144).

37. *On the Sacred Disease* 4 (p. 144). Usually Thessalian witches are credited with the feat to call down the moon; for weather magic below n. 42.

38. *On the Sacred Disease* 3 (p. 144).

39. *On the Sacred Disease* 4 (p. 146).

40. G. E. R. Lloyd, *Magic, Reason, and Experience: Studies in the Origin and Development of Greek Science* (Cambridge/New York: Cambridge University Press, 1979), pp. 49–58.

41. Empedokles, Peter Kingsley, *Ancient Philosophy, Mystery, and Magic: Empedocles and Pythagorean Tradition* (Oxford: Clarendon Press, 1995).

42. Gorgias, in Diogenes Laertius VIII, 59. See Walter Burkert, *Lore and Science in Ancient Pythagoreanism* (Cambridge, Mass.: Harvard University Press, 1972), p. 153f.

43. Empedocles, DK 31 F 111. See G. S. Kirk, J. E. Raven, and M. Schofield, *The Presocratic Philosophers*, 2nd ed. (Cambridge: Cambridge University Press, 1983), p. 285f. (whose translation I follow); P. Kingsley, op. cit., pp. 217–227.

44. See also Theophrastus, *Characters* 16,7: the superstitious man calls a purifier to ritually cleanse his house, because he fears an *epagōgē* ("calling up a dead") of Hecate. Compare Bravo 1987, pp. 207f.

45. DK 31 B 112,4.

46. DK 31 B 12,5f.

47. Nilsson 1960, p. 430 (*Religion as Man's Protest Against the Meaning-*

lessness of Events [Bulletin de la Société Royale des Lettres à Lund 1953–1954: 2] [Lund: Gleerup, 1954], p. 37).

48. The Dirae Teorum in David Lewis (ed.), *A Selection of Greek Historical Inscriptions to the End of the Fifth Century* (Oxford: Clarendon Press, 1969), no. 30 A 1.

49. There is a rather extensive bibliography on magic in Rome, although most of the books are fairly old; it is found in Tupet, *La magie dans la poésie latine.* Two more recent articles of synthesis, which both attempt to show an important break in the Roman development, are Marcel LeGlay, "Magie et sorcellerie à Rome au dernier siècle de la république," in *Mélanges Jacques Heurgon* (Paris: Presses Universitaires de France, 1977), pp. 525–550; and esp. Raffaella Garosi, "Indagini sulla formazione del concetto di magia nella cultura romana," in Paolo Xella (ed.), *Magia: Studi di storia delle religioni in memoria di Raffaella Garosi* (Rome: Bulzoni, 1976), pp. 13–93.

50. Cicero, *De legibus* 2,26; *De divinatione* I, 46, 91.

51. Catullus, *Carmina* 90.

52. Xanthus, *Fragmente der griechischen Historiker* 765 F 31; compare Peter Kingsley, "Meetings with magi: Iranian themes among the Greeks, from Xanthus of Lydia to Plato's Academy," *Journal of the Royal Asiatic Society* 5, 1995, 173–209, esp. 179f.

53. Virgil, *Eclogue* 8, 66–69.

54. Romans do not burn *verbenae* but use them to adorn the altar; male frankincense is the best. Wendell Clausen, *A Commentary on Virgil: Eclogues* (Oxford: Clarendon Press, 1994), p. 257.

55. Laevius, frg. 27 Morel (Apuleius, *Apologia* XXX,13). Tupet, *La magie dans la poésie latine,* pp. 212–219, remains the most important analysis. I have reprinted the texts with the necessary corrections, particularly with *iunges* (1.3) instead of *ung<u>es* of the editors of Apuleius; Laevius does not speak of fingernails, but systemically groups magic paraphernalia, starting with mechanical devices, then going to the plant (4) and animal (5f.) world.

56. The iynx is a wheel, too, as its first description in Pindar, *Pythia* 4,213f. shows; see E. Tavenner, "Iynx and rhombus," *Transactions of the American Philological Association* 64, 1933, pp.109–127; A. S. F. Gow, "Ἴυγξ, rhombus, turbo." *Journal of Hellenic Studies* 54, 1934,

pp. 1–13; Vincianne Pirenne-Delforge, "L'iynge dans le discours mythique et les procédures magiques," *Kernos* 6, 1993, pp. 277–289; Christopher A. Faraone, "The wheel, the whip and other implements of torture: Erotic magic in Pindar, Pythia 4.213–19," *Classical Journal* 89, 1993, pp. 1–19; Sarah Iles Johnston, "The song of the iynx: Magic and rhetoric in Pythian 4," *Transactions of the American Philological Association* 125, 1995, (177–206). For Theocritus, *Idylls* II, 58 (lizard), see Chapter 6 of the present volume, n. 20.

57. Cicero, *Against Vatinius*, 14.

58. For example in the case of Apollonius of Tyana, Philostratus, *Life of Apollonius of Tyana* VIII, 7; or the story about S. Peter, Augustine, *De civitate Dei* XVIII, 53; see J. Hubaux, *Rome et Véies* (Paris: Les Belles Lettres, 1958), pp. 13–35; A. Henrichs, "Human Sacrifice in Greek Religion: Three Case Studies," in *Le Sacrifice dans l'antiquité* (Entretiens de la Fondation Hardt sur l'Antiquité classique: 27) (Geneva: Fondation Hardt, 1981), pp. 195–235. Without a divinatory function in Libanius, *Discours*, I,245, in a ritual *diabolé;* in erotic magic Zacharias, erotic defixion, *Vita Severi* 58f. (sacrifice of a slave). Legislation: Paulus, *Sententiae,* 5,23,15f. (FIRA 2,409f.): "(15) qui sacra impia nocturnave, ut quem obcantarent defigerent obligarent, fecerint faciendave curaverint, aut cruci affiguntur aut bestiis obiciuntur. (16) qui hominem immolaverint exve eius sanguine litaverint, fanum templumve polluerint, bestiis obiciuntur vel, si honestiores sunt, capite puniuntur."

59. Dio Cassius 49,43,5. Jerome, *Chronicon, Ad annum* 28 (p. 163, 25 Helm): "Anaxilaus Larissaeus Pythagoricus et magus ab Augusto urbe Italiaque pellitur."

60. Seneca, *Natural Questions* IV, 7, 2; Pliny the Elder, *Natural History* XXVIII, 17.

61. Virgil, *Eclogue* VIII, 99 ("I saw (Moeris) transport the crops to another field"); Servius ad loc. Augustine, *De civitate Dei* 8,19 uses this same verse and the facts known to him through Cicero, in order to condemn magic.

62. John Scheid, "Le délit religieux dans la Rome tardo-républicaine," in *Le délit religieux dans la cité antique* (Round Table, Rome, 6–7 April 1978), Rome, 1981, pp. 117–171, correctly insists on this point.

63. Cicero, *Republic*, IV, 12 ("for him who sang or composed a poem

of a nature to disgrace others by a scandal." See also Anna Maria Addabbo, "*Carmen* magico e *carmen* religioso," *Civiltà Classica e Cristiana* 12, 1991, pp. 11–28, notably for the Plinian usage.

64. Cato, *On Agriculture*, 160 (see also Pliny the Elder, *Natural History*, XXVIII, 21: *Cato prodidit luxatis membris carmen auxiliare*). Aside from the edition of G. Mazzarino (Leipzig: Teubner, 1912) see primarily the commentaries of Paul Thielsch, *Des Marcus Cato Belehrung über die Landwirtschaft* (Berlin: Duncker and Humblot, 1963), pp. 383–392; and of Raoul Goujard, *Cato: De l'agriculture* (Paris: Les Belles Lettres, 1975), pp. 319–321 ("the whole process . . . involves magic").

65. Mauss, 1973, 47f.

66. In general, Mauss, 1973, p. 50; Thomas, 1971, p. 179f.; and Tambiah, 1985, p. 18f.; for healing, see Hendrik S. Versnel, "Die Poetik der Zaubersprüche: Ein Essay über die Macht der Worte," in *Die Macht der Worte* (Eranos-Jahrbuch, Neue Reihe 4) (München: Fink, 1996), pp. 233–297.

67. Cicero, *Brutus*, 217; Plautus, *Amphitruo*, 1043; *Pseudolus*, 870 (*medicamento et suis veneris:* M. M. Willcock, in his edition of the comedy, Exeter 1987, p. 126 correctly translates *venenis* by "magical potions"). In the common version of the myth, Medea would have killed Pelias instead of rejuvenating him by the mere omission of the correct herbs.

68. *Digestae*, ed. T. Mommsen and P. Krueger, in *Corpus iuris civilis*, I, 1954[10], reprinted Dublin/Zürich, 1966, XLVIII, 8,3, after Marcianus, *Institutiones*, 14 ("venena ad sanandum, ad occidendum, amatoria"); ibid. 13, after Modestinus ("ex SC eius legis poena damnari habetur, qui mala sacrifia fecerit habuerit").

69. *Digestae* XLVIII, 8,7 "in hac lege dolus pro facto accipitur."

70. Livy VIII, 18, 1–10. See Luigi Monaco, "Veneficia matronarum: Magia, medicina e repressione," in *Sodalitas: Scritti in onore di A. Guarino* (Naples: Jovene, 1984), pp. 407–428; Jean-Marie Pailler, "Les matrones romaines et les empoisonnements criminels sous la République," *Comptes-rendus de l'Academie des Inscriptions et Belles-Lettres*, 1987, pp. 111–128.

71. Cato, *On Agriculture*, V, 4.

72. Livy XXXIX, 8–19. See the (almost too extensive) synthesis of Jean-Marie Pailler, *Bacchanalia: La répression de 186 av. J.C. à Rome et*

en *Italie: vestiges, images, tradition* (Bibliothèque des Écoles françaises d'Athènes et de Rome 270), Rome: École Française, 1988.

73. Pliny the Elder, *Natural History,* XXX, 1–14 (XXX, 1: *magicas vanitates saepius quidem antecedente operis parte . . . coarguimus*). See esp. Bidez and Cumont 1938: vol. 2, 1ff. (text and important commentary); A. Ernout, "La magie chez Pline l'Ancien," in Marcel Renard and Robert Schilling (eds.), *Hommages à Jean Bayet* (Brussels: Collection Latomus, 1964), pp. 190–195; Garosi 1976, pp. 17–30.

74. See Jerry Stannard, "Herbal medicine and herbal magic in Pliny's time," in J. Pigeaud and J. Orozio (eds.), *Pline l'Ancien, témoin de son temps* (Salamanca/Nantes: s.n., 1987), pp. 95–106.

75. The same reproof is found in the edict of the governor of Egypt against divination in 199 A.D.; see Georg M. Parassoglou, "Circular from a prefect: Sileat omnibus perpetuo divinandi curiositas," in Ann Ellis Hanson (ed.), *Collectanea Papyrologica: Texts Published in Honor of H. C. Youtie* (Bonn: Habelt, 1976), vol. 1, nr. 30 (262ff) 1, 7. It must also be noted that, very often in his discussion of the remedies in books 28 and 29, Pliny reports some opinions of the (deceptive) magi, but only in order immediately to dismiss them.

76. Pliny, *Natural History,* XXX, 2. For "religion" and *religio,* see Wilfred Cantwell Smith, *The meaning and end of religion* (San Francisco: Harper, 1978); Maurice Sachot, "Religio/superstitio: Historique d'une subversion et d'un retournement," *Revue de l'Histoire des Religions* 208, 1991, pp. 355–394; and the congress volume edited by Ugo Bianchi, *The Notion of "Religion" in Comparative Research,* Selected Proceedings of the XVIth Congress of the International Association for the History of Religions (Rome, 3rd–8th September, 1990) (Storia delle Religioni 8) (Rome: Ateneo, 1994), esp. Kurt Rudolph, "Inwieweit ist der Begriff 'Religion' eurozentrisch?," pp. 131–139.

77. For the Telmessians, see also Cicero, *On Divination,* I, 94.

78. From the child sacrifice blamed on Apollonius of Tyana (see earlier, n. 58) to those Druid sacrifices of which Strabo speaks, *Geographica* IV, 4–5; see Cicero, *For M. Fonteius* 31.

79. At least according to the *Digestae* XLVIII, 8,3, after Marcianus, *Institutiones,* 14: of the three "venena—ad sanandum, ad occidendum, amatoria"—only the second must be punished. This cannot

have been universal; otherwise, the trial of Apuleius would make no sense; a responsum of Constantine from 321 A.D. (*Codex Iustinianus* 9,18,4) orders punishment not only against those who practiced magical rites "contra salutem hominum," but also against those who had been found out "pudicos animos ad libidinem deflexisse"; the same responsum allows weather rites (*suffragia*) in the countryside.

80. Pliny, *Natural History,* XXVIII, 28f.

81. Pliny, *Natural History,* XXVIII, 19 "durat in pontificum disciplina id sacrum."

82. Garosi 1976, pp. 81–83. See also Ramsay MacMullen, *Enemies of the Roman Order: Treason, Unrest, and Alienation in the Empire* (Cambridge, Mass.: Harvard University Press, 1966), pp. 95–162.

83. Tacitus, *Annals,* IV, 22 (Numatia: "accusata iniecisse carminibus et veneficiis vecordiam marito"); XVI, 30f. (Servilia: "quod pecuniam magis dilargita esset," compare 31 "pecuniam faciendis magicis sacris").

84. Tacitus, *Annals,* XII, 22 (Paulina: "Chaldaeos, magos interrogatumque Apollinis Clarii oraculum super nuptiis imperatoris"); II,27 (Libo Drusus: "Chaldaeorum promissa, magorum sacra, somniorum etiam interpretes," to which II, 28,2 adds necromancy, "infernas umbras carminibus elicere"); the political background in Barbara M. Levick, *Tiberius the Politician* (London: Croom Helm, 1976), p. 41f.; Geraldine Herbert-Brown, *Ovid and the "Fasti": An Historical Study* (Oxford: Clarendon Press, 1994), pp. 208–211.

85. Paulus, *Sententiae* V, 23,17s. (FIRA 2, 410) [17] "magicae artis conscios summo supplicio adfici placuit, id est bestiis obici aut cruci suffigi; ipsi autem magi vivi comburuntur." [18] "libri magicae artis apud se neminem habere licet; et penes quoscumque reperti sint, bonis ademptis, ambustis his publice, in insulam deportantur, humiliores capite puniuntur. non tantum huius artis professio, sed etiam scientia prohibita est." (It is discussed whether the last sentence actually comes from Paul).

86. *Digestae* IX, 18,7 (Constantius, a. 358): "si quis magus vel magicis contaminibus adsuetus qui maleficus vulgi consuetudine nuncupatur"; see already Apuleius, *Apologia,* I, 5 ("insimulare magicorum maleficiorum") where the context gives a quasi-official tone to the term (see *Metamorphoses* 9, 29 "devotionibus et maleficiis," and

Apologia LI, 10: "magi et malefici hominis"; LXI, 1 "magica maleficia"; *Metamorphoses,* IX, 29 "devotionibus ac maleficis"); compare Abt, *Die Apologie des Apuleius,* p. 90ff; Butler and Owen, *Apulei Apologia Sive Pro Se De Magia,* p. 3 (below, p. 257n5).

87. Isidore, *Etymologiae* VIII, 9; see Kieckhefer 1989, p. 11f.

88. Later, this changes; see Paulus, *Sententiae* V, 21 (FIRA 2, 406), who attacks the "vaticinatores, qui se deo plenos adsimulant, qui novas sectas vel ratione incognitas religiones inducunt, qui de salute principis vel summa rei publicae mathematicos hariolos haruspices vaticinatores consulit: non tantum divinatione quis, sed ipsa scientia eiusque libris melius fecerit abstinere."

89. Tacitus, *Annals,* II, 27; XII, 22.

90. The Marsi are attested to since the annalist C. Gellius, frg. 9 Peter (ap. Solin. 2, 27–30); see Tibullus I, 8,20 and the commentary of Kirby Flower Smith, p. 347.

91. This is also the opinion of Marcel LeGlay and Raffaella Garosi; see n. 49.

92. See Tamsyn Barton, *Ancient Astrology* (London: Routledge, 1994), pp. 32–63.

93. Virgil, *Eclogue* VII, 97ff.

94. Herodotus IV, 105.

95. Paolo Poccetti, "Su due laminette plumbee iscritte nel Museo di Reggio Calabria," *Klearchos* 101–104, 1984, pp. 73–86; id., "Nuova laminetta plumbea osca dal Bruzio," in *Crotone e la sua storia tra il IV e III secolo A.C.* (Naples: Arte Tipografica, 1993), pp. 213–232; more texts come from the 4th cent., id., in M. Gualtieri (ed.), *Roccagloriosa* vol. 1 (Naples: Centre Jean Bérard, 1990), pp. 141–150.

96. Pliny the Elder, *Natural History,* XXVIII, 19: "Moreover there is not one who does not fear being spellbound by maleficent prayers."

97. Cicero, *Brutus,* 217; see Gager 1992, 120. The same story shorter in *The Orator,* 129.

98. Helmut Engelmann, *The Delian Aretalogy of Sarapis* (Leyden: Brill, 1975), p. 9 Z. 85ff.

99. Cicero, *Laws,* II, 21.

100. Paulus, *Sententiae* V, 23,15 (FIRA 2, 410) "qui sacra impia nocturnave, ut quem obcantarent defigerent obligarent, fecerint facien-

dave curaverint, aut cruci affiguntur aut bestiis obiciuntur." *Codex Theodosianus* 9, 16, 7 "ne quis deinceps nocturnis temporibus aut nefarias preces aut magicos apparatus aut sacrificia funesta celebrare conetur."

3. PORTRAIT OF THE MAGICIAN, SEEN FROM THE OUTSIDE

1. Mauss, 1973, p. 24: "C'est . . . l'opinion qui crée le magicien et l'influence qu'il dégage . . . Les individus, auxquels l'exercice de la magie est attribué, ont déjà . . . une condition distincte à l'intérieur de la société qui les traite de magiciens."

2. Piso, *Historicorum Romanorum Fragmenta*, ed. H. Peter, Frg. 33 (Pliny the Elder, *Natural History*, XVIII, 41–43). Fundamental Garosi: 1976, pp. 33–36.

3. Servius, *On Virgil, Eclogue* 8,99: "TRADVCERE MESSES: magicis quibusdam artibus hoc fiebat unde est in XII tabulis NEVE ALIENAM SEGETEM PELLEXERIS."

4. Paulus, *Sententiae* V, 23 ["ad legem Corneliam de sicariis et veneficis"] (FIRA 2, 405–410) mentions the death penalty (by fire, by crucifixion, by the circus animals, or, for the *honestiores*, a more discreet form of death) as the normal punishment; the deportation to the island is imposed only on the possessor of magic books who did not practice the art.

5. The best critical edition is still that of R. Helm in the Bibliotheca Teubneriana (vol. 2:1 of the Works of Apuleius), 2nd ed. (Leipzig: Teubner, 1912, often reprinted); critical edition with French translation by Paul Valette in the Édition Budé (Paris: Les Belles Lettres, 1960). Still important remains the commentary of H. E. Butler and A. S. Owen, *Apulei Apologia sive pro se de magia liber* (Oxford: Clarendon Press, 1914; repr. Hildesheim: G. Olms, 1967); and the thesis of Adam Abt, *Die Apologie des Apuleius von Madaura und die antike Zauberei; Beiträge zur Erläuterung der Schrift de magia*. RGVV 4:2 (Giessen: Toepelmann, 1908; repr. Berlin: De Gruyter, 1967). See also the analysis in Clerc 1995, esp. pp. 45–49.

6. The edict figures on the P. Yale inv. 299, published by George M. Parassoglou, "Circular from a Prefect: Sileat Omnibus Perpetuo Divinandi Curiositas," in Ann Ellis Hanson (ed.), *Collectanea*

Papyrologica: Texts Published in Honor of H. C. Youtie (Bonn: Habelt, 1976), vol. 1, p. 262, no. 30; again in G. H. R. Horsley (ed.), *New Documents Illustrating Early Christianity* vol. 1 (Macquairie University: 1984), p. 47, no. 12. For Paul, see n. 4.

7. *Apology*, LXXXIII, 1.
8. For Apuleius the philosopher, see primarily John Dillon, *The Middle Platonists: A Study of Platonism* 80 B.C. to A.D. 220 (Ithaca: Cornell University Press, 1977), pp. 306–340; and Claudio Moreschini, *Apuleio e il Platonismo* (Florence: Olschki, 1978). The reference to Sextus is found in *Metamorphoses*, I, 2.
9. St. Gsell, *Inscriptions latines de l'Algérie*, vol. 1 (Paris: Leroux, 1922), no. 2115; *[Ph]ilosopho [Pl]atonico [Ma]daurenses cives ornament[o] suo d(e)d(icaverunt) p(ecunia) p(ublica)*.
10. *Apology*, LXXVIII, 1 "aquariolus iste uxoris suae ita ira extumuit, ita exarsit furore, ut in feminam sanctissiman et pudicissimam praesente filio eius digna cubiculo suo diceret, amatricem eam, me magum et veneficum clamitaret multis audientibus quos, si voles, nominabo: se mihi sua manu mortem allaturum."
11. *Apology*, I, 3 "gratulor medius fidius quod mihi copia et facultas te iudice optigit purgandae apud imperitos philosophiae et probandi mei."
12. *Apology*, III, 5.
13. *Apology*, IV, 4.
14. *Apology*, XXV, 10; XXXVIII, 1; XLI, 4; LX, 2.
15. *Apology*, XIX, 2 "virum tam austerae sectae tamque diutinae militiae"; see Butler and Owen 1914, p. 56 (for Stoicism); p. 11. A. Stein, *PW* 3, 1899, 2772 nr. 238 (the philosopher); E. Groag, ibid. 2773 nr. 239 hesitates on the identification of governor and philosopher; in E. Groag and A. Stein, *Prosopographia Imperii Romani*, (Berlin: Walter de Gruyter, 1936), Part 2 no. 933 and 934—Groag is more optimistic.
16. For the philosopher in later Greek and Roman society, see Johannes Hahn, *Der Philosoph und die Gesellschaft. Selbstverständnis, öffentliches Auftreten und populäre Erwartungen in der höheren Kaiserzeit* (Stuttgart: Steiner, 1989).
17. Glen Warren Bowersock, *Greek Sophists in the Roman Empire* (Oxford: Clarendon Press, 1969).
18. Useful indications are found in Ramsay MacMullen, *Enemies of the*

Roman Order: Treason, Unrest, and Alienation in the Empire (Cambridge, Mass.: Harvard University Press, 1966), pp. 95–127; and esp. Graham Anderson, Sage, Saint, and Sophist: Holy Men and Their Associates in the Early Roman Empire (London/New York: Routledge, 1994), pp. 65–68. For a model at least partially derived from Apuleius, see Paola Zambelli, L'ambigua natura della magia, Filosofi, streghe, riti nel Rinascimento (Milan: Il Saggiatore, 1991).

19. Apology, XXIX, 1.

20. Greek $\tau\rho\acute{\nu}\gamma\omega\nu$, D'Arcy W. Thompson, A Glossary of Greek Fishes (Oxford: Clarendon Press, 1947), p. 270f.; Pliny the Elder, Natural History, IX, 155; Philostratus, Life of Apollonius of Tyana, VI, 32.

21. Apology, XL, 5.

22. Apology, XXXIV, 4.

23. Pliny the Elder, Natural History, XXVII, 131 "Circa Ariminium nota est herba quam resedam vocant. discutit collectiones inflamma-tionesque omnes. qui curant ea, addunt haec verba: 'reseda, mor-bos reseda, / scisne scisne quis hic pullus egerit radices? / nec caput nec pedes habeat.' haec ter dicunt totiensque despuunt." See Maria Cristina Martini, Piante medicamentose e rituali magico-re-ligiosi in Plinio (Rome: Bulzoni, 1977).

24. Origen, Against Celsus, I, 24 (vol. 1, pp. 134–136, Borret); for Herodotus, see Walter Burkert, "Herodot über die Namen der Götter: Polytheismus als historisches Problem," Museum Helveticum 42, 1985, 121–132.

25. Apology, XXXVIII, 7.

26. Apology, XLII, 3; PGM IV 850, Charm of Salomon that produces a trance; Abt 1908, p. 240.

27. Plotinus, II, 9, 14: the only difference is that Plotinus confirms for us that by their powers, the sorcerers would have great renown with the crowd.

28. Apology, XLIII, 7 "carmine . . . initiare."

29. Butler and Owen, 1914; p. 108ff; Juvenal, VI, 551s.

30. Heraclitus, DK 12 B 14, see this volume, Chapter 2.

31. Asclepius: Emma J. and Ludwig Edelstein, Asclepius: A Collection and Interpretation of the Testimonies (Baltimore: Johns Hopkins University Press, 1948, repr. Salem, N. H.: Ayer Co., 1988), vol. 1, pp. 296–299; documents 523–531. Magic: e.g., PGM IV, 30 (white

rooster). XIII, 377 (in order to prove one's initiation) Audollent 1904, LXIIs. (defixiones); see Abt 1908, ad loc.; see also Aeneas of Gaza, in Hopfner 1990, p. 562f. (vol.2, § 339; sacrifice of a rooster typical for necromantic rituals among Chaldaeans, Egyptians, and Greeks).

32. *Apology,* XLVIII, 1.

33. *Apology,* LI, 10.

34. See C. Bonner, "The Technique of Exorcism," *Harvard Theological Review,* 1943, pp. 39–49; id., "The Violence of Departing Demons," *Harvard Theological Review,* 1944, pp. 334–336; K. Thraede, "Exorzismus," *Reallexikon für Antike und Christentum* vol. 7, 1969, pp. 44–117; Peter Brown, "The Rise and Function of the Holy Man in Late Antiquity," *Journal of Roman Studies* 61, 1971, pp. 80–101.

35. For the *Acts* and *Gospels,* see esp. Smith 1978 passim; for the papyri PGM IV, 1228; V, 125; XIII, 243.

36. Lucian, *The Lover of Lies,* 16.

37. *Apology,* LIII–LVI.

38. *Apology,* LVII–LX.

39. *Apology,* LXI, 2.

40. PGM VIII 13; Abt 1908, 302.

41. Suetonius, *Nero 56.*

42. Abt 1908: ad loc.

43. PGM I, 163ff.

44. Abt 1908, p. 297f. (also on PGM IV, 2130); Martin S. Smith (ed.), *Petronius: Cena Trimalchionis* (Oxford: Clarendon Press, 1975), p. 74; Katherine M. D. Dunbabin, "Sic erimus cuncti . . : The skeleton in Graeco-Roman art," *Jahrbuch des Deutschen Archaeologischen Instituts* 101, 1986, 185–255.

45. *Apology,* LIV 7.

46. Henrik S. Versnel, "Religious Mentality in Ancient Prayer," in H. S. Versnel (ed.), *Faith, Hope and Worship: Aspects of Religious Mentality in the Ancient World* (Studies in Greek and Roman Religion, vol. 2) (Leiden: E. J. Brill, 1981), pp. 1–64, esp. pp. 25–28, who refers to Cicero, *De divinatione,* I, 129 and to the amorous prayer in Roman elegy; Pieter W. van der Horst, "Silent prayer in antiquity," *Numen* 41, 1994, pp. 1–25.

47. Thomas 1971: p. 179.

48. *Seneca: Letter to Lucilius,* 41, 2; see also fragment 36 Hasse of the treatise *De superstitione* (Jupiter Capitolinus).

49. Lucian, *The Lover of Lies,* 20, see Otto Weinreich, *Antike Heilungswunder: Untersuchungen zum Wunderglauben der Griechen und Römer,* RGVV VIII: 1, (Giessen: Toepelmann, 1909), pp. 137ff.

50. See later, Chapter 5, n. 26.

51. *Apology,* XXVI, 6 "sin vero more vulgari eum isti proprie magum existimant, qui communione loquendi cum dis immortalibus ad omnia, quae velit, incredibili quadam vi cantaminum polleat . . ."

52. As a literary figure, e.g., Tibullus, I, 5,11; Ovid, *The Art of Loving,* II, 329; Aesopus, *Fabula* 91; mythical transformation Diodorus of Sicily, III, 58, 2 (Cybele); late antiquity John Chrysostomus, *Homily on Coloss., III* VIII (PG 62,358 B) (healing); Theodoretus, *History of the Monks of Syria,* XIII, 10 (erotic magic); Callinicus, *Life of Hypatius,* XXVIII, 1–3 (healing). See Jan N. Bremmer, "The old women in ancient Greece," in Josine Blok and Peter Mason (eds.), *Sexual Asymmetry: Studies in Ancient Society* (Amsterdam: J. C. Gieben, 1987), pp. 191–215.

53. For Athens in the classical age, Adolf Wilhelm, "Über die Zeit einiger attischer Fluchtafeln," *Oesterreichische Jahreshefte* 7, 1904, pp. 113–125 (exemplary his conclusions, p. 118); Trumpf 1958, 99; Jordan 1988a: vol. 4, pp. 273–377; F. Willemsen, in W. K. Kovacsovics, *Die Eckterrasse an der Gräberstrasse des Kerameikos* (Kerameikos. Ergebnisse der Ausgrabungen 14) (Berlin/New York: De Gruyter, 1990), 142 (trierach), 148 (the orators Hyperides and Lycurgus). For Delos (um 100 v. Chr.) *Inscriptions de Délos,* vol. 5, no. 2534.

54. Plato, *Republic* 364 B.C., see earlier, Chapter 2, n. 9.

55. Curio: Cicero, *Brutus,* 217; Vatinius: Cicero, *In Vatinium,* 14; Nigidius Figulus: Apuleius, *Apology* XLII, 3; Germanicus: Tacitus, *Annals,* II, 69; the other cases IV, 52,1 (26 A.D., *venefica in principem et devotiones*); VI, 29,4 (34 A.D. *magorum sacra*); XII, 59 (53 A.D., *magicae superstitiones*); XII, 65,1 (54 A.D., *devotiones* against the empress).

56. Libanius: C. Bonner, "Witchcraft in the Lecture Room of Libanius," *Transactions of the American Philological Association* 63, 1932, pp. 34–44; Sopater: Eunapius, *Vitae sophistarum* VI, 2,9–11 (the philosopher was offered as a scapegoat during a crisis); see also

Zosimos, *Historia* II, 40,3; Boethius: his own *Consolation of Philosophy* I, 4,134–148; and Pierre Rousseau, "The death of Boethius: The charge of maleficium," *Studi Medievali* 20, 1979, pp. 871–889. Extensive, but sometimes rambling, discussions in Clerc 1995, esp. pp. 153–237.

57. Andreas Alföldi, "Stadtrömische heidnische Amulett-Medaillen aus der Zeit um 400 n. Chr.," in *Mullus: Festschrift Theodor Klauser* (Jahrbuch für Antike und Christentum, suppl. 1) (Münster: Aschendorff, 1964), pp. 1–9; an exciting amulet represents a scene of necromancy (5, Taf. 1,4), another one a Bacchic dance in front of Hecate (7, Taf. 2,6), which combines magic and mysteries.

58. Zacharias, *Life of S. Severus*, 61.

59. Paulus, *Sententiae*, 5,23,18 "libri magicae artis . . . penes quoscumque reperti sint, bonis ademptis, ambustis his publice in insulam deportantur, humiliores capite puniuntur."

60. Kieckhefer 1989: 12f.

61. See the arguments of Peter Brown, *The Cult of the Saints: Its Rise and Function in Latin Christianity* (Chicago: University of Chicago Press, 1981); Natalie Zemon Davis, "Some Tasks and Themes in the Study of Popular Religion," in Charles Trinkaus and Heiko A. Oberman, *The Pursuit of Holiness in Late Medieval and Renaissance Religion* (Leiden: Brill, 1974), pp. 307–336; Dario Rei, "Note sul concetto di religione popolare," *Lares* 40, 1974, pp. 262–280.

62. *Apology*, XXVII, 1–3 "qui providentiam mundi curiosius vestigant."

63. *Apology*, XL, 1.

64. *Apology*, XL, 3.

65. Later cases in Brown 1972: pp. 124–127 (Boethius, Mummolus of Bordeaux); and Hypatia of Alexandria, according to Maria Dzielska, *Hypatia of Alexandria* (Cambridge, Mass.: Harvard University Press, 1995).

66. Mauss 1973: 24 "Toute condition sociale anormale prépare à l'exercice de la magie."

4. HOW TO BECOME A MAGICIAN

1. E.g., John Chrysostomus, *Homely on Matthew* VIII 4; see Fowden 1986: pp. 79–87.

2. Lucian, *The Lover of Lies*, 34–36.

3. Fowden 1986: p. 166f. wishes to identify him with the magician and priest Pachrates of Heliopolis, mentioned in PGM IV, 2446–2455; but Heinz J. Thissen, "Ägyptologische Beiträge zu den griechischen magischen Papyri," in U. Verhoeven and E. Graefe (Hrsgg.), *Religion und Philosophie im alten Ägypten: Festgabe für Philippe Derchain* (Louvain: Peeters, 1991), p. 296 tries an Egyptian etymology for the latter name: Pa-hrt, "he who belongs to the (divine) child."

4. Caesar, *Bellum Galllicum* VI, 14.

5. Pseudo-Cyprian, *Confessions* 12, see Hopfner 1983: p. 22f. For another sorcerer taught in Memphis, Jerome, *Vita Hilarionis eremitae* 12; and already the powerful divinities of the Delian Serapeum came from Memphis, Helmut Engelmann, *The Delian Aretalogy of Sarapis* (Leiden: Brill, 1975); in a Demotic text, it is the capital of sorcery, G. Maspero, *Popular Stories of Ancient Egypt*, trans. A. S. Johns (New Hyde Park, N. Y.: University Books, 1967) (orig. Paris, 4th ed. 1911, p. 425f.).

6. Arnobius, *Against the Gentiles*, I, 43 1, 43: "magus fuit, clandestinis artibus omnia illa perfecit, Aegyptiorum ex adytis angelorum potentium nomina et remotas furatus est disciplinas."

7. Dio Cassius LXXV, 13,2.

8. PGM VIII 41ff. The Christians told a story about how the emperor Julian underwent initiation in an *aduton*: Sozomenus, *Historia Ecclesiastica* V, 2, and the Coptic Christians suspected magic in all Egyptian temples; see the story of the Coptic saint Shenute in Trombley 1993: vol. 2, 211.

9. Origen, *Against Celsus* I, 25. Hopfner 1974: pp. 64–82 (§§ 135–162); for a *defixio* Audollent 1904: no. 74; Daniel and Maltomini: 1992, no. 97b.

10. Celsus (in Origen, *Against Celsus* I, 28) follows Jewish sources in his account of how young Jesus had been forced through poverty to look for work in Egypt, where he learned magic. For all this, Smith 1978: pp. 45–80; still interesting is E. M. Butler, *The Myth of the Magus* (Cambridge: Cambridge University Press, 1948), pp. 66–73.

11. Zalmoxis: Herodotus IV, 96; Hellanicus, *FGrHist* 4 F 73; Pythagoras Diogenes Laertius 8,41, following Hermippus frg. 20 Wehrli *Die Schule des Aristoteles*. Suppl. 1 (Basel/Stuttgart: Schwabe,

1974). See Walter Burkert, *Lore and Science in Ancient Pythagoreanism* (Cambridge, Mass.: Harvard University Press, 1972), pp. 156–161.

12. Clarus: W. W. Parke, *The Oracles of Apollo in Asia Minor* (London: Croom Helm, 1985), pp. 137–39. Trophonius: P. and M. Bonnechère, "Trophonios à Lébadée: Histoire d'un oracle," *Etudes Classiques* 57, 1989, pp. 289–302.

13. Thus the reconstruction of the ritual from a magic ritual in PGM LXX, offered by Hans Dieter Betz, "Fragments from a catabasis ritual in a Greek magical papyrus," in Betz 1990: pp. 147–155 (orig. *History of Religions* 19, 1980, pp. 287–295); but see Jordan 1988b: pp. 245–259, who draws attention to parallels with a binding spell.

14. See Hans Dieter Betz, *Lukian von Samosata und das Neue Testament* (Berlin: De Gruyter, 1961).

15. The 1958 synthesis by Mircea Eliade, *Rites and Symbols of Initiation: The Mysteries of Birth and Rebirth,* trans. Willard R. Trask (Dallas: Spring Publications, 1994) remains as superficial as it is dogmatic; for the Christian world, see Victor Saxer, *Les rites de l'initiation chrétienne du IIe au VIe siècle: Esquisse historique et signification d'après leurs principaux témoins* (Spoleto: Centro Italiano di studi sull'alto Medioevo, 1988).

16. Thessalus of Tralles, *De virtutibus herbarum,* I, 13–14; see Hans-Veit Friedrich, *Thessalos von Tralles: griechisch und lateinisch* (Meisenheim am Glan: Hain, 1968); Armand-Jean Festugière, "L'expérience religieuse du médecin Thessalos," *Revue Biblique,* 1939, p. 45ff; Jonathan Z. Smith, *Map is not Territory: Studies in the History of Religions* (Chicago: University of Chicago Press, 1993); Fowden 1986: pp. 162–165.

17. PGM III, 440.

18. *Pythian Odes,* IV, 213–218. See Vinciane Pirenne-Delforge, "L'iynge dans le discours mythique et les procédures magiques," *Kernos,* 6, 1993, pp. 277–89; Christophe A. Faraone, "The wheel, the whip, and other implements of torture: Erotic magic in Pindar, Pythian 4, 213–19," *Classical Journal* 89, 1993, pp. 1–19. For the earrings, see the catalog by Dyfri Williams and Jack Ogden, *Greek Gold: Jewelry of the Classical World* (New York: Metropolitan Museum, 1994), 96f. no. 49f. (330–300 B.C.).

19. The case of Orpheus, who comes closest to it, is more complicated; see Fritz Graf, "Orpheus: A Poet Among Men," in Jan
Bremmer (ed.), *Interpretation of Greek Mythology* (London: Routledge,
1988), pp. 80–106.

20. On the theory of culture and on the "inventors of culture,"
A. Kleingünther, ΠΡΩΤΟΣ ΕΥΡΕΤΗΣ *Untersuchungen zur
Geschichte einer Fragestellung* (Philologus. Supplementband 26:1)
(Leipzig: Teubner, 1933).

21. For some initiatory aspects of the myth of Jason, see Alain
Moreau, "Introduction à la mythologie X–XIX: Les mille et une
facettes de Médéee," *Connaissance hellénique* 24–33, 1985–1987; id.,
Le mythe de Jason et Médée: Le va-nu-pied et la sorcière (Paris: Les Belles
Lettres, 1994); Fritz Graf, "Medea, the enchantress from afar:
Remarks on a well-known myth," in James J. Clauss and Sarah
Iles Johnston, *Medea* (Princeton N. J.: Princeton University Press,
1996), pp. 21–43.

22. Plato, *The Republic*, 364 B.C. Compared with the translation given
in the text, the alternative that connects ϑυσίαις τε καὶ
ἐπῳδαῖς with ἀκεῖσθαι ("heal . . . through sacrifices and incantations") is less natural.

23. It has been discussed whether Plotinus had already practiced it.
Philip Merlan offered good arguments in favor of this hypothesis,
"Plotinus and magic," in *Kleine philosophische Schriften* (Hildesheim,
New York: Olms, 1976), pp. 388–95 (*Isis* 44, 1954, pp. 341–48).
For a recent discussion, see G. Fowden, "The Platonist Philoso-
pher and His Circle in Late Antiquity," *Philosophia/Athen* 7, 1977,
pp. 359–383; G. Shaw, "Theurgy: Rituals of Unification in the
Neoplatonism of Jamblichus," *Traditio* 41, 1985, pp. 1–28; Georg
Luck, "Theurgy and Forms of Worship in Neoplatonism," in
Neusner, Frerichs, and Flesher 1989: pp. 185–225.

24. On the charismatics in general, see Ludwig Bieler, ΘΕΙΟΣ
ANHP: *Das Bild des "göttlichen Menschen" in Spätantike und Frühchris-
tentum* (Vienna: Oskar Hoefels, 1935/1936); see also G. Fowden,
"The Pagan Holy Man in Late Antique Society," *Journal of Hellenic
Studies* 102, 1982, pp. 33–59; G. Anderson, *Sage, Saint, and Sophist:
Holy Men and Their Associates in the Early Roman Empire* (London:
Routledge, 1994). For Apollonius at Aegae, see Fritz Graf, "Maxi-
mos von Aigai: Ein Beitrag zur Uberlieferung über Apollonios

von Tyana," *Jahrbuch für Antike und Christentum* 27/28, 1984–1985, pp. 65–73.

25. Irenaeus, *Against the Heresies*, I,13,3. On accusations of magic brought forward against gnostics, see Kurt Rudolph, *Die Gnosis* (Göttingen: Vandenhoeck & Rupprecht, 3rd ed., 1990), p. 187f.; on μαγεία in gnostic texts, Ioan P. Coulianou, *The Tree of Gnosis* (San Francisco: Harper, 1992) p. 106f.

26. Richard Reitzenstein, *Poimandres: Studien zur griechisch-ägyptischen und frühchristlichen Literatur* (Leipzig: Teubner, 1904), pp. 146–160.

27. For the formula *egō eimi*, known especially from the aretalogies of Isis, and the cults of Isis, see Jan Bergman, *Ich bin Isis: Studien zum mephitischen Hintergrund der griechischen Isisaretalogien* (Upsala, 1960). Examples later in n. 104.

28. Leyden papyrus: *PGM* XII, 87–95. Moses: *PGM* V, 110. Amulet: a copper tablet, edited in Kotansky 1994; no. 32; other amulets Louis Robert, "Amulettes grecques I: Théophanies sur les montagnes," *Journal des Savants* 1981, pp. 3–27 (*Opera Minora Selecta* vol. 7 [Amsterdam: Hakkert, 1990], pp. 465–489).

29. Tat: *Corpus hermeticum*, 13, 1; Reitzenstein 1904: Chapter 7. Jesus: Smith 1976, p. 121.

30. Hesiod, *Theogony*, 23. See also the exorcism P. Carlsberg 52 (7th century A.D.), in William M. Brashear, *Magica Varia* (Papyrologica Bruxellensia 25) (Brussels: Fondation Égyptologique Reine Élisabeth, 1991), pp. 16–62 (the exorcist represents himself as a demon on top of Mt. Sinai).

31. Martin P. Nilsson, "Greek mysteries in the 'Confession' of St. Cyprian," *Harvard Theological Review* 40, 1947, pp. 167–176, repr. in Nilsson 1960: pp. 106–116.

32. A synthesis in Hans Dieter Betz, "Magic and mystery in the Greek magical papyri," in Betz 1990: pp. 209–229, and in Faraone and Obbink 1991: pp. 244–259. The vocabulary is collected in Festugière 1932: pp. 303–306.

33. Μυστήριον e.g., *PGM* IV, 476. XIXa, 52, see A. D. Nock, *Journal of Egyptian Archeology* 11, 1925, p. 158.—Τελετή e.g., *PGM* XII, 95. See C. Zijderveld, Τελετή: Bijdrage tot de kennis der religieuze terminologie in het Grieksch (Diss. Utrecht: 1934).

34. E.g., *PGM* IV, 746 (magic ointment); 794 (amulet in the shape of a scarab); XII, 331, 333 (amulets).

35. *PGM* XII, 322.

36. *PGM* IV, 733 συνμύσται, compare IV, 479 μύσται. XIII, 57, 380, 427 ἀμνστηρίαστοι. IV, 172 μυσταγωγός.

37. *PGM* IV, 475–829; μύστης ΙΩ, 479; συνμύστης 733. See primarily Dieterich 1923 and Merkelbach 1992, but also Festugière 1932: pp. 310–313; and Marvin W. Meyer, *The "Mithras Liturgy"* (Missoula, Montana: Scholars Press, 1976). In a still unpublished paper, Sarah Iles Johnston understands it rather as a theurgical ritual.

38. *PGM* LXX, 12–19, τετελεσμένος, see Hans Dieter Betz, "Fragments from a catabasis ritual in a Greek magical papyrus," in Betz 1990: pp. 147–155.

39. Euripides, *Hercules* 613: "have been successful, because I saw the rites of the initiates."

40. The texts in Giovanni Pugliese-Carratelli, *Le lamine d'oro 'orfiche'* (Milan: Scheiwiller, 1993); in emblematical the scene on the leaf from Hipponium, p. 20 (and already id., *Parola del Passato* 29, 1974, p. 108f.).

41. *PGM* V, 110, see earlier, n. 27.

42. Eleusis: George E. Mylonas, *Eleusis and the Eleusinian Mysteries* (Princeton: Princeton University Press, 1961), pp. 224–226.— Magic: *PGM* XII, 315–322. See Betz 1995: pp. 153–175, esp. 154–160.

43. *PGM* XII, 403–408.

44. On the growing ignorance of the hieroglyphs under the empire, see Pieter W. van der Horst, "The secret hieroglyphs in classical literature," in Jan den Boeft and A. H. M. Kessels (eds.), *Actus: Studies in Honour of H. L. W. Nelson* (Utrecht: Instituut voor Klassieke Talen, 1982) pp. 115–123; and Fowden 1986: pp. 63–65. See the symptomatic testimony of Olympiodorus, *De arte sacra*, in M. Berthelot (ed.), *Collection des anciens alchimistes grecs* (Paris: Steinheil, 1887), pp. 87f. (repr. London: Holland Press, 1963); or Iamblichus, *De mysteriis Aegyptiorum* VIII, 5,267f. On the other hand, the Christians who destroyed the Alexandrian Serapeum still recognized the *ankh* as a sign for life (though now referring to Christ, the eternal life), Socrates, *Historia* V, 17 (PG 67,608A–609A), Rufinus, *Historia Ecclesiastica* XI,29.

45. Magicians: e.g., Claudianus, *In Rufinum* I, 145ff. (the witch

Megaera knows "quid signa sagacis / Aegypti valeant"). Christians: Rufinus *Historia Ecclesiastica* XI, 16 (the sacerdotal school of Canopus and their "litterae sacerdotales" is "magicae artis publica schola").

46. For the many copies used by a magician to constitute his text, see *PGM* V, 51; XII, 407.

47. Nock 1972: p. 193 formulated the difference between hermeticists and magicians: "The authors and readers of the Pistis Sophia (like Neoplatonist students of theurgy) were passionately eager to know how the wheels went round, the authors and readers of the magical papyri desired simply to be able to make them turn." This is too simplistic, as will be shown.

48. See Porphyry, *Life of Plotinus* X, 1–9; Eunapius, *Life of the Sophists*, 410–413 (Maximos von Tyrus); Marinus, *Life of Proclus* XXVIII (theurgy, fabrication of amulets, weather magic, divination); Psellus, *Explanationes in Oracula Chaldaica*, PG 122, 1133 AB (weather magic of Proclus).

49. For magic ecstasy, see, e.g., *PGM* IV, 738.

50. Homer, *Hymn to Demeter*, 480ff.; Apuleius, *Metamorphoses*, XI, 30.

51. Underscored by Burkert, 1987.

52. Reinhold Merkelbach, *Mithras* (Königstein/Ts.: Hain, 1984), p. 160ff; see the implicit reservations of Robert Turcan, *Les cultes orientaux dans le monde romain* (Paris: Les Belle Lettres, 1989), pp. 234–239.

53. Apuleius, *Apology*, LV, 8; *Metamorphoses* XI, passim.

54. According to Marinus, *Life of Proclus* XXVIII, the philosopher had been taught theurgy by Asclepiogenia, who had been taught by her father Plutarch, who had learned it from his father Nestorius. For similar chains of transmission in the middle ages, see Kieckhefer 1989: p. 59.

55. *PGM* XIII, 342f., compare 213 (τέκνον: Moses VIII). Other examples are *PGM* I, 42 (Pnouthis to Keryx); IV, 152 (Nephotes to King Psammetichos); 2006 (Pitys to King [sic] Ostanes), compare 475 (addressed to the daughter).

56. *PGM* IV, 733–747.

57. *PGM* IV, 172–176.

58. *PGM* IV, 210–215.

59. Like the sequel of *múesis* and *epópteia* in Eleusis or the very elaborated hierarchy of rites in the mysteries of Mithra, see Burkert 1987: p. 42f.

60. Pliny the Elder, *Natural History*, XXX, 16: "magicis etiam cenis eum initiaverat." (W. Burkert, *Griechische Religion der archaischen und klassischen Epoche*, Stuttgart, 1977, 163 no. 46.)

61. Version A of Moses VIII: *PGM* XIII, 1–230; the "introduction to the gods of the hours of the day," ibid., 29–39. For those gods (genuinely Egyptian), see G. Soukiassian, *Lexikon der Aegyptologie* vol. 6, 1986, p. 102f; they are mainly the aides of Osiris.

62. For these *antitheoi*, see Arnobius, *Adversus Nationes* IV, 12 "magi, haruspicum fratres, suis in actionibus memorant antitheos saepius obrepere pro accitis, esse autem hos quosdam materiis ex crassioribus spiritus, qui deos se fingant nesciosque mendaciis et simulationibus ludant."

63. Which shows that such commentaries contained not only explanations but also additional rites.

64. Sarah Iles Johnston, "Crossroads," *Zeitschrift für Papyrologie und Epigraphik* 88, 1991, 217–224.

65. We find a comparable series in the rather enigmatic formula of the Bacchic, "Orphic" eschatological texts. For a long time we have known the acclamation, "Kid, you fell into the milk"; a new text discovered in Thessaly now gives more—bull and ram, both fallen (or, in the case of the bull, having jumped) into the milk. See my articles in Philippe Borgeaud (ed.), *Orphisme and Orphée: En l'honneur de Jean Rudhardt* (Geneva: Droz, 1991), pp. 87–102; and in Thomas H. Carpenter and Christopher A. Faraone (eds.), *Masks of Dionysus* (Ithaca: Cornell University Press, 1993), pp. 239–258.

66. Arnold van Gennep, *Les rites de passage* (Paris: Nourry, 1909).

67. Porphyry, *Life of Plotinus* X.

68. Irenaeus, *Against the Heresies* I, 13,3.

69. *PGM* I, 96–130.

70. Origen, *Against Celsus I*, 68. See Eugen V. Gallagher, *Divine Man or Magician? Celsus and Origen on Jesus* (Society of Biblical Literature. Dissertation series 64), (Chico, Calif.: Scholars Press, 1982).

71. *PGM* XII, 161; compare XIII, 289.

72. *Passio Perpetuae* XVI, 2.

73. *PGM* IV, 3080. For demons and air, see Porphyry, Frg. 327 Smith (in Eusebius, *Praeparatio Evangelica* IV, 23): the Egyptians (and other knowledgeable people) whip the air, before they sacrifice, in order to drive away the demons. Smith 1978: p. 113 recalls John XX, 22 (Christ breathes the spirit on the disciples).

74. *PGM* I, 1–42.

75. Milk, magic, and other ritual liquids: e.g., PGM III 694 (milk, wine); IV 2192 (milk, wine, honey, oil); XII 215 (milk, wine, honey); XIII 135 (milk, wine); 1015 (milk, wine, water). Fritz Graf, "Milch, Honig und Wein: Zum Verständnis der Libation im griechischen Ritual," in *Perennitas: Studi in onore di Angelo Brelich* (Rome: Edizioni dell'Ateneo, 1980), pp. 209–221; A. Henrichs, "The Eumenides and wineless libation in the Derveni Papyrus," in *Atti del XVII congresso internazionale di papirologia* (Naples, 19–26 May 1983), Naples: Centro Internazionale per lo Studio dei Papiri Ercolanesi, 1984, pp. 255–268.

76. *PGM* XIII, 131–139; 413–440; 683–693; compare *PGM*, XIII, 890, in which a tablet of gold must be licked; Wortmann 1968: 102 no. 5 publishes a magical papyrus (with a recipe against an illness) which twice reproduces the same text but whose first version was rinsed with water; Wortmann supposes that one dipped a stele of Horos in this water, unless this water was drunk.

77. Ritner 1993: pp. 95–102 (licking); pp. 102–110 (drinking). The Egyptian tale in Fowden 1986: p. 59f. with n. 48.

78. *Ezekiel*, 2,8–3,3.

79. Ginzburg 1989: p. 21 (northern Italy); p. 288 (Berne, Switzerland).

80. See the commentaries in PGMTr ad loc.; for the role Egyptian solar mythology played in late antiquity, see Wolfgang Fauth, *Helios Megistos: Zur synkretistischen Theologie der Spätantike* (Religions in the Graeco-Roman World 125) (Leiden: Brill, 1995).

81. Porphyry, *Life of Plotinus*, X, discussed in Philip Merlan, "Plotinus and magic," *Kleine Schriften* (Berlin: De Gruyter, 1976), pp. 388–395 (originally published in *Isis*, 44, 1954, pp. 341–348).

82. The cardinal text is satire 15 of Juvenal; the necessary information in J. Gérard, *Juvénal et la réalité contemporaine* (Paris: Belles Lettres, 1976), pp. 385–387.

83. Cambyses: Herodotus III, 27; Antiochus: Plutarch, *Isis and Osiris* 11; the Hyksos and the Jews: Manetho, *FGrHist* 609 F 10, from Flavius Josephus, *Against Apion*, I, 248.

84. See *PGM* IV, 26–51; 2442–2495; XXXVI, 264–274.

85. *PGM* IV, 160.

86. *PGM* IV, 219.

87. *PGM* IV, 28. Another pure place is the temple, Porphyry, *Life of Plotinus* X.

88. Mircea Eliade, *Birth and Rebirth* (New York: Harper & Row, 1955). Burkert 1987: pp. 99–101.

89. Porphyry, *Life of Plotinus* X; Sokrates' daimonion: Plutarch, *De genio Socratis*; Apuleius, *De deo Socratis*.

90. See the demonstration of Peter Brown, *The Cult of the Saints: Its Rise and Function in Latin Christianity* (Chicago: University of Chicago Press, 1981), Chapter 3; add Lothar Kolmer, "Heilige als magische Helfer," *Mediaevistik* 6, 1993, pp. 153–175.

5. CURSE TABLETS AND VOODOO DOLLS

1. We do not have available a recent bibliography, but see Karl Preisendanz, art. "Fluchtafeln (Defixion)," in *Reallexikon für Antike und Christentum* 8, 1972, cols. 1–29; Christopher. A. Faraone, "The Agonistic Context of Early Greek Binding Spells," in Christopher A. Faraone and Dirk Obbink, *Magika Hiera: Ancient Greek Magic and Religion* (New York: Oxford University Press, 1991), pp. 2–32; and Gager 1992: pp. 3–41; for the magical dolls (or rather images), Christopher A. Faraone, "Binding and burying the forces of evil: The defensive use of 'voodoo dolls' in ancient Greece," *Classical Antiquity* 10, 1991, 165–205 (based on his Stanford thesis of 1988, *Talismans, Voodoo Dolls and Other Apotropaic Statues in Ancient Greece*, University Microfilms Nr. 8826138).

2. Richard Wünsch, "Appendix continens defixionum tabellas in Attica regione repertas," in *Inscriptiones Graecae: II/III Corpus Inscriptionum Atticarum* (Berlin: Reimer, 1897). Wünsch himself added more texts, "Neue Fluchtafeln," *Rheinisches Museum* 55, 1900, pp. 62–85, 232–271, with important discussions of Ziebarth 1899.

3. Auguste Audollent, *Defixionum tabellae* (Paris: Fontemoing, 1904).

4. John G. Gager (ed.), *Curse Tablets and Binding Spells from the Ancient World* (New York/Oxford: Oxford University Press 1992; 168 texts); David R. Jordan, "A survey of Greek defixiones not included in the special corpora," *Greek, Roman and Byzantine Studies* 26, 1985, pp. 151–197; this index contains bibliographic data for one hundred issues, and also mentions a much greater number of texts as yet unpublished. See also Jordan's *Contributions to the Study of Greek Defixiones*, University of Michigan, 1985; and among earlier publications, Erich Ziebarth, "Neue Verfluchungstafeln aus Attika, Böotien und Euboia," *Sitzungsberichte der Preussischen Akademie der Wissenschaften*, phil.-hist. Klasse 1934, 1022–1050; Werner Peek, *Inschriften, Ostraka, Fluchtafeln* (Kerameikos, Ergebnisse der Ausgrabungen, Bd. 3) (Berlin: De Gruyter, 1941); Wortmann 1968: pp. 56–111; and the index of Latin texts in the appendix of Heikki Solin, *Eine neue Fluchtafel aus Ostia* (Comment. Hum. Litt. Soc. Sc. Fenn. 42:3), Helsinki, 1968; Wortmann 1968, pp. 56–111.

5. Aeschylus, *Agamemnon* 306. See Jacqueline de Romilly, *Magic and Rhetoric in Ancient Greece* (Cambridge, Mass.: Harvard University Press 1975), p. 13; and Christopher A. Faraone, *Classical Journal* 89, 1993, p. 4f.; see id., "Aristophanes, 'Amphiarau,' fr. 29 (Kassel-Austin): Oracular response or erotic incantation?," *Classical Quarterly* 42, 1992, pp. 320–327.

6. Pliny the Elder, *Natural History* XXVIII, 19; Tacitus, *Annals* II, 69f. (Germanicus); IV, 52 (*devotiones* against the prince); XII, 65 (*devotiones* against the empress); XVI, 31 (*devotiones* in Caesarem); add IV, 22 (a woman who drove her husband mad "by spells and witchcraft," *carminibus et veneficiis*); Cicero, *Brutus* 217.

7. Plato, *Republic* 364 B.C.; see the catalog in Ovid, *Metamorphoses* X, 397–399.

8. Plato, *Laws* XI, 992E–993A. The theory is missing in the short survey in R. A. Markus, "Augustine on magic: A neglected semiotic theory," *Revue des Études Augustiniennes* 40 (1994), 375–388, esp. 376f.

9. Harpocration and Suidas, s. v. *katadein*.

10. *PGM* V, 321–331.

11. More recent research has adopted this terminology by making it

more subtle; see Faraone, in Faraone and Obbink, *Magika Hiera*, pp. 3–32.

12. Attested well into pagan and Christian late antiquity: Libanius, *Declamations* XLI, 29 lists, among the many misdeeds of sorcerers, their faculty to bind tongues; in a similar list, Arnobius, *Adversus nationes* I, 43 writes of "binding in silence," "ora silentio vincire"; Zacharias, *Life of S. Severus* 69 lists the content of magical books sequestrated in 490 A.D. in Beirut—among other things, recipes to "commit adultery, murder and theft, and to be acquitted in a trial"—the combination has its obvious charm.

13. Sophocles: Christopher A. Faraone, "Deianira's mistake and the demise of Heracles: Erotic magic in Sophocles' Trachiniae," *Helios* 21, 1994, pp. 115–136; in general, John J. Winkler, *The Constraints of Desire: The Anthropology of Sex and Gender in Ancient Greece* (New York/London: Routledge, 1990), see id., "The constraints of Eros," in Faraone & Obbink 1991: pp. 214–243. In the preceding lists: "uxoribus et liberis alienis sive illi mares sunt sive feminei generis inconcessi amoris flammas et feriales inmittere cupiditates," Arnobius I, 43; "to break marriages, to make a woman love against her will," Zacharias, loc. cit.

14. Arnobius, loc. cit., "in curriculis equos debilitare incitare tardare." See Henriette Pavis d'Escurac, "Magie et cirque dans la Rome antique," *Byzantinische Forschungen* 12, 1987, 447–467.

15. From Delos, Philippe Bruneau, *Recherches sur les cultes de Délos à l'époque hellénistique et à l'époque impériale* (Paris: E. de Boccard, 1970), pp. 650–655; from an unknown place in Asia Minor Christiane Dunant, "Sus aux voleurs! Une tablette en bronze à inscription grecque du Musée de Genève," *Museum Helveticum* 35, 1978, pp. 241–244. To Hendrik S. Versnel, these texts are not a matter of *defixio*, but of "judicial prayer": "Beyond cursing. The appeal to justice in judicial prayers," in Faraone and Obbink 1991: pp. 60–106, see Versnel's papers "Les imprécation et le droit," *Revue historique du droit français et étranger* 65, 1987, pp. 5–22 and "Πεπρη-μένος. The Cnidian curse tablets and ordeal by fire," in Hägg 1994: 145–154.

16. Wünsch 1897: no. 45; καταδῶ καί οὐκ ἀναλύσω: Athens, 400–350 B.C.; A. Wilhelm, *Oesterreichische Jahreshefte* 7, 1904, 120–122. For the exorcist, ἀναλύτης, see later n. 155.

17. Audollent 1904: 49 (Gager [1992] no. 44). In the presentation, I have tried to structure it.
18. For Sicily, López Jimeno 1991: no. 3ff.; for the imperial epoch, see earlier, n. 12.
19. Audollent 1904: no. 111.
20. Audollent 1904: no. 93a.
21. Sicily: López Jimeno 1991: p. 89f. Attica, e.g., Ziebarth 1899: p. 127, no.24 καταγράφω καὶ κατατίθω.
22. In early Sicilian texts, López Jimeno 1991: p. 71 (ἐγγράφω). 120 (ἀπογράφω).
23. Robert 1936, no. 13 (Jordan 1985a; p. 64), (Gager 1992: p. 19).
24. Audollent 1904: no. 2B.
25. Audollent 1904: no. 129.
26. The sanctuary of Demeter in Corinth, R. Stroud, "Curses from Corinth," *American Journal of Archaeology* 77, 1973, p. 228; of Demeter Malophoros in Selinus: J. Heurgon, *Kokalos* 18/19, 1972/73, pp. 70–74 (*Bulletin Epigraphique* 1976, p. 824); of Demeter on the acropolis of Mytilene, Caroline and Hector Williams, "Excavations at Mytilene 1984," *Échos du Monde Classique* 32, 1988, p. 145; a whole series comes from the sanctuary of the divinity of the thermal springs of Bath, Minerva Sulis, see H. S. Versnel, in Faraone and Obbink 1991: pp. 85–88; the temple of Mercurius at Uley, M. W. C. Hassall and R. S. Tomlin, "Roman Britain in 1978: II: Inscriptions," *Britannia* 10, 1979, 340; a sanctuary at Dahlheim (Luxemburg): Lothar Schwinden, *Hémecht* 44, 1992, 83–100.
27. Well of the Agora of Athens: G. Elderkin, "An Athenian maledictory inscription on lead," *Hesperia*, 1936, pp. 43–49; and "Two curse inscriptions," *Hesperia* 6, 1937, pp. 382–395; discussed again by David R. Jordan, "A curse tablet from a well in the Athenian agora," *Zeitschrift für Papyrologie und Epigraphik* 9, 1975, pp. 245–248 and in " Ἑκατικά," *Glotta* 38, 1980, pp. 62–65; see also Jordan 1985b: pp. 205–255. Well of the Athenian Ceramicus: D. Jordan, "Two inscribed lead tablets from a well in the Athenian Kerameikos," *Mitteilungen des Deutschen Archaeologischen Instituts (Athen. Abt.)* 95, 1980, pp. 225–239. Well on Delos: Philippe Bruneau, *Recherches sur les cultes de Délos à l'époque hellénistique et à l'époque impériale* (Paris: E. de Boccard, 1970), p. 649ff. A still unpublished hoard of 50

texts in a well in Caesaera Palaestinae, found during excavations of a team from Cincinnati in the place of Herod the Great. See the more general accounts of W. S. Fox, "Submerged Tabulae Defixionum," *American Journal of Philology* 33, 1912, pp. 301–310 and of Jordan 1985b: p. 207.

28. PGM VII, 450.

29. Philostratus, *Life of Apollonius of Tyana*, VII, 7: "What is the magician who would invoke Hercules? For the poor people ascribe their exploits to the sacrificial pits that they dig and to the action of the infernal gods"—confirmed by the great wizard Mithrobarzanes in Lucian's *Menippus or Necromancy*, who digs a sacrificial pit and invokes the infernal powers, the Poinai, Erinyes, Hecate, Persephone.

30. From Audollent 1904: p. LIf. to Louis Robert, *Journal des Savants* 1981, p. 35 (*Opera Minora Selecta* vol. 7 [Amsterdam: Hakkert, 1990], p. 497).

31. Hendrik S. Versnel, "Die Poetik der Zaubersprüche: Ein Essay über die Macht der Worte," in *Die Macht der Worte* (Eranos-Jahrbuch, Neue Reihe 4) (Munich: Fink, 1996), pp. 233–297.

32. We still lack a collection of the relevant ritual texts; for the literary ones, see Lindsay Watson, *Arae: The Curse Poetry of Antiquity* (Leeds: Francis Cairns, 1991).

33. Audollent 1904: pp. xxxi–xliii.

34. P. Herrmann, "Teos und Abdera im 5. Jahrhundert v. Chr. Ein neues Fragment der Teiorum Dirae," *Chiron*, 11, 1981, pp. 1–30.

35. See, for Herodes Atticus, Walter Ameling, *Herodes Atticus* (Subsidia Epigraphica 11) (Hildesheim: Olms, 1983) (with the earlier bibliography) and the supplement by the same author, "Eine neue Fluchinschrift des Herodes Atticus," *Zeitschrift für Papyrologie und Epigraphik* 70, 1987, p. 159. We still lack a comprehensive modern study of funerary imprecations, which should also contain the texts, but see J. H. M. Strubbe, "Cursed be he that moves my bones," in Faraone and Obbink 1991: pp. 33–59; still interesting are André Parrot, *Malédictions et violations de tombes* (Paris: 1939); Paul Moraux, *Une imprécation funéraire à Néocésarée* (Bibliothèque archéologique et historique de l'Institut Français d'Archéologie d'Istanbul 4), (Paris: E. de Boccard, 1959); Louis Robert, "Malédictions funéraires grecques I-IV," *Comptes-Rendus de l'Académie*

des Inscriptions et Belles-Lettres 1978, pp. 241–289 (*Opera Minora Selecta* vol.5 [Amsterdam: Hakkert, 1989], pp. 697–745).

36. Plutarch, *Roman Questions* XLIV, 275 D.

37. Homer, *Iliad* I, 35f.

38. Audollent 1904: no. 43 (Gager 1992: p. 43).

39. Faraone, in Faraone and Obbink, 1991: p. 7f.; see also Amor López Jimeno, "Las cartas de maldición," *Minerva* 4, 1990, pp. 134–144.

40. Wünsch 1897: no. 102. Other examples are Audollent 1904: nos.43/44 (Arcadia, 3rd cent. B.C.); Wünsch 1897: no. 103 (taken up again in *Oesterreich: Jahreshefte* 7, 1904, pp. 122–125); Bravo 1987, p. 206 (Olbia, 4th/3rd cent. B.C.); López Jimeno Nr. 27 (Jordan 1985a: 109 [Lilybaeum, late Hellenistic]).

41. E.g., *PGM* IV, 330; V, 381f; VII, 225, 429ff.

42. Spelled out in a text form Pannonia, Dorottya Gáspár, "Eine griechische Fluchtafel aus Savaria," *Tyche* 5, 1990, 13–16: "Abrasarx, I dedicate to you this Deiectus, son of Cumita, that he may be unable to act as long as [this text] is lying in this way; in the same way as you are a corpse, he may be with you, as long as he lives." Compare *PGM* IV, 2954f.; V, 325.

43. For the ἄωροι, see later, nn. 96–98; on whether all the graves with *defixiones* belonged to young people Jordan 1985a.

44. Audollent 1904: no. 139 (*Corpus Inscriptionum Latinarum* I² 1012 [*Inscriptiones Latinae Selectae* 8749]; Rome, late Republican or early Augustean). See also Audollent 1904: no. 192 (Oscan, from Capua). Ziebarth 1934: 1040 Nr. 23 (Boeotia).

45. Audollent 1904: no. 68 (Gager 1992: p. 22). Inscribed on both sides, only side A is quoted; for a closer analysis, see below, n. 96.

46. Wünsch 1897: no. 67.

47. Rudolf Münsterberg, "Zu den attischen Fluchtafeln," *Oesterreichische Jahreshefte* 7, 1904, p. 143; Caroline and Hector Williams, "Excavations at Mytilene 1988," *Échos du Monde Classique* 32, 1988, p. 145 with fig. 10.

48. Not only in magic, see Plutarch, *De sera numinis vindicta* 30, 567 C: three infernal lakes, one of boiling gold, one of ice-cold lead, and one of iron.

49. Wünsch 1897: no. 55 (ἀφανία); nos. 106 and 107 (both 4th cent. B.C.).

50. Extensive argumentation in E. G. Kagarow, "Form und Stil der Texte der Fluchtafeln," *Archiv für Religionswissenschaft* 21, 1922, pp. 494–497; id., *Griechische Fluchtafeln* (Eos. Supplementa 4), (Leopoli/Lvov, 1929).

51. *PGM* V, 305.

52. Plato, *Laws* 933 A; Ovid, *Amores* III, 7,29; more in Audollent 1904: p. XLVIIf., CXIIf.; C. A. Faraone, in Faraone and Obbink 1991: p. 7.

53. A business letter from 4th century Athens in Adolf Wilhelm, "Der älteste griechische Brief," *Oesterreichische Jahreshefte* 7, 1904, pp. 94–105, a private letter from 6th century north coast of the Black Sea, Benedetto Bravo, *Annali della Scuola Normale Superiore di Pisa* 10, 1980, pp. 880–885. Pausanias, IX, 31, 4 knows a "very old" text of the works of Hesiod engraved on lead; Pliny, *Natural History* XIII, 69, 88, remembers that earlier, public texts were written on lead scrolls and private ones on linen scrolls and wax tablets (*plumbea, lintea volumina, cerae*); in a mythical narration, the characters send each other "a letter on lead," Parthenius, *Erotica* IX, 4.

54. See the list of *PGM* VII, 450, earlier in n. 28.

55. *PGM* V, 304f.

56. Wünsch 1897: no. 49 τούτους ἅπαντας καταδῶ ἀφανίζω κατορύττω καταπασσαλεύω.

57. Publication and interpretation Trumpf 1958: pp. 94–102; the grave also in Karl Kübler, *Die Nekropole von der Mitte des 6. bis Ende des 5. Jahrhunderts* (Kerameikos. Ergebnisse der Ausgrabungen 7:1) (Berlin: De Gruyter, 1976), 48 no. 148; the text also Gager 1992: p. 41.

58. Jordan 1988a. Names on such figurines are relatively rare; there are two Etruscan examples from the 4th/3rd century B.C., from the same grave in Sovanna, B. Nogara and R. Mariani, *Ausonia* 4, 1909: pp. 31–47; the texts also in *Corpus Inscriptionum Etruscarum* nos. 5234, 5235; a drawing in Ambros Pfiffig, *Religio Etrusca* (Graz: Akademische Verlagsanstalt, 1975), p. 365 (and fig. 141); and on eight figures of uncooked clay from a grave in Pozzuoli, Audollent 1904: nos. 200–207. See also the novel of Pseudo-

Callisthenes (Iulius Valerius, *Historia Alexandri Magni* I, 5), where the magician Nectanebus writes his own name onto a wax figurine that he hides in the bedroom of Queen Olympias in order to make her dream about him.

59. Some lists were drawn up by Robert 1936 no. 13; Trumpf 1958: 96f; Georges Posener, *Cinq figurines d'envoutement* (Cairo: Institut Français d'Archéologie Orientale du Caire, 1987); a complete list in Christopher A. Faraone, *Talismans, Voodoo Dolls and Other Apotropaic Statues in Ancient Greece,* dissertation Stanford University, 1988 (University Microfilms, number 8826138); and his "Binding and burying the forces of evil: The defensive use of 'voodoo dolls' in ancient Greece," *Classical Antiquity* 10, 1991, pp. 165–205; for the bonds, see also the figurines of Delos, Philippe Bruneau, *Recherches sur les cultes de Délos à l'époque hellénistique et à l'époque impériale* (Paris: E. de Boccard, 1970), p. 649f.

60. Audollent 1904: no. 112.

61. Some examples in Trumpf 1958; H. S. Versnel, "A Twisted Hermes: Another View of an Enigmatic Spell," *Zeitschrift für Papyrologie und Epigraphik* 72, 1988, 287–292. See also what Libanius tells us about the disfigurements of a chameleon, *Oratio* I, 243–250.

62. The figurine of the Louvre: P. du Bourguet, "Ensemble magique de la période romaine en Egypte," *La Revue du Louvre* 25, 1975, pp. 255–257; S. Kambitsis, "Une nouvelle tablette magique d'Egypte. Musée du Louvre, inv. E27145 (III/IVe siècle)," *Bulletin de l'Institut Français pour l'Ancien Orient,* 76, 1976, pp. 211–223; two figurines from Delos, with three nails in the head, in Philippe Bruneau, op. cit. p. 649ff.

63. For example, *PGM* III, 296ff; Audollent 1904: no.222b; Juvenal, *Satires,* 6551f; for the cat, the rooster, and Egyptian magic, see also O. Rubensohn, *Archaeologischer Anzeiger,* 44, 1929, p. 216.

64. Wortmann 1968: 85 no. 4 (Daniel and Maltomini 1990: 162 no. 45).

65. *PGM* IV, 296–466.

66. ἤ πηλόν is missing in the papyrus, but the supplement is indispensable.

67. See, for example, Ernesto di Martino, *Sud e magia* (Milan: Feltrinelli, 1959, repr. 1978); and the opposed, but exaggerated,

position of Wolfgang Brueckner in the volume edited by Leander Petzoldt, *Magie und Religion: Beitraege zu einer Theorie der Magie* (Wege der Forschung; 337) (Darmstadt: Wissenschaftliche Buchgesellschaft, 1978), pp. 404–419.

68. Already noticed by Mauss 1973, p. 61f., who talks about "travail d'interprétation et d'abstraction."

69. Robert 1936 no. 13 (Jordan 1985a: p. 64; Gager 1992: no. 67, with fig. 110).

70. Jordan 1985b: p. 251.

71. *PGM* IV, 435, 447.

72. *PGM* IV, 49.

73. See Ziebarth 1934: 1042 no. 24 (Athens, fever); Fritz Graf, "An oracle against pestilence from a Western Anatolian town," *Zeitschrift für Papyrologie und Epigraphik* 92, 1992, pp. 267–278 (a magical figurine provoking the pest). In the Cnidian texts Audollent 1904: nos. 1ff. fever is threatened as a punishment, see Hendrik S. Versnel, "Πεπρημένος. The Cnidian curse tablets and ordeal by fire," in Hägg 1994: pp. 145–154.

74. Ovid, *Amores* III, 7, 27–29: "num mea Thessalico languent devota veneno / corpora? num misero carmen et herba nocent? / sagave poenicea defixit nomina cera?" Hipponax, frgs. 78 and 92 West, see Kurt Latte, "Hipponacteum," in *Kleine Schriften* (Munich: Beck, 1968), pp. 464–466 (*Hermes* 64, 1929, pp. 385–388). Ancient Orient: Robert D. Biggs, *Sà.ziga: Ancient Mesopotamian Potency Incantantions* (Texts from Cuneiform Sources 2) (Locust Valley, N.Y.: J. J. Augustin, 1967); Thomsen 1987: pp. 54–56.

75. Sophronius, *Narratio miraculorum SS Cyri et Ioannis sapientium Anargyrorum* 35 (Natalio Fernandez Marcos, ed., *Los Thaumata de Sofronio: Contribución al estudio de la incubatio cristiana*, Madrid: Instituto "Antonio de Nebrija," 1975); see Gager 1992: p. 165.

76. Jerome, *Vita S. Hilarionis eremitae*, XII, 10. The sheet of bronze from Cyprus, *aeris Cyprii lamina*, perhaps refers to Venus Cypria; a *defixio* on a piece of copper was, however, found in the necropolis of Rheneia (around 100 B.C.), *Inscriptions de Delos* no. 2534 (from about 100 B.C.), an amulet on copper from Sicily in Kotansky 1996: no. 32. Plato, *Laws* XI, 933 B: statuettes in wax under the doors or in the tombs.

77. Some symptoms of an at least partially Dionysiac ecstasy.
78. See Wolfgang Helck, art. "Gliedervergottung," *Lexikon der Aegyptologie*, vol.2, 1977, pp. 624–627.
79. See also the binding spell for all 365 (!) parts of the body. Audollent 1904: no. 15, and Daniel and Maltomini 1990: no. 53, discussed again by David R. Jordan, "Magica Graeca Parvula," *Zeitschrift für Papyrologie und Epigraphik* 100, 1994, p. 321f.
80. Plato, *Laws* 11, 933b; Theocritus, *Idyls*, II, 38; Horace, *Satires*, I, 8,30; Virgil, *Eclogue*, VIII, 73f.; Ovid, *Fasti* II, 575 (*Amores* III, 7,30 on the other hand, means a wax tablet); see Audollent 1904: lxxv–lxxi; Gager 1992: p. 15. The figurine in the Louvre, fabricated after *PGM* IV, 296ff., is of sun-dried clay, Gager 1992: p. 98, fig. 12; wax statuettes Wortmann 1968: p. 85, no. 4 (Gager 1992: p. 102, fig. 14).
81. Ludwig Wittgenstein has similar misgivings, which hinge too on the concept of emotional satisfaction; see Chapter 7, n. 5.
82. Plato, *Republic* 364 BC; Theocritus, *Idyls* II, 90, 161; Virgil, *Bucolics* VIII, 95; *Codex Iustinianus* IX, 18,4. See the discussion in Audollent 1904: XLV–XLVII.
83. The text in Daniel and Maltomini 1990: nos. 46–51.
84. From Sophocles, *Oedipus Rex* 397f. to Philostratus, *Life of Apollonius of Tyana* VIII, 6.
85. Athens already, Wünsch 1900: p. 8; then Jordan 1985b: 21f.("we may wonder if he was A's apprentice"). Cyprus (Amathus): David R. Jordan, in Hägg 1994: p. 132. Agonistic *defixio* from the circus of Beirut, with mistakes due to the copying from a book, David R. Jordan, "Magica Graeca Parvula," *Zeitschrift für Papyrologie und Epigraphik* 100, 1994: 325–333.
86. *PGM* IV, 336–345.
87. The Greek text contains a long series of magical words that here are understood as epithets of Hermes; they are too unwieldy for the translation.
88. *PGM* IV, 345f.
89. *PGM* IV, 384.
90. *PGM* IV, 436–465.
91. Variants of this hymn are used several times in the papyri: *PGM* I, 315–327 (divination, to Helios-Apollo); IV, 1957–1989 (spell

of King Pitys); VIII, 74–84 (request for a dream); a reconstruction of the original text in *PGM Hymnus* 2.

92. See in general Franz Joseph Dölger, *Sol Salutis* (Münster: Aschendorff, 1925), 1–60. Proclus prays also to the rising moon, Marinus, *Vita Procli* XI.

93. Erwin Rohde, *Psyche: The Cult of Souls and Belief in Immortality Among the Greeks*, trans. W. B. Hillis (London: Routledge and Kegan Paul, 1950); still useful the art. of H. Waszink, *Reallexikon für Antike und Christentum*, vol. 1, 1950, pp. 1167–1170 (see also Waszink's remarks in his commentary on Tertullian, *De anima*, Amsterdam: Gieben, 1947, pp. 564–567).

94. Audollent 1904: no. 68 (Gager 1992: 22).

95. ἐπ᾽ ἀτελείαι López Jimeno 1991, nos. 7, 10, 18; no. 1 (Selinus about 550 B.C.) has the formula "let words and deeds be unsuccessful."

96. There are three different interpretations: (1) Audollent 1904: no. 68 follows Ziebarth, who compares Plato, *Phaedo* 69 C and understands the term as uninitiated; (2) Liddell-Scott-Jones s.v. translate "unmarried"; Gager 1992: no. 22 follows; (3) Michael Jameson, David Jordan, and Roy Kotansky, *A Lex Sacra from Selinous* (Durham, N. C.: University of North Carolina Press, 1993), p. 130f., understand *telos* not as "goal," but like *teleté* as "ritual" and suppose them to be dead persons who were not properly buried and who therefore are angry.

97. I did not mark the plausible supplements.

98. *Kernos* 7, 1994, 352 no. 32.

99. See earlier, n. 83.

100. Faraone in Faraone and Obbink 1991, pp. 3–32.

101. A. Abt, *Archiv für Religionswissenschaft* 14, 1911, p. 155, no. 5: "I make disappear and I bury the trial that he is going to hold in the month of Maimacterion." For the scholarly debate, see E. Ziebarth, *Sitzungsberichte der Preussischen Akademie der Wissenschaften*, phil.-hist. Klasse 1934, pp. 1029–1032 (which this text does not make entirely convincing).

102. The two trials: Delos, against Apollonius, priest of Sarapis; Helmut Engelmann, *The Delian Aretalogy of Sarapis* (Leiden: Brill, 1975), 9 Z. 85ff.; Rome, Curio: Cicero, *Brutus* 217.

103. Audollent 1904: no. 68 (Gager 1992: no. 22).

104. *Supplementum Epigraphicum Graecum* 30, 353.

105. The magic papyri call these rites διάκοποι, "Destroyers of harmony," e.g., *PGM* XII, 365. The accusation in the lists Arnobius, *Adversus nationes* I, 43,5 *(familiarium dirumpere caritates)*; Zacharias, *Life of S. Severus* 69f.; neither Zacharias nor the papyri confine this dissension to love and marriage.

106. Jordan 1985b: p. 222f. drew up the list; the examples range from the fourth century B.C. to late antiquity.

107. A list of the rare homosexual defixions in Daniel and Maltomini 1990: 162.

108. "I bind the shop and the work," Wünsch 1897: 71; "I bind Dionysios the maker of helmets, their family, their work, their products, and their life," Wünsch 1897: no. 69; "I bind his art and his tools," Wünsch 1897: no. 73.

109. *Supplementum Epigraphicum Graecum* 34, 1175, Gager 1992: no.81.

110. Wrestlers (Athens, High Empire), Jordan 1985b: p. 214, no.1– p. 219, no. 5; a racer (Egypt, High Empire) Wortmann 1968: no. 12.

111. Large groups come from Beirut, see G. Mouterde, *Mélanges Beyrouth* 15, 1930/31, pp. 106–123 *(Supplementum Epigraphicum Graecum* 7,213); A. Maricq, *Byzantion* 22, 1952, pp. 360–368; and from Carthage, D. Jordan, "New Defixiones from Carthage," in J. H. Humphrey (ed.), *The Circus and a Byzantine Cemetery at Carthage*, vol. 1 (Ann Arbor: University of Michigan, 1988), 117–34. For the texts of Kourion, already in Audollent, now see Terence Bruce Mitford, *The Inscriptions of Kourion* (Philadelphia: Memoirs of the American Philosophical Society, v. 83, 1971), nos. 127–142; compare Th. Drew-Bear, *Bull. Am. Soc. Papyrologists* 91, 1972, pp. 85–107; for the corresponding recipes in the papyri *PGM* III, 1; VII, 390, 436. See also Henriette Pavis d'Esturac, "Magie et cirque dans la Rome antique," *Byzantinische Forschungen* 12, 1987, 447–467.

112. Audollent 1904: no. 233.

113. Audollent 1904: no. 234, Carthage.

114. *Codex Theodosianus* VIII, 16,1 (August 16, 389 A.D.).

115. A characteristic story is in Jerome, *Vita S. Hilarionis eremitae* 11.

116. Brown (1972) 128f.

117. Jerome, *Vita Hilarionis eremitae*, 20, see *Aufstieg und Niedergang der Römischen Welt* 2:18:4, 2419a. Another, less spectacular case of a Christian fallen victim to the *defixio* of a competitor in Callinicus, *V. Hypatii* 22, Trombley 1993: vol. 2, 92.

118. For the potters, see Pliny the Elder, *Natural History*, XXVIII, 19; the potters of the classical era already attributed such incidents to demons and sought protection from them; see Fritz Graf, "Religionen und Technik in den frühen Hochkulturen des Vorderen Orients und des Mittelmeerraums," in Ansgar Stoecklein and Mohammed Rassem, *Technik und Religion* (Düsseldorf: VDI-Verlag, 1990), pp. 65–84.

119. For magic and social crisis, see Max Marwick (ed.), *Witchcraft and Sorcery* (Harmondsworth: Penguin, 1982); criticism in Charles Stewart, *Demons and the Devil: Moral Imagination in Modern Greek Culture* (Princeton: Princeton University Press, 1991), pp. 14–16. M. Titiev, "A Fresh Approach to the Problem of Magic and Religion," in W. A. Lessa and E. Z. Vogt (eds.), *Reader in Comparative Religion: An Anthropological Approach* (New York: Harper & Row, 1979), pp. 316–319, followed by T. Abusch, "The Demonic Image of the Witch in Standard Babylonian Literature: The Reworking of Popular Conceptions by Learned Exorcists" in Neusner, Frerichs, and Flescher 1989, pp. 27–58, considers the individual crisis as a characteristic feature of magic that distinguishes it from religion; for classical antiquity in any case, the criterion is too narrow.

120. *PGM* IV, 2375: "when you have done so, you will become rich"; ibid., 2439; one prays: "Give me silver, gold, clothing, blissful wealth."

121. νικητικόν *PGM* VII, 528ff.; νικητικὸν δρόμεως ibid., 390.

122. *Oxyrhynchus Papyri* 12, 1916, 237 (*PGM* XXVII).

123. Published by Louis Robert, "Amulettes grecques I–IV," *Journal des Savants* 1981, pp. 3–44.

124. *PGM* III, 574ff., a systasis where a human meets a god. "Memory" means that posterity remembers him, rather than a good memory, requested in the prayers of divination.

125. Bernand 1991, followed by Clerc 1995, has made jealousy the central motive of all magic; this explanation is too narrow, although it is useful in some cases.

126. *Année Epigraphique,* 1978, 455 (H. Solin, *Arctos* 21, 1987, pp. 130–133): "Q. Domatius C.f. bonum tempus mihi meaeque aetati. / Id ego mando remandata / quo apud eos inferos ut pereant / et defigantur quo ego heres sim: / pupillus C. Grani C.f. C. Poblicius populi l(ibertus) / Aprodis(ius), L. Cornelius, meo sumptu / defigo illos quos pereant."

127. Wells: see the list dressed earlier in n. 27. Source: *Année Epigraphique,* 1975, no. 497 (Italica, addressed to *Domna Fons Fore*[——]; ibid., 1978 no. 739 (Bath, addressed to the goddess Suli). Sanctuaries: see the list earlier in n. 26.

128. Often, the formula used expresses this uncertainty, as, for example, "si liber si servus si libera si serva si puer si puella" (*Année Epigraphique* 1979 no. 739). See E. Garcia Ruiz, "Estudio linguistico de las defixiones latinas no incluidas en el corpus de Audollent," *Emerita* 35, 1967, pp. 55–89, pp. 219–248; but there are also examples in which the perpetrator of the crime is known but elusive.

129. *PGM* V, 70, 175; Gager (1992): 175–199.

130. Audollent 1905: no.1.

131. Cicero, *Pro Caelio* 61.

132. For the punishment which consists in a fit of fever and for the background, see Hendrik S. Versnel, "Πεπρημένος. The Cnidian curse tablets and ordeal by fire," in Hägg 1994: pp. 145–154. Sometimes, the stolen object is dedicated to the divinity and goes into his possession, which will prompt him to care more about it; but this is not always the case: if the object is too costly, like a bull or cow, *iumentum*—one prefers to keep it oneself, *Année Epigraphique* 1979 no. 383.

133. See Christopher A. Faraone, "Molten wax, spilt wine and mutilated animals: Sympathetic magic in Near Eastern and Early Greek oath ceremonies," *Journal of Hellenic Studies* 113, 1993, pp. 60–80.

134. See the fascinating study of the French ethnologist Jeanne Favre-Saada, *Deadly Words: Witchcraft in the Bocage,* trans. Catherine Cullen (Cambridge: Cambridge University Press, 1980).

135. Sophronius, *Narratio miraculorum SS Cyri et Ioannis Anargyrorum* 35.

136. Jerome, *Vita Hilarionis eremitae,* 12,10.

137. Kotansky 1994: no. 67.

138. Ibid. no. 68.

139. Tacitus, *Annals*, II, 69.

140. See the funerary inscription of Alexandria in the Froehner Collection, Robert 1936 no. 77, to which Robert adds the earlier dossier; the important inscriptions of Rheneia, calling for avenging the death of a "poor young woman" killed by "murderers or clandestine sorcerers," are republished in *Inscriptions de Délos* 2532 I and II; see also F. Dölger, *Jahrbuch für Antike und Christentum* 5, 1936, pp. 138–149; see also Robert 1936 no. 45.

141. *Corpus Inscriptionum Latinarum* VIII, 2756 (Lambaesis): "carminibus defi/xa iacuit per tempora muta."

142. *Corpus Inscriptionum Latinarum* VI, 3,19747; *Carmina Latina Epigraphica* no. 987: "In quartum surgens comprensus deprimor annum / cum possem matri dulcis et esse patri, / eripuit me saga[e] manus crudelis ubique, / cum manet in terris et nocet arte sua. / vos vestros natos concustodite, parentes, / ni dolor in toto pectore finis eat."

143. Libanius, *Oratio* I, 243–250; see also his apologia *Oratio* 36 (*De veneficiis*, 368 A.D.); still important is C. Bonner, "Witchcraft in the Lecture Room of Libanius," *Transactions of the American Philological Association* 63, 1932, pp. 34–44.

144. For these students, Paul Petit, *Les étudiants de Libanius* (Paris: Nouvelles Editions Latines, 1956).

145. Dreams like that are also known to Artemidorus I, 77.

146. Libanius, *Oratio* I, 41 (Libanius had an astrologer as a sort of bodyguard); 98 (the accusation of having killed two girls and used their heads for malevolent magic). See Brown 1972: p. 127f.

147. The inscription was published, rather summarily, by D. Knibbe, and reprinted by R. Merkelbach, *Zeitschrift für Papyrologie und Epigraphik* 88, 1991, p. 71f; see my analysis, "An Oracle Against Pestilence from a Western Anatolian Town," *Zeitschrift für Papyrologie und Epigraphik* 92, 1992, pp. 267–278; an addition in Hägg 1994, p. 95f.

148. Eunapius, *Vitae sophistarum* 6, 2, 9–12; the author shows that the philosopher was victim of court machinations.

149. See Roy Kotansky, "Incantations and Prayers for Salvation on Inscribed Greek Amulets," in Faraone and Obbink 1991: pp. 107–137, esp. p. 117ff.

150. Pliny, *Natural History* XXX, 98, "in quartanis medicina clinice propemodum nihil pollet. quam ob rem plura magorum remedia ponemus," cited by Jerry Stannard, "Herbal medicine and herbal magic in Pliny's time," in J. Pigeaud and J. Orozio (eds.), *Pline l'Ancien, témoin de son temps* (Salamanca/Nantes: Bibliotheca Salmaticensis, 1987), pp. 95–106 (97); the vulgate tradition of Pliny, however, writes *eorum* instead of *magorum*.

151. See *PGM* V, 340; Audollent 1904: no. 262; see ibid. cxvii. *PGM* VII, 435–438 (binding spell, tied to a cord; countermeasure: ἀπολύειν); IV, 2954 (marking the spot); for the *defixio* from Savaria (Szombathely) Dorottya Gáspár, "Eine griechische Fluchtafel aus Savaria," *Tyche* 5, 1990, pp. 13–16, earlier in n. 42.

152. Plotinus: Porphyry, *Life of Plotinus* 10; Maximus: Eunapius, *Lives of the Sophists* VI, 9, 1–10.

153. Jerome, *Vita S. Hilarionis eremitae* 12,9. See the similar case of S. Macedonius, Theodoretus, *Historia religiosa* 13; Brown 1972: 137.

154. Audollent 1904: no. 137 "ne quis solvat nisi nos qui fecimus"; see also the Attic text earlier in n. 16.

155. ὀνειροκρίταισιν, ἀναλύταις Magnes, *Lydoi* frg. 4, in R. Kassel and C. Austin (eds.), *Poetae Comici Graeci* (Berlin/New York: De Gruyter, 1986). Hesychius, II 1722. The material already in August Lobeck, *Aglaophamus* (Königsberg: Borntraeger, 1829), p. 644 n. f, see also Dodds 1951: p. 205, n. 99; for λύειν, ἀναλύειν, and ἀπολύειν see also earlier n. 16. A dream also helped Libanius against magic, *Oratio* 1, 245.

156. The original excavator: Trumpf 1958, pp. 94–102; the final publication: Karl Kübler, *Die Nekropole von der Mitte des 6. bis Ende des 5. Jahrhunderts* (Kerameikos. Ergebnisse der Ausgrabungen 7:1) (Berlin: De Gruyter, 1976), p. 48, no. 148 ("Skelett in Rückenlage, Beine ausgestreckt, Hände seitlich am Körper, Kopfende nach Nordosten, Rumpf und Oberschenkel stark nach dem Kopfende verrutscht.") In the French edition of this book, I fell victim to Trumpf's (and my own) imagination.

157. The position of Jonathan Z. Smith, *Drudgery Divine: On the Comparison of Early Christianity and the Religions of Late Antiquity* (Jordan Lectures in Comparative Religion 14) (Chicago: Chicago University Press, 1990) is too narrow in this case.

158. After a phase of Pan-orientalism, classical studies for too long did

not look East (see Martin Bernal, *Black Athena: The Afroasiatic Roots of Classical Civilization.* Bd. 1: *The Fabrication of Ancient Greece 1785– 1985* [New Brunswick: Rutgers University Press, 1987] who over-reacts). Fundamental Walter Burkert, "Itinerant Diviners and Ma-gicians: A Neglected Element in Cultural Contacts," in R. Hägg (ed.), *The Greek Renaissance of the Eighth Century* B.C.: *Tradition and Innovation* (Acta Instituti Atheniensis Regni Sueciae, vol. 30) (1983), pp. 115–119; and Burkert 1992: pp. 41–87; see also Christopher A. Faraone, "Hephaestus the Magician and Near Eastern Parallels to Alcinous's Watchdogs," *Greek, Roman, and Byz-antine Studies,* 28, 1987, pp. 257–280; id., "Clay Hardens and Wax Melts: Magical Role-reversal in Virgil's Eighth Eclogue," *Classical Philology,* 84, 1989, pp. 294–300.

159. Syntheses: J. Bottéro, "Magie A. In Mesopotamien," in *Reallexikon der Assyriologie* 7 (1987–1990), pp. 200–234; Charles Fossey, *La magie assyrienne: Etude suivie de textes magiques transcrits, traduits et com-mentés* (Paris: Leroux, 1902); id., "Textes magiques assyriens," in *Recueil de travaux relatifs à la philologie et à l'archéologie égyptiennes et assyriennes (Recueil Maspero)* 26, 1904, pp. 179–218; Erica Reiner, "La magie babylonienne," in *Le monde du sorcier* (Sources Orientales 7), Paris: Seuil, 1966, pp. 69–98; M.-L. Thomsen, *Zauberdiagnose und Schwarze Magie in Mesopotamien* (The Carsten Niehbur Institute of Ancient Near Eastern Studies, Publications; 2), Copenhagen: Museum Tusculanum Press, 1987; a description of the texts in R. Borger, *Handbuch der Keilschriftliteratur,* vol. 3, Leiden: Brill, 1975, pp. 85–93; W. Röllig, art. Literatur 4.8: "Akkadische magische Literatur," in *Reallexikon der Assyriologie* 7 (1987–1990) pp. 61–64; V. Haas, *Magie und Mythen in Babylonien,* Gifkendorf, 1986; some exemplary analyses in J. Bottéro, *Mythe et rites de Babylone* (Ge-neva/Paris: Droz, 1985), esp. pp. 65–112 ("Le manuel de l'exor-ciste et son calendrier") and pp. 163–219 ("Une grande liturgie exorcistique").

160. Tacitus, *Annals,* II, 69,3; Libanius, *Oratio* I, 249. Maqlû (Gerhard Meier, *Die assyrische Beschwörungssammlung Maqlû.* Archiv für Orient-forschung. Beiheft 2, Berlin: Horn, 1937) 4, 30 "Figuren von mir habt ihr in der Mauer verschlossen"; 35 "Figuren von mir habt ihr im Mauereingang verschlossen." W. Lambert, *Archiv für Orientfor-schung,* 18, 1957/58, p. 292; "that man—figurines were sealed in

a partition": R. C. Thompson, *Assyrian Medical Texts* (London: Luzac, 1923), 86,1 (III 1); see Thomsen 1987: 36.

161. *PGM* IV, 26–51, undetermined rite of initiation: "on the banks of the river where no man's foot has trod, it is necessary to build an altar to offer sacrifices to Helios; before sunrise, one moves around the altar; when the sun rises, one sacrifices a white rooster; all dressed, one takes a bath in the river, one leaves it backing out and puts on new clothes . . ." Erich Ebeling, "Beschwörungen gegen den Feind und den bösen Blick aus dem Zweistromlande," *Archiv für Orientwissenschaft* 17:1, 1949, pp. 172–211, to combat a whole gamut of difficulties: "In the morning, on the banks of the river, where no man's foot has trod, one builds three altars; one sacrifices some food to Shamash, Ea, Marduk; one makes a libation of milk, beer, and wine; after a prayer, one undresses, one puts the clothes on a scale and says an incantation; then one puts on new clothes, one prays to Shamash, one purifies oneself by an inhalation and one leaves."

162. *PGM* IV, 337, 1417, 2484, 2749, 2913; V, 340; VII, 984; XIV, 23; XIXa, 7; LXX, 5; W. H. Roscher, *Ausführliches Lexikon der griechischen und römischen Mythologie* (Leipzig: Teubner, 1890–1894), vol. 2, 1, pp. 1584–1587: "Kore Persephone Erschigal"; Burkert 1992: p. 68.

163. Maqlû 2, 135–146 ("wie diese Figuren zertropfen, zerrinnen und zerfliessen, / so mögen Zauberer und Zauberin zertropfen, zerrinnen und zerfliessen!"); 5, 152 ("Zertropft, zerrinnt, [zerfliesst]!").

164. Synthesis by Chr. Daxelmüller and M.-L. Thomsen, "Bildzauber im alten Mesopotamien," *Anthropos* 77, 1982, pp. 27–64; see also O. R. Gurney, "Babylonian Prophylactic Figures and Their Ritual," *Annals for Archaeology and Anthropology* (Liverpool) 22, 1935, pp. 21–96; A. Ungnad, "Figurenzauber für den kranken König Shamash-shumu-ukîn," *Orientalia* 12, 1943, pp. 293–310.

165. Hair: A. Falkenstein, "Sumerische Beschwörung aus Boghazköy," *Zeitschrift für Assyriologie* 45, 1939, pp. 8–41; Jordan 1985b: 251. Cloth: Maqlû: II, 182; Theocritus, II, 53; Virgil, *Eclogue* VIII, 91–93.

166. Assyrian erotic magic V. Scheil, *Revue d'Assyrologie* 18, 1921, 21

no. 17; binding spell Maqlû 4,105–115 and 9,73; 5,117–119; Greco-Roman world Virgil, *Eclogue* VIII, 72.

167. Graves in general: Maqlû 2,182ff; 4,14ff.; wells Maqlû 4,38. Graves of the family: Maqlû 4,19 "you delivered me to a spirit of my family"; Plato, *Laws* XI, 933b, wax figurines at the crossroads or under the doors or on the tombs of the parents.

168. Erotic charms Robert D. Biggs, *Sà.zi.ga: Ancient Mesopotamian Potency Incantations* (Locust Valley, N. Y.: J. J. Austin, 1967), 70–75 (KAR 61,11–21. KAR 69,25f.; right hip KAR 69,17–19). Hittites V. Haas, *Reallexikon der Assyriologie* 7 (1987–1990) 241 (KUB 40,83). Attica: Jordan 1988b: 273–277. Etruria: Ambros Pfiffig, *Religio Etrusca*, (Graz: Akademische Verlagsanstalt, 1975) 365 Abb. 141.

169. Maqlû 4,30 ("Figuren von mir habt ihr auf der Schwelle niedergelegt"); Plato, *Laws* XI, 399C; Jerome, *Vita S. Hilarionis eremitae* 12; Sophronius, *Narratio miraculorum SS Cyri et Ioannis Anargyrorum* 55; see *PGM* XII 99–103 for a commercial amulet.

170. Syntheses: J. Bottéro, *Mythes* (n. 159), pp. 100–108, after Ungnad 1941/44.

171. I. Tzvi Abusch, "Dismissal by Authorities: Shushkunu and Related Matters," *Journal of Cuneiform Studies* 37, 1985, pp. 91–100. In the papyri, this procedure is called "Charm to restrain anger," θυμοκάτοχος; or "Charm to procure favor," χαριστήριον, e.g., *PGM* IV 469; VII 186; X 24; XII 179, 395; XIII 250.

172. Ungnad 1941/44, pp. 251–282; for a family of such priests, p. 255.

173. For Burkert, earlier n. 158; Plato, *Republic* 364 B.C.

174. Gerhard Meier, *Die assyrische Beschwörungssammlung Maqlû* (Archiv für Orientforschung. Beiheft 2) (Berlin: Horn, 1937); Israel Tzvi Abusch, *Babylonian Witchcraft Literature: Case Studies* (Atlanta: Scholars Press, 1987); Erica Reiner, *Surpu: A Collection of Sumerian and Akkadian Incantations* (Archiv für Orientforschung. Beiheft 11) (Graz: E. Weidner, 1958).

175. Love: "Love of a man for a woman"; "love of a woman for a man"; "love of a man for a man": Ungnad 1941/44, II.5–8. Practical examples: H. Zimmern, "Der Schenkenliebeszauber. Berl. VAG 9728 (Assur) (Lond. K3464 + Par. N.3554 [Niniveh])," *Zeitschrift*

für Assyriologie 32, 1918/19, pp. 164–184; E. Ebeling, *Liebeszauber im Alten Orient* (Mitteilungen der Deutschen Orientgesellschaft 1:1), Leipzig: Pfeiffer 1925; R. D. Biggs, *Sà.zi.ga: Ancient Mesopotamian Potency Incantations;* reconciliation of a married couple V. Scheil, *Revue d'Assyriologie* 18, 1921 No. 17; Joan and Aage Westenholz, "Help for Defected Suitors: The Old Akkadian Love Incantation MAD V8," *Orientalia* 46, 1977, pp. 203–215; a Sumerian example, A. Falkenstein, "Sumerische religiöse Texte. 6: Ein sumerischer Liebeszauber," *Zeitschrift für Assyriologie* 56, 1964, pp. 113–129. Success: "To provide success for an innkeeper"; "depositing of money," that is, the discovery of a treasure; "reporting a fugitive slave," Ungnad 1941/44, II, 19, 20, 25, 47. The "Schenkenliebeszauber" promises the success of a cabaret (and its girls) thanks to an erotic charm; and the rite for capturing a fugitive slave E. Ebeling, *Orientalia* N. S. 23, 1954, pp. 52–56. Social status: "To enter the palace"; "to calm the anger"; "that the king in his palace mentions the name for the good"; "let him who sees you rejoice to see you." Ungnad 1941/44, II, 12–16. See also T. Abusch, *Journal of Cuneiform Studies* 37, 1985, pp. 91–100; and O. R. Gurney, "A Tablet of Incantation Against Slander," *Iraq* 22, 1960, pp. 221–227.

176. Synthesis in Thomsen 1989: 58; see Codex Hammurapi 2, in Hugo Gressmann, *Altorientalische Texte aum Alten Testament* (Berlin: De Gruyter, 1926), p. 383; J. B. Pritchard (ed.), *Ancient Near Eastern Texts Relating to the Old Testament* (Princeton: Princeton University Press, 1969), p. 163; Assyrian laws 47 (Gressmann 420).

177. Sicily: López Jimeno 1991; the practice in Magna Graecia is indirectly attested, through the Oscan texts that start in the later 6th century, earlier in Chapter 2, n. 95.

178. Fritz Graf, *Eleusis und die orphische Dichtung Athens in vorhellenistischer Zeit* (RGVV 31) (Berlin/New York: De Gruyter, 1974).

179. As Dodds had it, 1951: 194f., writing about "regression taking an even cruder form."

6. LITERARY REPRESENTATION OF MAGIC

1. Among others, Jacques Annequin, *Recherches sur l'action magique et ses représentations: Ier et IIème siècle après J.C.* (Paris: Les Belles Lettres,

1973); and Georg Luck, *Arcana Mundi: Magic and the Occult in the Greek and Roman Worlds* (Baltimore: Johns Hopkins University Press, 1985); much more conscious of the problems is Anne-Marie Tupet, *La magie dans le poésie latine I: Des origines à la fin du règne d'Auguste* (Paris: Les Belles Lettres, 1976).

2. As A. S. F. Gow in his authoritative *Theocritus* (Cambridge/New York: Cambridge University Press, 1988), vol 2, p. 25; see the justified protest of Tupet 1967: p. 52.

3. I cannot share A. D. Nock's conviction that it would be possible to interpret the difference between Theocritus's and Lucan's texts as an indication of a historical development in magic: A. D. Nock, "Greek Magical Papyri," in A. D. Nock (ed.), *Essay on Religion and the Ancient World* (Oxford: Clarendon Press, 1972), pp. 183–187 (originally published in *Journal of Egyptian Archaeology*, 15, 1929).

4. See *Anthologia Palatina*, 5,277 (Agathias); 3,71 (Dioscurides).

5. There is a small textual problem: in the three occurrences—v. 3, v. 10, v. 159—the manuscript tradition unanimously writes καταθύσομαι; it is the *Scholia Vetera* that attest to the already ancient variant καταδήσομαι, undoubtedly (and all the modern editors think so) the correct text.

6. John J. Winkler drew up a list of these, in "The Constraints of Eros," in Faraone and Obbink 1991: pp. 214–243.

7. *PGM* IV, 1496.

8. *PGM* IV, 2455–2464.

9. *PGM* III, 224 (prayer to Helios-Apollo who enjoys fumigations of laurel), 309 (divination). Pods, πίτυρα, are parts of a sacrificial cake in *PGM* LXX, 20, and they are used in a cathartic ritual in Demosthenes, *De corona* (18) 259.

10. For the magic essence (οὐσία), earlier in Chapter 5, n. 71; cloth in this function is already present in the Near East, Maqlû 2,185 ("Wer bist du, Zauberin, die . . . im Haus des Gerbers abgeschnitten hat [meinen Gewandsaum] . . .?").

11. See A. S. F. Gow, *Journal of Hellenic Studies* 54, 1934, pp. 1–13; Loretta Baldini Moscadi, "Osservazioni sull'episodio magico del VI libro della Farsaglia di Lucano," *Studi Italiani di Filologia Classica* 48 (1976) 140–199, Appendix 193–199; for the oldest attestation, G. W. Nelson, "A Greek Votive Iynx-wheel in Boston," *American*

Journal of Archaeology 44, 1940, pp. 443ff.; the earrings Dyfri Williams and Jack Ogden, *Greek Gold Jewelry of the Classical World* (New York: Metropolitan Museum, 1994), p. 96f., nos. 49f.

12. For this traditional structure, see C. Ausfeld, "De Graecorum precationibus quaestiones," *Jahrbücher für Classische Philologie* Supplement 28, 1903, pp. 502–547; H. S. Versnel, "Religious Mentality in Ancient Prayer," in H. S. Versnel (ed.), *Faith, Hope and Worship: Aspects of Religious Mentality in the Ancient World* (Leiden: E. J. Brill, 1981), pp. 1–64; for the magic prayers, see Fritz Graf, "Prayer in Magic and Religious Ritual," in Faraone and Obbink 1991: pp. 188–213.

13. *PGM* IV, 2575–2584. The papyrus does not mention the common laurel: what is important for the reversed ritual is the color of the black laurel.

14. Ritner 1993: p. 97 and p. 173f.

15. *PGM* IV, 2594–2596, 2475–2482.

16. Libanius, *Oratio,* I, 245.

17. *PGM* IV, 2504–2509.

18. Eleusis: Apollodorus, FGrHist 244 F 110; Velleius Paterculus, *Roman History* I,4,1: other parallels in Walter Burkert, *Homo Necans: The Anthropology of Ancient Greek Sacrificial Ritual and Myth,* trans. Peter Bing (Berkeley: University of California Press, 1983). Trumpet: Fritz Graf, *Nordionische Kulte* (Rome: Schweizer Institut in Rom, 1985), p. 245.

19. *PGM* IV, 1854, "hits the door with the statuette."

20. See Arthur Darby Nock, "The Lizard in Magic and Religion," in Nock 1972, pp. 271–276; in a fragment of magic papyrus, published by Wortmann 1968, 109 no. 13, the eye of a lizard must be used; unfortunately, the context has been lost.

21. *PGM* XIII, 318. The same *PGM* XIII, 320, recommends the use of the statuette of a crocodile to prevent a wife's infidelity. A drink plays a rather enigmatic role in an Attic defixion, Wünsch 1897: no.99,10: "when she drinks this drink on my behalf . . ."

22. *PGM* VII, 861–918 (lunar rite of Claudianus).

23. Lucian, *Lover of Lies* 13–15; I owe this story (like other suggestions contained in this paragraph) to J. Winkler, see earlier n. 6.

24. See Kenneth Dover, *Greek Homosexuality* (Cambridge, Mass.: Har-

vard University Press 1978); and Harald Patzer, *Die griechische Knabenliebe* (Wiesbaden: F. Steiner, 1982), pp. 112–114.

25. A list of homosexual defixions from Egypt has been drawn up by Daniel and Maltomini 1990, p. 132 (there are examples of relations between men as well as between women); an Athenian example can be added from the High Empire, Jordan 1985b, 225 no. 8 (two men; this whole group of texts belongs to the world of the ephebes).

26. Arnobius, *Adversus nationes* I, 43,5.

27. See J. Winkler, loc cit. (earlier n. 6).

28. Lucan, *Pharsalia*, VI, 507–830. See, among others, Wolfgang Fauth, "Die Bedeutung der Nekromantieszene in Lucans Pharsalia," *Rheinisches Museum für Philologie* 118, 1975, pp. 325–344; Loretta Baldini Moscadi, "Osservazioni sull'episodio magico del VI libro della Farsaglia di Lucano," *Studi Italiani di Filologia Classica* 48, 1976, pp. 140–199; Richard Gordon, "Lucan's Erictho," in Michael Whitby, Philipp Hardie, Mary Whitby (eds.), *Homo Viator: Classical Essays for John Bramble* (Oak Park, Ill.: Bolchazy-Carducci, 1987), pp. 231–241 and, for the literary analysis, W. R. Johnson, *Momentary Monsters: Lucan and his Heroes* (Ithaca/London: Cornell University Press, 1987), pp. 19–33.

29. Lucan VI, 527f. "omne nefas superi prima iam voce precantis concedunt carmenque timent audire secundum." "The heavenly gods allow her all the heinous crimes at the first words of her prayer, and they fear hearing a second charm."

30. Modern commentaries refer to the nine knots of three colors in Virgil, *Eclogues* VIII, 78; more to the point is the contrast with the plain dress of the Roman matron. The *virus lunare* is found in other writers of the era; see the commentary of Pierre-Auguste Lemaire (Paris: N. E. Lemaire, 1832), on VI, 505.

31. See earlier, n. 12.

32. VI, 695f. "Eumenides Stygiumque Nefas Poenaeque nocentum / et Chaos . . ." (700f.) "nostraeque Hecates pars ultima, per quam / manibus et mihi sunt tacitae commercia linguae." "Hecate, by whom the Manes and I exchange secrets."

33. PGM XXIII, 1–70, following the *Kestos* 18 of Iulius Africanus (third century A.D.); for the latter, see the thesis of Francis C. T.

Thee, *Julius Africanus and the Early Christian View of Magic* (Tübingen: Mohr, 1984).

34. For Greek and Roman necromancy, see Erwin Rohde, *Psyche: Seelencult und Unsterblichkeitsglaube der Griechen,* 2nd ed. (Freiburg i.B./Leipzig/Tübingen, 1898), vol. 2, pp. 362–365. Ancient Orient and Israel: J. Tropper, *Nekromantie. Totenbefragung im Alten Orient und im Alten Testament* (Alter Orient und Altes Testament 223), (Neukirchen-Vluyn: Neukirchener Verlag, 1989); Brian B. Schmidt, *Israel's Beneficent Dead: Ancestor Cult and Necromancy in Ancient Israelite Religion and Tradition* (Forschungen zum Alten Testament 11) (Tübingen: Mohr, 1994). Middle ages: Richard Kieckhefer, "La necromanzia nell'ambito clericale nel tardo Medioevo," in Agostino Paravicini Bagliani and André Vauchez (eds.), *Poteri carismatici e informali: Chiesa e società medioevali* (Palermo: Sellerio, 1992), pp. 210–223.

35. Arnobius, *Against the Gentiles* I,43,5. "Quis enim hos nesciat aut imminentia studere praenoscere, quae necessario velint nolint suis ordinationibus veniunt aut mortiferam immittere quibus libuerit tabem aut familiarium dirumpere caritates aut sine clavibus reserare quae clausa sunt aut ora silentio vincire aut in curriculis equos debilitare incitare tardare aut uxoribus et liberis alienis sive illi mares sunt sive feminei generis inconcessi amoris flammas et feriales inmittere cupiditates aut, si utile aliquid videantur audere, non propria vi posse, sed eorum quos invocant potestate?" Similar lists in Libanius, *Declamations* XLI, 29, and Zacharias, *Vita S. Severi* 69; see earlier Chapter 5, n. 12.

36. The list of defixions in Jordan 1985b, p. 222; the *diakopos PGM* XII, 365. See earlier Chapter 5, n. 105.

37. Arnobius, loc. cit. 4,12 "magi, haruspicum fratres"; Isidorus, *Etymologiae* VIII, 9; Tacitus, *Annales* 2,27f. and 12,22.

38. Apollonius: Philostratus, *Life of Apollonius of Tyana,* VIII, 5; *Passio Perpetuae* XVI, 2; ἄνοιξις *PGM* XIII, 327, 1065; δεσμόλυτον XII, 161, see earlier, Chapter 4, n. 72.

39. *PGM* IV, 2145–2240.

40. *PGM* III, 263–275 (with the title πρόγνωσις).

41. *autoptos* in *PGM* V, 55–69; the term is used by mistake to refer to lecanomancy, and *PGM* IV, 930–1114, combines it with lychnomancy.

42. For example, *PGM* IV, 850. The accusers reproach Apuleius to have practiced similar divination, *Apologia* XLII (other means—lamp, vase—can come into play, too).

43. ὀνειραιτηο in όν τ *PGM* VII; ὀνειροθαυπτάνη in *PGM* IV, 3174, a word that Preisendanz explains by ὀνειρ-αυτ-ὑπτάνη, "immediate vision in the dream"; Pythagoras and Democritus, *PGM* VII, 795–845; a statuette of Hermes in *PGM,* V, 370–446. See the synthesis by Samson Eitrem, "Dreams and Divination in Magical Ritual," in Faraone and Obbink 1991: pp. 175–187.

44. Apuleius, *Metamorphoses,* II, 11; immediate vision and lamp: *PGM* V, 1–53; immediate vision and lamp: V, 55–69.

45. *PGM* IV, 1928–2006 (first version); 2007–2139 (second version); 2140–2144 (third version).

46. Pliny the Elder, *Natural History* XXX, 8–11, see Bidez and Cumont 1938: I, pp. 167–212; II, 267–356. Heinz J. Thissen, "Ägyptologische Beiträge zu den griechischen magischen Papyri," in U. Verhoeven and E. Graefe (eds.), *Religion und Philosophie im alten Ägypten: Festgabe für Philippe Derchain* (Orientalia Lovanensia Analecta 39) (Louvain: Peeters, 1991), 285f., identifies Pithys with Bithys in Iamblichus and proposes an Egyptian etymology: this does not explain why the papyri call him a Thessalian.

47. Pliny the Elder, *Natural History* XXVIII, 82; Iamblichus, *The Mysteries of Egypt* VIII, 5; VIII, 10.

48. *PGM* XII, 278 ἔγερσις νεκροῦ, "the awakening of a dead body."

49. *PGM* IV, 2145–2177.

50. XIII, 139f.

51. For those ancient observers, see the fun that Lucian, *Menippus* IX, pokes at "barbarian, meaningless and polysyllabic words," and the dead-serious criticism of Plutarch, *De superstitione* III, 166 B, "their strange and barbarian expressions are shameful and unjust with respect to the gods."

52. *PGM* IV, 1035–1047.

53. *PGM* II, 50–53; another text that exhibits a sign of the almost-philological work of these collectors of magic recipes, see earlier, Chapter 1.

54. A. D. Nock, moreover, insisted on the quality of Lucan's sources and thought of Statilius Taurus or another platonist as a source,

"Greek Magical Papyri," in Nock 1972, p. 186ff. (originally *Journal of Egyptian Archaeology* 15, 1929).

7. WORDS AND ACTS

1. See Tamsyn Barton, *Ancient Astrology* (London: Routledge 1994), p. 103f, who underscores that the term was important in ancient medicine already before the Stoa.
2. Quotation taken from Bidez and Cumont, 1938: I, p. 193ff.
3. Plotinus, *Enneads* 4,4,40. See Philip Merlan, "Plotinus and magic," in *Kleine Schriften* (Berlin: De Gruyter 1976), pp. 388–395 (urspr. *Isis* 44, 1954, 341–348) and esp. his own polemics against the magicians in *Enneads* 2,9, for which see Karin Alt, *Philosophie gegen Gnosis: Plotins Polemik in seiner Schrift II 9* (Abhandlungen der Akademie Mainz 1990:7) (Wiesbaden: Steiner, 1990).
4. See the synthesis Tambiah 1985, pp. 123–166, "A performative approach to ritual." The discussion about ritual is immense, a first sensible help in Daniel de Coppet (ed.), *Understanding Rituals* (London: Routledge, 1992) and Catherine Bell, *Ritual Theory, Ritual Practice* (New York/Oxford: Oxford University Press, 1992).
5. Tambiah 1990, p. 58. Ludwig Wittgenstein's discussion is published in "Bemerkungen über Frazers 'The Golden Bough,'" *Synthese* 18, 1965, pp. 236–258.
6. Victor Turner, *Dramas, Fields, and Metaphors: Symbolic Action in Human Society* (Ithaca: Cornell University Press, 1974) and id., *From Ritual to Theatre: The Human Seriousness of Play* (New York: PAJ Publications, 1982).
7. S. J. Tambiah, "The Magical Power of Words," *Man* 3, 1968, pp. 175–208; reprinted in Tambiah 1985: pp. 17–59.
8. Stanley J. Tambiah, "Form and Meaning of Magical Acts: A Point of View," in Robin Horton and Ruth Finnegan (eds.), *Modes of Thought: Essays on Thinking in Western and Non-Western Societies* (London: Faber, 1973), pp. 199–229; reprinted in Tambiah 1985: pp. 60–86.
9. Christopher A. Faraone, "Molten wax, spilt wine and mutilated animals: Sympathetic magic in Near Eastern and Early Greek oath ceremonies," *Journal of Hellenic Studies* 113, 1993, pp. 60–80.

10. *Supplementum Epigraphicum Graecum* IX, no. 3 (lines 44ff.; the mani-kins are called κολοσσοί).

11. Livy, *Roman History*, I, 24; see Georg Wissowa, *Religion und Kultus der Römer*, 2nd ed. 1912 (repr. Munich: Beck, 1971).

12. Jean-Pierre Vernant, *Myth and Thought Among the Greeks* (London/Boston: Routledge & Kegan Paul, 1983); id., *Figures, idoles, masques. Conférences, essais et leçons du Collège de France* (Paris: Julliard, 1990), pp. 25–30.

13. Quoted by Burkert 1987: p. 62.

14. Frantiszek Sokolowski, *Lois sacrées des cités grecques: Supplément* (Paris: E. de Boccard, 1962), no. 115.

15. A synthesis of this discussion in S. Sharot, "Magic, Religion, Science, and Secularization" in Neusner, Frerichs, and Flesher 1989: pp. 261–283; not very helpful is the thesis of I. M. Arkin, *Roman Magism at the End of the Republic: A Reevaluation in the Light of the Degeneration Theory of Wilhelm Schmidt*, Dissertation St. Louis University, 1964 (See *Dissertation Abstracts* 25, 1965, 5915).

16. Synthesis: F. Graf, "Dionysian and Orphic eschatology: New texts and old questions," in Thomas Carpenter and Christopher Faraone (eds.), *Masks of Dionysos* (Ithaca, N.Y.: Cornell University Press, 1993), pp. 239–258. For the significantly earlier date of the first Sicilian curse tablet, see earlier, Chapter 5, n. 176.

17. Audollent 1904: no. 22 (Gager 1992; no. 45), line 39, "I deposit with you this charge to make Ariston silent, and you give over his name to the infernal gods." Similar phrases in no. 26, line 27; no. 27, line 23.

18. Apuleius, *Apologia* XXVI, 6; Jamblichus, *The Mysteries of Egypt*, VII, 5. An anecdote introduces Jamblichus during such a dialogue, Eunapius, *Life of the Sophists* V,2,2; see Michel Tardieu, *Les paysages reliques* (Louvain/Paris: Peeters, 1990), pp. 11–13.

19. See Libanius, *Oratio* I, 248, and Plutarchus, *On Superstition* III, 166 B; both Pliny, *Natural History* XXX, 18, and Tacitus, *Annals* XII, 59, use the term *magicae superstitiones*.

20. That is why E. Heitsch, a specialist in late Greek poetry, became interested in them, "Zu den Zauberhymnen," *Philologus* 103, 1959, pp. 215–236; "Drei Helioshymnen," *Hermes* 88, 1960, pp. 150–158; see also Paolo Poccetti, "Forma e tradizione dell'inno magico nel mondo classico," in Albio Cesare Cassio and Giovanni Cerri

(eds.), *L'inno tra rituale e letteratura nel mondo antico*. Atti di un colloquio (Napoli 21–25 ottobre 1991) (A.I.O.N. 13, 1991) (Rome: GEI, 1993), pp. 179–204. The previous bibliography *PGM* vol. 2, p. 264.

21. Richard Reitzenstein, *Poimandres: Studien zur griechisch-ägyptischen und frühchristlichen Literatur* (Leipzig: B. G. Teubner, 1904), p. 14: "die Gebete . . . die zum Teil ohne Rücksicht auf den Zweck der magischen Handlung aus älteren Quellen übernommen und für sie nur durch Aufnahme unverständlicher Formelm erweitert sind"; Martin P. Nilsson, *Die Religion in den griechischen Zauberpapyri* (Lund: Gleerup, 1949).

22. See the communication of M. J. Vermaseren to the Congress of Rome, "La sotériologie dans les Papyri Graecae Magicae," in Ugo Bianchi and Maarten J. Vermaseren (eds.), *La soteriologia dei culti orientali nell'Impero Romano: Atti del Colloquio Internazionale* (Leiden: E. J. Brill, 1982), pp. 17–30: 'The magician does not implore the gods, he wishes to constrain them; he does not wish to obey the gods or subject himself on his knees in all simplicity of the heart." The magician's behavior was meant despite everything to transmit to the gods the evidence of his soteriological search ("cries of the heart")—at the cost of a *salto mortale*: the magicians did not, in fact, succeed in formulating in friendly terms what they felt, but they expressed themselves "like impudent boys." The strategy that consists in comparing with childish behavior those cultural facts that are unacceptable according to the criteria of one's own culture, but that one does not for all that wish to find fault with, goes back at least to Fontenelle.

23. Dieterich 1923; Festugière 1981, pp. 281–326. ("Excursus E: La valeur religieuse des papyrus magiques"; his position: "A magic action . . . is of a magical essence . . . It is not a prayer, a request, but a summons. One forces the divinity to act.")

24. Further details in Fritz Graf, "Prayer in Magic and Religious Rituals," in Faraone and Obbink 1991: pp. 188–213.

25. Josep Corell, "Defixionis tabella aus Carmona (Sevilla)," *Zeitschrift für Papyrologie und Epigraphik* 95, 1993, pp. 261–268; another example in a spell from Cremona, Heikki Solin, *Arctos* 21, 1987, pp. 130–133, see earlier chap. 5, n. 128; more D. Maltomini, *Zeitschrift für Papyrologie und Epigraphik* 107, 1995, p. 297, n. 3.

26. Audollent 1904: no. 22 (Gager 1992: no. 45)(Amathus).

27. Sappho, frg. 1 Lobel-Page.

28. *PMG* VIII, 1–60 (what is translated as "sexual attractiveness," is ἐπαφροδίσια in the Greek text. The wish to "come like babies in the belly of their mother" refers to the wish of a peaceful possession by the god; the sacred wood of Hermes is ebony; see also Apuleius, *Apologia* LXI.

29. Euripides, *Iphigenia among the Taurians* 1336f.

30. Plinius, *Naturalis historia* 28,20, "neque est facile dictu externa verba atque ineffabilia abrogent fidem validius an Latina et inopinata, quae inridicula videri cogit animus semper aliquid immensum exspectans ac dignum deo movendo, immo vero quod numini imperet."

31. Jamblichus, *De mysteriis Aegyptiorum* 7,5. See John M. Dillon, "Jamblichus of Chalcis (c. 240–325 A.D.)," in *Aufstieg und Niedergang der römischen Welt* II: 36:2 (Berlin/New York: De Gruyter 1987), pp. 862–909; Beate Nasemann, *Theurgie und Philosophie in Jamblichs "De Mysteriis"* (Stuttgart: Teubner, 1991). Jerome, the Christian, makes fun of those "names meant to excite the spirits of the ignorant and women" and taken "in some way from Hebraic sources," *Letters* 75,3.

32. Origen, *Against Celsus* I, 24; see also Clement of Alexandria, *Stromateis* I, 143, 1.

33. Tambiah 1985: pp. 18–21.

34. Greek in Latin spells: a fine example from Autun, from the 1st century A.D. J. Marcillet-Jaubert, *Zeitschrift für Papyrologie und Epigraphik* 33, 1979, p. 185f.; ead., *Mém. Soc. Éduenne* 54, 1979, pp. 1–25; there are entire Greek spells from the Latin west, see Dorottya Gáspár, "Eine griechische Fluchtafel aus Savaria," *Tyche* 5, 1990, pp. 13–16. Latin in England: Thomas 1971: p. 179.

35. Jerome, *Letters* 75,3.

36. Examples Audollent 1904: no. 231 (Carthago); 252 (id.); 270 (Hadrumetum); Kotansky 1994: no. 7.

37. *PGM* VII, 742, a charm for receiving dreams.

38. *PGM* VIII, 1f. (Astrapsoukhos); I, 40 (*sústasis*); III, 574–583 (*sústasis*).

39. The citation from M. J. Vermaseren, "La sotériologie dans les Papyri Graecae Magicae," earlier n. 22, p. 21. For the connection

with Frazer see, among others, John Skorupski, *Symbol and Theory: A Philosophical Study of Theories of Religion in Social Anthropology* (Cambridge/New York: Cambridge University Press, 1976), pp. 130–134; or Stanley J. Tambiah, *Magic, Science, Religion, and the Scope of Rationality* (Cambridge/London: Cambridge University Press, 1990), p. 52f.

40. *PGM* IV, 155–222 (letter of Nephotes).

41. *PGM* IV, 65–70.

42. Proteus: Homer, *Odyssey* IV, 383ff.; Virgil, *Georgics*, IV, 387ff; Faunus and Picus: Ovid, *Fasti* III, 291ff; Silenus: Theopompus, *FGrHist* 115 F75 and the references in the commentary of G. Bömer to Ovid's *Fasti*.

43. *PGM* XII, 1ff. .

44. See Robert K. Ritner, *The Mechanics of Ancient Egyptian Magical Practice* (Chicago: Oriental Institute of the University of Chicago, 1993).

45. *PGM* II, 45–50.

46. *PGM* IV, 1438.

47. *PGM* IV, 1472–1481.—Another *historiola* about Isis in the coptic text *PGM* IV, 95; a third one in the spell of the Syrian woman from Gadara, *PGM* XX, 6f., see Ludwig Koenen, "Der brennende Horusknabe: Zu einem Zauberspruch des Philinna-Papyrus," *Chronique d'Égypte* 37, 1962, pp. 167–174; a fourth one on the spell against headache Kotansky 1994, no. 13. See Anthony A. Barb, "Antaura: The Mermaid and the Devil's Grandmother," *Journal of the Warburg and Courtauld Institutes* 29, 1966, pp. 1–23.

48. Homer, *Odyssey*, VIII, 266–367; once again, thus, we note the mixture of Greek and Egyptian.

49. *PGM* IV, 2900–2907; for Adonis in Egypt, see *PGMTr* 93 n. 363.

50. See also H. Philsooph, "Primitive Magic and Mana," *Man* 6, 1971, pp. 182–203.

51. *PGM* XII, 117f.

52. *PGM* IV, 1035f.

53. A. F. Segal, "Hellenistic Magic: Some Questions of Definition," in R. Van den Broek and M. J. Vermaseren (eds.), *Studies in Gnosticism and Hellenistic Religion Presented to Gilles Quispel* (Leiden: Brill, 1981), pp. 349–375.

54. *On the Sacred Disease* IV.

55. Pagans: Seneca, *Oedipus*, 561–563; Pliny the Elder, *Natural History*, XXVIII, 20 (earlier n. 30); Pseudo-Quintilian, *Declamations*, 10,19; more examples in *Thesaurus Linguae Latinae* VIII, 587,7. Christians: for example, Eusebius, *Evangelical Preparation*, V,8,6 (referring to *Oracula Chaldaica* 220, 221, 223 Des Places); Hippolytus, *Refutation* VII, 32; Irenaeus, *Against the Heresies*, I,25,3.

56. Jamblichus, *On the Mysteries of the Egyptians*, I, 14.

57. Apuleius, *Apologia*, XXVI, 6.

58. The concept has been used esp. by Max Gluckman and Victor Turner; see the introductions by Peter Weidkuhn, "The quest for legitimate rebellion: Towards a structuralist theory of rituals of reversal," *Religion* 7, 1977, pp. 167–188; A. Barbara Babcock (ed.), *The Reversible World: Symbolic Inversion in Art and Society* (Ithaca, N.Y./London: Cornell University Press, 1978); Brian Morris, *Anthropological Studies of Religion: An Introductory Text* (Cambridge/London: Cambridge University Press, 1987), pp. 246–263.

59. Cato, *On Agriculture*, 156 (see earlier, Chapter 2, n. 57); *Tibullus* I, 4,11f.

60. Still exemplary are the remarks of Claude Lévi-Strauss, "The Sorcerer and His Magic," in Claude Lévi-Strauss, *Structural Anthropology* (Chicago: University of Chicago Press, 1976); Peter Brown, *The Cult of the Saints: Development and Function in Latin Christianity* (Chicago: University of Chicago Press, 1981), pp. 71–73.

61. *PGM* VII, 199f.

62. *PGM* VII, 201f.

63. The same holds true for the Middle Age, Kieckhefer 1989: pp. 3f. and 57–75.

64. Fumigation with disgusting substances as a rite of reversal plays a role in the medieval "fête des fous," a festival belonging to the New Year cycle: "thurificare de fumo fetido ex coreo veterum sotularium" in a letter from the Theological faculty of the Sorbonne of 1445; see Heinrich Denifle, *Chartularium Universitatis Parisiensis 1* (Paris: Erères Delalavia, 1889), no. 2595.

65. *PGM* IV, 26–51, a τελετή, a ritual of initiation (at the end, "you will be an initiate," τετελεσμένος).

66. *PGM* XII, 201–269 (ὁλοκαυστῶν 213).

67. Plato, *Republic* 364 B.C.

68. See Renate Schlesier, "Olympian versus chthonian religion," *Scripta Classica Israelica* 11, 1991/92, pp. 38–51; ead., "Olympische Religion und chthonische Religion," in Ugo Bianchi (ed.), *The Notion of "Religion" in Comparative Research.* Selected Proceedings of the XVI IAHR Congress (Rome: L'Herma di Bretschneider, 1994), pp. 301–310.

BIBLIOGRAPHY

Abt, Adam. 1908. *Die Apologie des Apuleius von Madaura und die antike Zauberei: Beiträge zur Erläuterung der Schrift de magia* (RGVV 4:2). Giessen: Töpelmann.

Audollent, Auguste. 1904. *Defixionum Tabellae*. Paris: Fontemoing.

Bernand, André. 1991. *Sorciers grecs*. Paris: Fayard.

Betz, Hans Dieter. 1990. *Hellenismus und Urchristentum. Gesammelte Aufsätze* vol.1. Tübingen: Mohr.

————. 1995. "Secrecy in the Greek magical papyri," in Hans G. Kippenberg and Guy G. Strousma (eds.), *Secrecy and Concealment: Studies in the History of Mediterranean and Near Eastern Religions*. Leyden: Brill, 153–175.

Bidez, Joseph, and Franz Cumont. 1939. *Les mages hellénisés*. Paris: Les Belles Lettres.

Bravo, Benedetto. 1987. "Une tablette magique d'Olbia pontique, les morts, les héros et les démons," in *Poikilia: Études offertes à Jean-Pierre Vernant*. Paris: École des Hautes Études en Sciences Sociales, 185–218.

Brown, Peter. 1972. "Sorcery, demons and the rise of Christianity: From late antiquity into the Middle Ages," in *Religion and Society in the Age of Augustine*. London: Faber & Faber, pp. 119–146 (orig. in Mary Douglas, ed., *Witchcraft Confessions and Accusations*. London, 1970, 17–45).

Burkert, Walter. 1987. *Ancient Mystery Cults*, Cambridge, Mass./London: Harvard University Press.

————. 1992. *The Orientalizing Revolution: Near Eastern Influence on Greek Culture in the Early Archaic Age,* Cambridge, Mass.: Harvard University Press (trans. and rev. ed. of *Die orientalisierende Epoche in der griechischen Religion und Literatur,* Sitzungsbericht Heidelberg 1984:1).

Butler, H. E., and A. S. Owen. 1914. *Apulei Apologia Sive Pro Se De Magia Liber: With Introduction and Commentary.* Oxford: Clarendon Press.

Clerc, Jean-Benoît. 1995. *Homines magici: Étude sur la sorcellerie et la magie dans la société romaine impériale* (Publications Universitaires Européennes 3: Histoire et sciences auxiliaires de l'histoire 673). Bern/Berlin/Paris: Peter Lang.

Daniel, Robert W., and Franco Maltomini (eds.). 1990. *Supplementum Magicum* 1 (Abhandlungen der Nordrhein-Westfälischen Akademie, Sonderreihe Papyrologica Coloniensia 16:1). Opladen: Westdeutscher Verlag.

————. 1992. *Supplementum Magicum* 2 (Abhandlungen der Rheinisch-Westfälischen Akademie. Sonderreihe Papyrologica Colonensia 16:2). Opladen: Westdeutscher Verlag.

Dieterich, Albrecht. 1923. *Eine Mithrasliturgie,* 3rd ed. by Otto Weinreich. Leipzig/Berlin: Teubner (1. Aufl. 1903).

DK: *Die Fragmente der Vorsokratiker,* 5th to 7th ed., H. Diels, ed., with additions by W. Kranz.

Dodds, Eric Robertson. 1951. *The Greeks and the Irrational* (Sather Lectures 25). Berkeley/Los Angeles: University of California Press.

Faraone, Christopher A., and Dirk Obbink (eds.). 1991. *Magika Hiera: Ancient Greek Magic and Religion.* New York/Oxford: Oxford University Press.

Festugière, André-Jean. 1932. *L'idéal religieux des Grecs et l'Évangile.* Paris: Les Belles Lettres.

FIRA: Iohannes Baviera. *Fontes Iuris Romani Anteiustiniani.* Florence 1940.

Fowden, Garth. 1986. *The Egyptian Hermes: A Historical Approach to the Late Pagan Mind.* Cambridge: Cambridge University Press.

Hägg, Robin (ed.). 1994. *Ancient Greek Cult Practice from the Epigraphical Evidence.* Proceedings of the Second International Seminar on Ancient Greek Cult, organized by the Swedish Institute at Athens, 22–24 November 1991 (Acta Instuti Atheniensis Regni Sueciae XIII). Stockholm: Svenska Institutet i Athen.

Hopfner, Theodor. 1974. *Griechisch-ägyptischer Offenbarungszauber.* Amsterdam: Hakkert (orig. *Studien zur Palaeographie und Papyruskunde,* vol.21. Leipzig: H. Haessel, 1921).

————. 1983. *Griechisch-ägyptischer Offenbarungszauber. Seine Methoden.* Teil 1, Amsterdam: Hakkert (orig. *Studien zur Palaeographie und Papyruskunde,* vol.23:1. Frankfurt: H. Haessel 1924).

————. 1990. *Griechisch-ägyptischer Offenbarungszauber. Seine Methoden.* Teil 2, Amsterdam: Hakkert (orig. *Studien zur Palaeographie und Papyruskunde,* vol.23:2. Frankfurt: H. Haessel 1924).

Jordan, David R. 1985a. "A survey of Greek defixiones not included in the special corpora," *Greek, Roman and Byzantine Studies* 26, 151–197.

————. 1985b. "Defixiones from a well near the southwest corner of the Athenian Agora," *Hesperia* 54, 205–255.

————. 1988a. "New archaeological evidence for the practice of magic in classical Athens," in *Praktika of the 12th International Congress of Classical Archaeology, Sept. 4–10, 1983,* vol.4, Athens, 273–277.

————. 1988b. "A love charm with verses," *Zeitschrift für Papyrologie und Epigraphik* 72, 245–259.

Kieckhefer, Richard. 1989. *Magic in the Middle Ages,* Cambridge: Cambridge University Press.

Kippenberg, Hans G., and Brigitte Luchesi, eds. 1978. *Magie: Die sozialwissenschaftliche Kontroverse über das Verstehen fremden Denkens.* Frankfurt a.M.: Suhrkamp (repr. 1987).

Kotansky, Roy. 1994. *Greek Magical Amulets: The Inscribed Gold, Silver, Copper, and Bronze Lamellae.* Part 1: *Published Texts of Known Provenance* (Abhandlungen der Rheinisch-Westfälischen Akademie der Wissenschaften. Sonderreihe Papyrologica Coloniensia 22:3). Opladen: Westdeutscher Verlag.

Lloyd, Geoffrey E. R. 1979. *Magic, Reason, and Experience: Studies in the Origin and Development of Greek Science.* Cambridge: Cambridge University Press.

López Jimeno, Maria del Amor. 1991. *Las tabellae defixionis de la Sicilia Griega.* Amsterdam: Hakkert.

Martinez, David G. 1991. *A Greek Love Charm from Egypt (P.Mich.757)* (American Studies in Papyrology 30. Michigan Papyri vol. 16). Atlanta, Georgia: Scholars Press.

Mauss, Marcel. 1973. "Esquisse d'une théorie générale de la magie."

Année Sociologique 7, 1902/03, again in M. M., *Sociologie et anthropologie*, introduction par Claude Lévi-Strauss. Paris: Presses Universitaires de France, 1–141.

Merkelbach, Reinhold. 1992. *Abrasax. Ausgewählte Papyri religiösen und magischen Inhalts*, vol.3: *Zwei griechisch-ägyptische Weihezeremonien (Die Leidener Weltschöpfung. Die Pschai-Aion-Liturgie)* (Abhandlungen der Rheinisch-Westfälischen Akademie der Wissenschaften. Sonderreihe Papyrologica Coloniensia 17:3). Opladen: Westdeutscher Verlag.

Merkelbach, Reinhold, and Maria Totti. 1990. *Abrasax: Ausgewählte Papyri religiösen und magischen Inhalts*, vol.1: *Gebete* (Abhandlungen der Nordrhein-Westfälischen Akademie, Sonderreihe Papyrologica Coloniensia 17:1). Opladen: Westdeutscher Verlag.

———. 1991. *Abrasax. Ausgewählte Papyri religiösen und magischen Inhalts*, vol.2: *Gebete (Fortsetzung)* (Abhandlungen der Nordrhein-Westfälischen Akademie der Wissenschaften. Sonderreihe Papyrologica Coloniensia 17:2). Opladen: Westdeutscher Verlag.

Neusner, J., E. S. Frerichs, and P. V. M. Flesher (eds.). 1989. *Religion, Science, and Magic in Concert and in Conflict.* New York/Oxford: Oxford University Press.

Nilsson, Martin P. 1960. *Opuscula Selecta linguis anglica, francogallica, germanica conscripta* 3 (Acta Instituti Atheniensis Regni Sueciae, ser. 2, II:3). Lund: Gleerup.

Nock, Arthur Darby. 1972. *Essays on Religion and the Ancient World*, ed. by Zeph Stewart. Oxford: Clarendon Press.

PGM: Karl Preisendanz (ed.). *Papyri Graecae Magicae: Die griechischen Zauberpapyri*, 2nd ed. by Albert Henrichs. Stuttgart: Teubner 1973–1974 (1st ed. Leipzig/Berlin: Teubner 1928–1931).

PGMTr: Hans Dieter Betz (ed.). 1985. *The Greek Magical Papyri in Translation Including the Demotic Spells.* Chicago and London: The University of Chicago Press (repr. 1992).

Reitzenstein, Richard. 1904. *Poimandres: Studien zur griechisch-ägyptischen und frühchristlichen Literatur.* Leipzig: Teubner.

Ritner, Robert K. 1993. *The Mechanics of Ancient Egyptian Magical Practice.* Chicago: The Oriental Institute.

Robert, Louis. 1936. *Collection Froehner.* vol.1. *Inscriptions grecques.* Paris.

Smith, Morton. 1978. *Jesus the Magician.* San Francisco: Harper & Row.

————. 1984. "The eighth book of Moses and how it grew (P.Leid. J 395)," in *Atti del XVII Congresso Internazionale di Papirologia*. Naples: Centro Internazionale per lo Studio dei Papiri Ercolanesi, vol. 2, 683–693.

Tambiah, Stanley Jeyaraja. 1985. *Culture, Thought, and Social Action: An Anthropological Perspective*. Cambridge, Mass.: Harvard University Press.

————. 1990. *Magic, Science, Religion, and the Scope of Rationality*. Cambridge: Cambridge University Press.

Thomas, Keith. 1971. *Religion and the Decline of Magic: Studies in Popular Beliefs in Sixteenth and Seventeenth Century England*. London: Weidenfeld & Nicolson.

Thomsen, Marie-Louise. 1987. *Zauberdiagnose und Schwarze Magie in Mesopotamien*. Copenhagen: Museum Tusculanum Press.

Trumpf, Jürgen. 1958. "Fluchtafel und Rachepuppe," *Athenische Mitteilungen* 73, 94–102.

Tupet, Anne-Marie. 1976. *La magie dans la poésie latine* vol. I. *Des origines à la fin du règne d'Auguste*. Paris: Presses Universitaires de France.

Ungnad, Arthur. 1941/44. "Besprechungskunst und Astrologie in Babylon." *Archiv für Orientforschung* 14, 251–282.

Winkler, John J. 1991. "The constraints of Eros," in Faraone and Obbink 1991, 214–243.

Wortmann, Dierk. 1968. "Neue magische Texte," *Bonner Jahrbücher* 168, 56–111.

Wünsch, Richard. 1897. "Appendix continens defixionum tabellas in Attica regione repertas," in *Inscriptiones Graecae*. Vol. II/III *Corpus Inscriptionum Atticarum*. Berlin: Reimer.

————. 1990. "Neue Fluchtafeln," *Rheinisches Museum* 55, 62–85, 232–271.

Ziebarth, Erich. 1899. "Neue attische Fluchtafeln," *Nachrichten von der Gesellschaft der Wissenschaften zu Göttingen*. Philologisch-Historische Klasse, 105–135.

————. 1934. "Neue Verfluchungstafeln aus Attika, Böotien und Euboia," *Sitzungsberichte der Preussischen Akademie der Wissenschaften*. Philologisch-Historische Klasse, 1022–1050.

INDEX

Acts of the Apostles, 7
Aeschylus, 28, 119; *Persians*, 194
agōgai (attraction spells), 178–
    179, 181, 186, 188, 198, 199
Agonistic context, 152–161
Agonistic spell. *See defixiones*
    agonisticae (agonistic spells)
Agrippa, 40–41
agúretēs, 21, 22, 26, 27–28, 49
ahoroi, 150, 194
alligare, 125
Amulet, 158–159
amustēriastoí, 97
anieróō, 125
anatíthemi, 125
apánankoi, 223
apográpho, 125
Apollonius of Tyana, 21, 94–
    95, 196
Apuleius: *Apologia sive de magia*,
    65–88, 116; and communica-
    tion, 214, 228–229; and in-
    itiation, 101; and Laevius, 38–
    39; *Metamorphoses*, 101, 102,
    104; and philosophy, 51–52,
    67, 68, 69–70, 73, 76, 84,

86–88; and Plato, 20, 86;
    and society, 68–69, 70–71,
    72, 84–86, 88, 102, 187
Archangelike, 7
Arnobius, 195–196
Assistant. *See Parhedros*
Assurbanipal, 170
Assyria, 170, 173
Astrology, 50, 51, 54, 55, 57,
    205–206
Attraction spells. *See agōgai*
audiurare, 125
Augustus, 40–41, 48–49

Babylon, 173
Bacchic mystery, 23, 49, 98–99
basileus, 80–81
biaiothánatoi, 150, 194
Binding spells. *See defixiones*
    (binding spells)
Black magic, 41, 47, 53

cantio, 44
carmen, 41, 42, 48, 58
carmen auxiliare, 43–46
carmen malum, 41, 47, 52, 56

Cato, 43–46, 47, 49, 50
Catullus, 36–37
Celsus, 108
Chaldeans, 54, 57, 196
Charismatic, 94
Charm, 158
Charm of Astrampsychus, 218, 222
Christ, 90, 91, 96, 105, 108
Christianity, 117, 157, 162
Cicero: *Brutus*, 58–59; *De divinatione*, 36; *De legibus*, 36; and judicial spells, 58–59, 119, 123, 164; *Laws*, 59, 60; *Republic*, 42; and society, 85; *Against Vatinius*, 39–40; and *veneficium*, 46
Clement of Alexandria, 21
Coercion, 222–229
Commercial *defixiones*, 121, 154–155, 158
Commercial magic, 171
Communication, 209–214, 228–229
Consultation of a Skull According to Pitys the Thessalian, 198–199
Cosmology, 32
Crisis, 157–158, 160
Crop conveyance, 41, 42, 48, 57, 58, 62–65
Curse, 128–129
Cyprian, 96–97

daimones, 23–24
Death, 163–164, 166
dedicare, 125
Defense, 160–161
defigo, 125
defixiones (spells), 118–174; and Arnobius, 196; and divination, 194–195; and gender, 185–186; and Pliny, 53; and prayer, 207; and Rome, 58–59; and society, 156–157, 167, 213; and Theocritus, 178; and underworld, 82, 150,

232. *See also* Commercial *defixiones; defixiones agonisticae; defixiones amatoiae; defixiones iudicariae*
defixiones agonisticae (agonistic spells), 121, 155–156, 158, 196
defixiones amatoriae (erotic spells), 137–144; and Arnobius, 196; and attraction spells, 178; defined, 120; and gender, 185–186, 187; and *Life of St. Hilarion*, 162; and prayer, 148–149; and professionals, 147; and rivalry, 153–154. *See also* Erotic magic
defixiones iudicariae (judicial spells), 58–59, 119, 120, 122–125, 145, 153, 154, 158, 164
demandare, 125
Derveni papyrus, 21, 23, 32
devotio, 128–129
diabolé, 181, 183, 223
Dinarchus, 120, 121
Dio Cassius, 90
dirae, 128–129
Dirae Teorum, 35, 129
Disease, 165, 166
Divination, 26, 49, 51, 52, 55, 56, 57, 66, 158, 190–204
Divinity, contact with, 92–96, 100–101, 105–107, 116, 197, 213–214, 220–221, 222, 231, 232–233
Dream, 197

Egypt, 5–6, 89–92, 99–100, 107, 108–109, 114, 128, 145, 169
Eighth Book of Moses, 6, 7–8, 105–107, 112, 200, 201
Empedocles of Acragas, 33–34
engráphō, 125
epánankoi, 223–224
epaoidé, 28–29
Erictho, 190–194, 200–202, 203–204, 216

Erotic attraction spells. *See agōgai*
Erotic Attraction Spells of King Pitys, 198
Erotic binding spell. *See defixiones amatoriae*
Erotic magic, 53, 66, 73, 74, 92–93, 171, 176–190
Euripides, 98, 218; *Orestes*, 24
Evolutionism, 13–14, 15
excantare, 41, 42, 56, 57
exhorkízō, 125
Exorcism, 78–79, 109, 172
Ezekiel, 112, 113

Falcon, 109, 110, 111, 113, 114, 115, 116
Figurine, 136, 137, 138–147, 152, 171, 178, 212
Formula, 124–125, 135, 148–151. *See also* Ritual; Terminology
Frazer, Sir James George, 12–13, 14, 27, 35, 205–206
Furius Cresimus, 62–65, 68, 69

Gender, 185–187, 188, 189–190
Germanicus, 163, 170
Gnosticism, 94, 95, 101, 107, 232
God. *See* Divinity, contact with
goēs, 24, 28, 33, 46, 49
goēteia, 24, 26, 46
Gorgias: *Apology for Helen*, 26
Greece: and medicine, 30–32, 34, 35; and Mesopotamia, 170–174; and religion, 26–27, 30, 31–32, 34; and Rome, 36, 38, 40, 42, 50, 52, 53; and terminology, 20–35, 46, 49, 56
Harvest conveyance. *See* Crop conveyance
Hellenistic era, 56–57
Heraclitus, 21, 23, 27, 30

Hermetism, 96, 101, 104
Herodotus, 20, 58, 91
Hesiod: *Theogony*, 96
Hierarchy, 226–227, 232, 233
Homer, 28, 197; *Hymn to Demeter*, 101; *Iliad*, 129–130, 208; *Nekyia*, 194, 203
Homosexuality, 188–189, 196
horkízō, 125
Hymn, 215–216

Iamblichus, 214, 228; *The Mysteries of Egypt*, 219–220
Imprecation, 208, 211
incantamentum, 63, 64
incantare, 41, 42, 56
Initiation: and clothing, 116; and gnosticism, 95; and meal, 112; and mystery cults, 98, 101, 102, 104–107, 117; and *parhedros*, 109; and Pindar, 93; and Plato, 94; and religion, 92
Inscription, 82, 83, 138, 143–144, 152, 171, 212–213
Insult, 181, 183
Intention, 14, 47, 48, 88, 101, 103, 152–161
Irenaeus: *Against Heresies*, 95, 107
Isidore of Seville, 55, 196
Iynx, 92–93, 179–180

Jerome, 220; *Life of Saint Hilarion*, 142–143, 157, 161–162, 168
Judicial spells. *See* defixiones iudiciarae
Julio-Claudian dynasty, 53–54, 56

katadeîn, 121
katadeîsthai, 121
katadeō, 125
katadesmós, 121
Kerameikos, 136, 139, 169
Key to Moses, 8, 106

Knowledge, 94, 96, 101, 220–221, 233

Laevius, 38–39
Language. *See* Terminology
Lead tablet, 118, 126–127, 133, 135, 175
Legislation, 35, 41–43, 46–47, 59–60, 156
Letter form, 130–131
Lex Cornelia, 46–47, 54, 56, 58, 59, 60, 64, 66, 69, 73
Libanius, 164–165, 170, 182
ligare, 125
Literature, 175–204
Lives of the Saints Cyrus and John the Pennyless, 142
Livy, 47–48, 49, 208
Lucan, 190–198, 200–204, 216
Lucian: *Philopseudes*, 78–79, 90, 91–92, 105, 187–188
Lucius Verus, 165, 166

mageía, 26, 29, 34, 53
magi, 21, 196. *See also* Persians
magia, 36, 39, 48, 56, 66
magica maleficia, 66, 68
magicus, 37–38, 49, 50
magiká, 29
Magnes, 168
magos, 20–30, 31, 34, 49
magus, 36–37, 39, 48–49, 55, 69
maleficus, 55
Malinowski, Bronislaw, 15–16
mántis, 21, 22
Marcion, 95, 107
Marriage, 186, 188
Mauss, Marcel, 15, 17, 61, 88
Maximus, 168
Meal, 111–114, 231
Medicine: and Apuleius, 87–88; and *carmen auxiliare*, 43–46, 48; and

epaoidḗ, 28–29; Greek, 30–32, 34, 35; and Hellenistic era, 57; and isolation, 229–230; and Plato, 28–29; and Pliny, 50, 52, 55; and Tacitus, 56. *See also* Science
megalomustḗrion, 97
Memory, 212–213, 221
Men, 185–187, 189
Mesopotamia, 170–174
Mithras, 102
"Mithras Liturgy," 97–98, 103–104, 216
Moses, 6–7, 96
mustagōgós, 97
mustḗria, 97
mustḗrion, 97
Mystery cult, 22–23, 26, 49, 59, 91, 96–117

Name, 95, 127–128, 162, 201, 218–220. *See also* Terminology
Nature, 32, 33
Necromancy, 54, 57–58, 82, 190–200
Neo-Platonism, 94, 101, 104, 232
Nero, 52, 105

Oath, 207–209, 212
obligare, 125
On the Sacred Disease, 30–32, 50, 77, 86, 87, 201, 221, 227, 229–230
Origen, 74–75, 108, 219
Ovid, 141

Pankrates, 89, 92, 105
parhedros, 81, 82, 105, 107–116, 117, 200
Paul (jurist), 55, 59, 66
Performative model, 16, 206–207
Persia, 20–21, 29, 36, 37, 51, 52, 169, 196
Persuasive analogy, 207, 209–210

phármaka dēlētēria, 35

phármakon, 28, 46

Philosophical theology, 30, 34, 35

Philosophy: and Apuleius, 51–52, 67, 68, 69–70, 73, 76, 84, 86–88; and *parhedros*, 117; and Pliny, 51, 52; and secrecy, 100

Philostratus, 94–95

Piercing, 139, 140–142, 145, 146

Pindar, 92–93

Plato: and Apuleius, 20, 86; and black magic, 53; and coercion, 227–228; and *defixiones*, 119–120, 121; and figurine, 171; *First Alcibiades*, 20, 29; and initiation, 94; and itinerant priests, 24–26; *Laws*, 25, 27, 30, 119; and medicine, 28–29; *Meno*, 25, 35; and philosophical theology, 30; and prayer, 216; and religion, 27; *Republic*, 21, 22, 25, 93–94, 105, 119, 146–147; and society, 25–26, 85; *Symposium*, 24

Plautus, 46

Pliny the Elder, 7, 41, 44, 58, 62–65, 119, 219; *Natural History*, 49–56

Plotinus, 107, 117, 168, 206

Poison, 28, 46, 47, 72, 73

Porphyry: *Life of Plotinus*, 114

Prayer, 148–150, 180–181, 184, 191–194, 201, 207, 215–222

Private *vs.* public, 55–56, 128–129

Professional, 21, 22, 146–147, 171–172

Property, 42, 48, 56, 57

Protection, 182–183

Psychology, 146–147, 211

Pythagorus, 91

religio, 50–51

Religion: and Apuleius, 83–84, 87; and coercion, 225–227; false, 31–32; Greek, 26–27, 30, 31–32, 34; and initiation, 92; and Lucan, 204; and magic, 14, 15, 16–17, 211, 215–222; Persian, 20–21, 29, 36, 37, 51, 52, 169, 196; and Plato, 27; Pliny on, 50–51; and society, 213

Republican era, 36–41, 50, 56

Reversal, 128, 224, 229–233

Rhombus, 179–180

Ritual, 134–151, 200–204, 210, 230–232. *See also* Formula; Terminology

Rivalry. *See* Agonistic context

Rome, 36–60, 72, 74–76

Science, 14, 15–16, 30–32, 34, 35, 55, 76–77, 86. *See also* Medicine

Scribonius Curio, 58, 119, 164

Secrecy, 99–100

Seneca, 41

Septimus Severus, 90

Servius, 41–42, 58

similia similibus formula, 125, 130–134, 151, 178, 211, 213

Slander, 121, 159, 160

Society: and Apuleius, 68–69, 70–71, 72, 84–86, 88, 102, 187; and spells, 156–157, 167, 213; and Cicero, 85; and Cresimus, 63–65; and erotic magic, 186, 188–190; and Mauss, 61; and mystery cults, 102–104; and Plato, 25–26, 85; and religion, 213; and ritual, 210

Sopater, 165–166

Sophocles: *Oedipus Rex*, 22

Sophronius, 161

Sosipatra, 168

Source material, 3–8

sústasis, 105–107; *Sustasis to Helios*, 115–116. *See also* Divinity, contact with
Sympathy, 134, 145–146, 205–215

Tacitus, 54, 56, 85, 128, 163
Tambiah, Stanley Jeyaraja, 16, 206–207
teletaí, 97
teleté, 97
Terminology: and binding spells, 121–123, 125–126, 150–151; Greek, 20–35, 46, 49, 56; and invocation, 220; and Lucan, 203; and mystery cult, 97–98; Roman, 36–60, 72, 74–76; and Theocritus, 203. *See also* Formula; Name; Ritual
Theatricality, 207, 211–212
Theocritus: *Pharmakeútriai (The Sorceresses)*, 38, 39, 84, 175–185, 202–203, 205, 211
Thesallus of Tralles, 92
Thief, 121, 159
Tiridates of Armenia, 105
Transmission, 151–152
Twelve Tables, 41–43, 53, 58, 62

Tylor, Sir Edward Burnett, 12–13, 15

Underworld: and Apuleius, 82; and binding spells, 82, 150, 232; and Germanicus, 163; and lead tablets, 127; and Lucan, 191–192, 193–194; and permanency, 131; and prayer, 148–149; and reversal, 232; and Theocritus, 183

veneficium, 46–49, 54–55, 56, 57, 66, 73, 189
veneficus, 46–49, 58, 69
venenum, 46–47, 56
Victim, 161–169
Virgil: *Eclogue* 8, 37–38, 39, 41–42, 49, 57–58, 84

Walking backward, 114–115, 183. *See also* Reversal
Weather, 53, 165
Women, 59, 60, 185–186, 188, 189–190

Xenophon, 20

Zalmoxis, 91

REVEALING ANTIQUITY

G. W. Bowersock, General Editor

1. *Dionysos at Large* by Maarcel Detienne,
   translated by Arthur Goldhammer

2. *Unruly Eloquence: Lucian and the Comedy of Traditions*
   by R. Bracht Branham

3. *Greek Virginity* by Giulia Sissa,
   translated by Arthur Goldhammer

4. *A Chronicle of the Last Pagans* by Pierre Chuvin
   translated by B. A. Archer

5. *The Orientalizing Revolution: Near Eastern Influence on Greek
   Culture in the Early Archaic Age* by Walter Burkert,
   translated by Margaret E. Pinder and Walter Burkert

6. *Actors in the Audience: Theatricality and Doublespeak
   from Nero to Hadrian* by Shadi Bartsch

7. *Prophets and Emperors: Human and Divine Authority from
   Augustus to Theodosius* by David Potter

8. *Hypatia of Alexandria* by Maria Dzielska, translated by F. Lyra

9. *The Craft of Zeus: Myths of Weaving and Fabric* by John Scheid and
   Jesper Svenbro, translated by Carol Volk

10. *Magic in the Ancient World* by Fritz Graf,
    translated by Franklin Philip